'A stimulating survey of Scottish cultural and political identity, from law to football, literature to architecture, education to religion, kail-yard to parliament and more. Gardiner reassesses in witty fashion what those often unexamined words "Britain" and "Scottish" might mean today, not to mention the status of that other stateless nation "England". His field is wide and from the Highland clearances to the "cultural clearances", from *Macbeth* to *Shallow Grave*, Gardiner offers a highly entertaining primer on the state of Scotland, backed up by probing questions and excellent lists of further reading. A lively book from start to finish, informed, insightful, quick and irreverent.'

Roderick Watson, University of Stirling

For Kyoko

Modern Scottish Culture

Michael Gardiner

Edinburgh University Press

© Michael Gardiner, 2005

Edinburgh University Press Ltd
22 George Square, Edinburgh

Typeset in 11/13 Monotype Ehrhardt
by Servis Filmsetting Ltd, Manchester, and
printed and bound in Great Britain by
MPG Books Ltd, Bodmin, Cornwall

A CIP record for this book is available from the British Library

ISBN 0 7486 2026 5 (hardback)
ISBN 0 7486 2027 3 (paperback)

The right of Michael Gardiner
to be identified as author of this work
has been asserted in accordance with
the Copyright, Designs and Patents Act 1988.

Every effort has been made to trace the copyright holders, but if any have been inadvertently
overlooked, the publisher will be pleased to make the necessary arrangements at the first
opportunity.

Contents

Acknowledgements

Many thanks to everyone at Edinburgh University Press, especially Sarah Edwards; to my colleagues at Chiba for placing importance on research; and to Ian Watson, Mee-Ching Ho, Glasgow Survival, Theo Seffusatti, the John Macmurray Society, Simon McKerrel, Anthony Guest-Scott, Robert Gardiner, William Hodges, Kyoko Gardiner, Duncan Petrie, Hector MacQueen, Kazuya Sato, Ben Crighton, Chris Jones, Chie Kawaragi, Yoko Ikehata, Saori Takahashi, Kirsti Wishart, Hiyona Kim, Keiko Sato, J. Derrick McClure, Jane Stuart-Smith, Karen Lupton, the University of St Andrews, the University of Aberdeen, and the staff of the National Library of Scotland.

Introduction

Scotland is not a country that gives the head of the United Nations sleepless nights. It has a tenth of the population of England, the home of the British state. There are provincial cities in China with a larger population than the entire Scottish nation. Public transport timetables are largely fictional; its politicians show an unwillingness to rethink a neocolonial foreign policy; its industries flap in a wind of globalisation which makes it an area of cheap labour for outsourcing third-rate jobs; the sun shines only on special occasions; and in its national sport, its great passion, football, it is currently 2,500–1 to win the World Cup. Why should we study the culture of this kind of nation? Or rather, why bother with Scotland *specifically*? Doesn't talking about a specific national culture imply the kind of narrow nationalism the world already has too much of?

The answer to this last question is no, not necessarily. Talking about a national culture does not make you a nationalist, and often, as we will see, talking about Scotland specifically as a nation has been an *anti-nationalist* tactic. To put the question a bit differently: why might small, unpowerful nations be important as independent entities?

Here I propose that we think of Scotland, borrowing the terminology of the French philosopher Gilles Deleuze, as a *minor* nation. For Deleuze, who talks of Franz Kafka's work as a 'minor literature', minor does not mean small or insignificant; it describes the function of iteration (speaking) working within a larger, *major* language or power – here, Standard English dialect or the British empire – and it implies an entity which is always *becoming* something else. Scotland, in Deleuzian terms, always has to *become* in the face of a more power-ful *being*, since, as a nation with no state, it has no official identity, outside of the images of an ethnic people (or even 'race') which have been described as its *being* by the rest of the world, by the UK and, especially, by itself.

The importance of *becoming* has to do with the way some nations are seen as simply somehow already there, and the way this 'coming before', this being *major*, seems to make them eternal. Britain is *major* – to most of the world it seems a unified body with '1,000 years of history' and a set of properties including gentlemanliness, afternoon tea, and the monarchy – yet these are all specifically *English* images. In Britain, the major continues to smother the minor, and British politi-cians need the major to keep them in office, even when it means offi-cially telling fibs. Britain's history, for example, is a mere 300 years old. And yet, it seems like every day another guide to 'British Culture' is published, ranging from travel guides to grown-up Cultural Studies books. What we should notice here is how the *minor* question of 'why Scotland?', which you might have asked yourself on seeing this book, always also forces the *major* question of 'why Britain?'. 'Why Britain' is a question with global implications. But then, given Scotland's cen-trality to empire, its position in Britain has *also* been a question with global implications. And since Scotland has no state, the question of what it is, is necessarily a cultural one.

My use of the *minor* therefore shows how Scottishness troubles the way in which that other adjective 'British' seems to describe a natural overarching being, despite the fact that Britain *as a nation* has been brief and fitful. This remains relevant to even the most cutting-edge collections, such as Robins and Morley's *British Cultural Studies* (OUP, 2001), which duly includes the compulsory 'Scotland chapter' but still gets away with not answering 'why Britain?' by stressing difference and hybridisation, and seeing Britain as an amalgam of properties. Why are some of the most articulate voices in Cultural Studies willing to stay under the umbrella category 'Britain' even though they know Britishness is, in cultural terms, over?

And we should be clear that British culture *is* over, leaving only administrative contexts (for which we talk of *states*, not *nations*, a differ-ence I will make clear throughout). British nationhood has tottered since the 1910s and 1920s, struggling with movements such as Irish Nationalism, the labour movement, and the Scottish Renaissance; it finally expired in the 1980s and 1990s with a swansong of Anglo-British nonsense encouraged by a government which, symptomatically, thought of itself as Unionist. While British culture might still be saleable to an extent in its tea-and-Shakespeare version in far-off countries, the national bonding of Britain is over. It is an ex-nation; it has ceased to be.

Even by the standards of the time of the devolution referendum (1997), when there was much talk of how quickly things were moving, subsequently things have moved even more quickly. The progress from Tom Nairn's speculative *After Britain* (Granta, 2000) to Eric Jo Murkens's more concrete *Scottish Independence: A Practical Guide* (EUP, 2003) shows how definitions that at first seemed quite abstract soon become critical in this field, and even have worldwide consequences. For the conception of a unified Britain was *always* primarily for export, allowing for participation in the greater goal of imperial gain. When the empire disappears, so does Britain's *raison d'état*. In this sense, we should be wary of the popular press's description of imagined ethnic awakenings in Scotland and Wales, since a look at the history of the empire shows that Scotland would have had to remake itself after Britain anyway. In fact, the remaking of Scotland as a distinct political entity (not a new process, by any means) has, thankfully, been markedly *un*-ethnic. News of anti-English attacks may help to sell newspapers, but in fact Scotland and England have a good relationship, one that I believe is being *strengthened* rather than weakened by the process of devolution. As the nations become more independent, they also rediscover how much they have in common.

Yet, as Tom Nairn has shown, the number one responsibility of any British prime minister is to keep Britain together. This is difficult when so many people north of the border are now sceptical about the union, and when so many people south of the border fail to understand what the question about union is. The difficulty of selling a British culture without a worldwide colonial empire was discovered by the Tony Blair administration after 1997 when, while delivering devolution, it also had to come up with a cultural rationale for keeping the union together. Most commentators agree that Blair's exercise, described as a 'rebranding' to fit the mood of privatisation and marketing, was unsuccessful; New Labour frequently had recourse to *old* motifs – union jacks, Victoriana, bulldogs and other Anglo-British imperial kitsch, in a way that would have been unbelievable to the

Scottish founder of Blair's Labour Party, Kier Hardie. A New Labour think-tank even reworked the (Scoto-British) song 'Rule, Britannia!' into the dubiously funny pun of 'Cool Britannia'. Laughing at your own past as coloniser: how cool is that?

Post-Britishness, then, has left a vacuum in which new national cultures must be negotiated. To return to the Deleuzian metaphor, Scotland is *minor* in the sense that it forces basic questions about the *terms* of civil society. And the legacy left by the muddling of England and Britain takes a lot of unpacking. The country from which this book is being written, for example, has no commonly-used word for England at all; the only word available is also the one used for Britain. It is, in other words, impossible to talk specifically about English culture here. Scottish culture, yes; English culture, no. Most worryingly, the English people themselves still show an extraordinary lack of interest in the location of their own nation, and the question of whether it has its own government. England, a part of the UK, is also a *minor* nation crippled by the idea of its own *majority*, but it is having a much harder time identifying a specific national culture. This is not surprising: as Krishan Kumar and others have reminded us, England's cultural centrality to the British empire was well served by this vagueness over borders. Imperial England could be everywhere and nowhere. Becoming *somewhere* is the challenge that now faces England; the hope is that this will be helped by Scotland's own process of becoming.

The other reason that Scotland's Britishness has worldwide implications is that the Scotland which participated in an eighteenth-century form of 'globalisation' after losing its state, at the same time exported a range of ideas about the universal progress of 'man', 'civilisation' and the centrality of communications. Scots' tendency to claim that they invented almost everything has become a bit of joke, but let's take a look at some of these inventions: logarithms (1614), steam engine for rail (end of the eighteenth century), bicycle (1844), facsimile (1846), telephone (1874), telephone switchboard (1883), tarmacadam (1907), television (1925), radar (1935), 3.5-inch disk drive (1983), single-cell cloning (1997). What strikes me about this very truncated list (there are lots more) is that they all relate to some development in communications; they all aim at overcoming a distance, like the one opened up between Scotland and the state capital. Glasgow became the British empire's prime shipbuilder. The country abounds with engineers and physicists; in the first series of *Star Trek*, the officer charged with keeping the ship up to multiples of light speed is 'Scotty'. From the time of union, Scots were always trying to go as fast as possible.

Another thread that emerges from the longer list of Scottish inventions (I'll spare you the details this time) is surveillance, or the ability to place individuals relative to some kind of visual map. This belongs, if we read David Hume, to an Enlightenment tradition of scepticism, of maintaining the rules by which something is known, and then placing them in categories. Even the idea of 'Western thought' itself largely arose in Scotland, as well as its specific categories of thought. But since Scotland has been so central to the empire's *types of possible knowledge*, the making and unmaking of these norms in a modern Scotland must also be a rethinking of how Scots have understood and felt history, while the 'national' identities of major nations like the UK often seem separated from history altogether.

On the other hand, we have to beware of confusing the growth of Scottish national consciousness with the growth of the Scottish National Party (SNP). The SNP is not the only expression of nationalism, far less of national consciousness. As we will see, national parties, Nationalist parties, national culture and nationalist culture all have a complex inter-relationship, sometimes aggregative and sometimes conflictual, and none can be used directly to measure another.

Nor, though, will this book rely on the language of multiculturalism; multiculturalism separates out discrete 'cultures' and requires them to behave as such. Despite the title of this book, which seems to point to 'a' culture, the policy is that culture is fluid and should not normally be made 'singular' in the name of a nation. And nations are *always* composed of multiple customs and 'cultures': there is no singular nation, no ethnic nation anywhere in the world, and there never has been. So, if Pakistanis move to Glasgow and take British citizenship, their customs become Scottish customs. This is a simple point, but one which is often missed by multiculturalism, with its obsession with compounding apparently singular terms: 'Asian Scottish'. One reason this book is being written is that in Scotland (and England) *no-one* is officially Scottish (or English); so not only is there no single Scottish or English culture, there is no citizenship attached to either of these terms. No-one has an English passport, England did not have a large empire, and England was not one of the parties of the Second

World War. What is England? The answer to this is also a cultural one, and to answer it we have to look to Scotland, which has been thinking about these questions for 300 years.

Put another way, there are two ways in which we use the national adjectives that precede the term *culture*. The first is very simple, and indicates a belonging backed up with citizenship and rights – and some of us believe that the only good reason for nationalism is to guarantee these rights relative to the people who live in a stateless nation, such as Scotland. The second use of the national adjective, the multicultural one, describes an imagined essence; it is in this sense that an ice-cream can 'taste very Italian', a manner of speech 'sound very French', or a chair 'look very Japanese'. The thing to notice is that some of the world's nations seem to be *restricted to* the second meaning; people who would get upset about the lack of multiculturalism in a phrase like 'he looks American' – America being already-diverse – often do not have a problem with 'he looks Vietnamese' – and they might even take a pride in being able to tell the difference between 'looks Vietnamese' and 'looks Chinese'.

It is like the way that some foods are described as 'ethnic' – Chinese, Bangladeshi, Moroccan – while others are imagined to have a universal, global range which makes them seem placeless and everywhere. Notice also how every UK/US military strike from Hiroshima to Baghdad has been immediately followed with highly ethnic descriptions of a rebuilding 'people' and the singularisation of their culture: they have effectively been shifted into the second category, the 'ethnic' one. The point is that exactly the same process occurs when a British newspaper describes 'the Scottish people' as rediscovering their ethnic pride.

The exasperating thing about Scottish culture, as we will see, is that the 'universalist' thinking that splits the world into basic properties that should be the same everywhere – justice, history, MacDonald's – versus one-off, ethnic flavours, was largely made by Scotland itself, particularly Edinburgh, during the Scottish Enlightenment, from the second half of the eighteenth century. Via the Enlightenment, which contrasted a 'unique' and highly visible Scotland to globalisation Anglo-British-style, Scotland created for itself its greatest difficulty. Much of the confusion over the very possibility of national cultures arises from a confusion between these two ways of using the national adjective – let's call them the concrete use ('British passport') and the multiculturalist use ('Scottish style'). Racism is inevitable if we slide between them. In other words, nations are forced into becoming 'essence' if they have no concrete body, no rights. So how do we give Scots basic rights, if there is nothing official about being Scottish? Some have recently tried to get round this by speaking of 'imagining' the nation, or the nation as 'mythology', negotiating between the absent concrete and the present essential. Whether ethnocentrism – the thinking of nations as discrete groups or 'races' – is lessening or increasing with the arrival of the Scottish Parliament is a question you may be better equipped to think about after reading this book.

It is in this sense that we should encourage a sense of national 'pride': if nations, like Scotland, become more democratic and inclusive than states which they leave (the UK, crippled by a reliance on 'precedent'), then there is a point to supporting national culture. In Scotland's case, there is good reason to assume that an emerging Scottish nation-state *would* be more inclusive and democratic: for one thing, the UK is something that even many people living there have trouble defining. Moreover, the UK has no properly written constitution, an electoral system based more on knowing a candidate's individual qualities than ethical stance, a narrow parliament which invests far too much power in the leading party and its leader, and little resistance to the privatisation of everything, laying its own 'national' culture open to the highest bidder. It is reasonable to assume that the Scottish nation, and even the English nation, could come up with more democratic answers than this. And we should clear this up as soon as possible: we could fill entire library shelves with the question of what makes a nation (civil society, sociolinguistics, consciousness, culture), but there is now no argument that Scotland is one. This is not a matter of opinion, but a matter of fact – and this is why Scots abroad will tend to get upset about the question, since they are often assumed to be proud nationalists by describing their own nationality as Scottish, whereas all they are doing is making a statement of fact. Nevertheless, this book takes *Modern* to mean 1707, the year of the enactment of the Act of Union – a dating that will doubtless annoy many nationalists – but this is not because Scotland only became modern through Britishness, but because ideas of what 'modern' itself means cannot easily be separated from 'advancement' via empire, and the empire was one reason Scotland participated in British union.

At the end of each chapter is a summary (which should not be seen as a substitute for the text itself), a carefully limited reading list, and questions for further thought. For the reading lists, I have concentrated on studies or editions that are fairly new; older studies or original editions are only there if they seem particularly apt for some reason. I have not gone to the level of recommending journal articles, but have at times listed journals which are likely to regularly carry papers of interest in the field. Any further research in any of these fields would require a journal search. The questions that end each chapter are supposed to be fairly typical of the key questions that scholars of Scottish Studies (at all levels) think about. They also raise some questions very basic to Cultural Studies as a whole; but then, as I said at the outset, a good reason for studying Scotland is that it does trigger fundamental cultural questions – not because it is a *major* nation, but because it is a *minor* one.

CHAPTER 1

What is Scotland?

Scotland is a small nation with a population of just over 5 million people, in the northern part of the United Kingdom. Dispensing with its own state, it was one signatory of the Act of Union in 1706 (the Act took effect in 1707), which today has absorbed all four nations of Scotland, England, Wales and Northern Ireland, all of which are different kinds of nation (many in Northern Ireland, for example, would not describe Northern Ireland as a nation at all, though I think that calling it one is possibly the best way forward). Scotland has a mixture of urban and rural landscapes, the urban ones being mostly in the central belt around and between Glasgow and Edinburgh. Edinburgh and the north-west of Scotland are the parts most familiar to visitors, the north-west as picturesquely empty, and Edinburgh as the 'historic' capital. 'Historic' is a word we should view with the highest suspicion (how can some places be more 'historic' than others?), and the Highlands' emptiness has only come in relatively recent times, and for the worst of reasons, as we shall see in Chapter 3. Scotland's climate is slightly less hospitable than that of England, the east coast being cold but relatively bright, and the west coast being mostly rainy and cloudy. The nation has four major cities – Aberdeen, Dundee, Glasgow and Edinburgh – of which the biggest is Glasgow, although Edinburgh tends to be more famous as the political capital, and, more contentiously, the 'cultural capital'. Off the west coast of the country are a collection of islands which remain culturally relatively distinct – the Western Isles – and to the far north, the Northern Isles, Orkney and Shetland. About half of Scotland's people live in

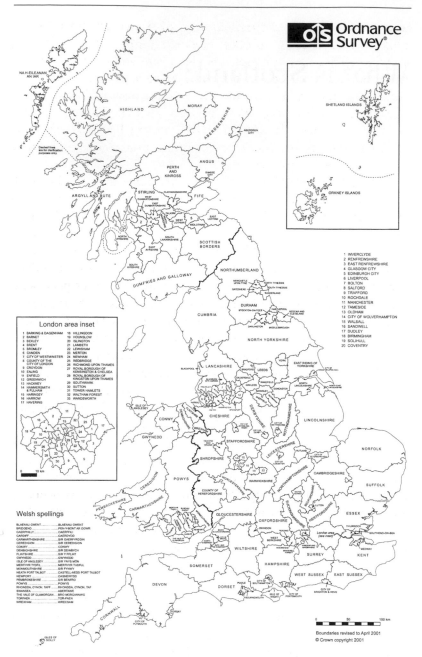

Figure 1.1   Map of Scotland. (Source: Ordnance Survey.)

what used to be called Strathclyde, a wide area around Glasgow. Edinburgh continues to appear to be a centre of power: as I write this, average salaries in Edinburgh are about one and a half times the national average, a whole new layer of bureaucrats are congregated around the new Parliament, the city is better marketed abroad, and house prices in Edinburgh have recently rocketed. (Think about this in relation to the anti-colonial activist Frantz Fanon's claim that nations emerging from a period of imperial culture tend to over-inflate the value of their capital city.)

Although the terrible image of the British diet is largely justified, Scotland also has some of the best natural foods in the UK; it is often used as the larder of high-profile restaurants in England and indeed Scotland itself, and occupies a position in the popular British imagination as a place for hunting and fishing. Economically, Scotland relies more than England on agriculture and fishing. It is a fairly mixed nation ethnically and culturally, compared to some other peripheral small nations, if not to England. This book deliberately refuses to imagine some kind of continuity from the ancient Scots and Picts: modern national culture is the sum of all of the interpretations of history by all the people living in the nation in modern times. If some of today's Scots have 'genetically' come from Ireland, then others have 'genetically' come from India. Creating a qualitative distinction between these two types of Scot is a disastrously bad idea, for reasons which I will come to later. There is a hint of colloquial anti-Englishness in Scottish culture, but incidents of violence are vastly overstated by the mass media, and the two nations have close and friendly relations. As Murray Pittock has astutely noted, those British newspapers that frequently talk of 'anti-English racism' in Scotland are often also those which themselves most exemplify terrible habits of xenophobia. In fact (and here I may as well paint a target on my chest), today Scotland is culturally closer to England than any other nation, including France and Ireland. It is just that being stuck in this unbalanced monstrosity of the United Kingdom prevents us from seeing those similarities, and encourages a silly kind of resentment.

Outside of Scotland, people tend to believe that refusing the description of Scotland as part of an imaginary state called 'England' is a sign of Scottish patriotism. This mistake is a general ethical problem, and even more for England than Scotland – for what happens when you really want to talk about England? Not the state of

Figure 1.2   Glasgow Celtic supporters' pub. (Photograph: Karen Lupton.)

Britain, but the nation of England? How do you convey Englishness? Correcting the mistake of calling England 'Britain' or vice-versa is not a matter of patriotism and pride, it is putting right a factual mistake. If we look at a map, we see that the names of Scotland, England, Northern Ireland and Wales are all printed in capital letters, and are separated by border-lines, indicating that each of these four units is a separate nation. The nation called England stops where Scotland begins; Scotland is not in the north of England any more than Spain is in the south of France. But the name of the United Kingdom is printed in capital and bold letters, and the border between Northern Ireland and the Republic of Ireland is indicated by a thicker line. This indicates that the United Kingdom is internationally recognised as a state. The four members of the United Kingdom – England, Scotland, Wales, and Northern Ireland – are *nations* but not *states*; the only state is that of the United Kingdom itself, often colloquially called Britain, missing out Northern Ireland. The fact that Scotland is a nation with no state has become common knowledge; we should also bear in mind, however, that England has exactly the same status, a nation without a state.

Here, as a kind of shorthand, a very short shorthand, we might say that a society culturally aware of itself as a discrete body *and* with a discrete civic structure – institutions like law, education, media and strong local government – can be called a nation. Scotland remained a nation even when it joined with England and Wales in the Act of Union in 1707. But unlike Scotland and England, most of the world's nations are also states, and the term 'state' is much easier to define: a state is a government exerting sovereign powers over its citizens, making decisions which directly concern their international presence. France, Germany, Nigeria, Thailand and the UK are all states. England and Scotland are unusual in being nations without states. Scotland does not even correspond to any of the stateless areas listed by the Scottish Parliament itself, such as Catalunya – a nation spread across two nation-states without modern experience of separate government – or the German *Länder* and Swiss Cantons, which are not really nations at all. In this sense, the UK's four nations are unique.

So the separation of nation and state has to be borne in mind when discussing Scotland or England. And although there are certainly other stateless nations in the world – Palestine, Taiwan, Kurdistan – there are few states that offer such a feeble basis for nationhood as does the United Kingdom, resting as it does on shared economic benefit, first through empire and then through a version of globalisation. The maintenance of national feelings (Scottish and so on) within the British state has led to an odd situation in which nation or state allegiance is divided *by context*; few Palestinians would see themselves as Israelis 'sometimes', yet this is the situation in modern Scotland. In Scotland, a child can go to school to receive an education which is highly British, being trained away from her native dialect, then go home, switch dialects and go back to talking about concerns more specific to herself as a Scot – effectively changing national orientation a number of times a day without even noticing. (Sociolinguistically, this doubling of dialects is called *diglossia*, and we will look at it in Chapter 8.)

All Britons have a double allegiance, or a 'dual nationality', if we see the UK as a nation. This is true even of English people, though in English life the doubleness is buried so deep that people don't often notice it. A book like this, but titled *Modern English Culture* instead of *Modern Scottish Culture* would have a much harder time justifying itself, since, even though it represented about ten times more people, it would struggle to describe England specifically. Many readers would even suggest that the term 'England' should be described more politically-correctly as 'Britain', missing the point of union. In this book this kind of Britain, inseparable from English norms, will be described as 'Anglo-Britain', a body in the ascendant from the early nineteenth century to the late twentieth, but now pretty much gone, for Scots at least.

Britain's peculiar off-centre situation has its origins in 1707, when the union of governments created the British state by joining the old Scottish state on the one hand, to England and Wales on the other. In theory, this was an alliance. In practice, the English state made little adjustment to the situation of union, which was widely viewed as an annexation. Parliament remained in London, and the constitution – a traditional balance of estates not written down in coherent form – remained English, as it does today (and in this very limited and specific sense one might argue that Scotland was 'colonised'). Conversely, the adjustment of Scotland to union was dramatic, especially from the 1740s, when anti-union rebellions were finally quashed (in the Disarming Act of 1746) and returns on colonial investments made the idea of Britain more attractive to Scots. While England remained relatively unchanged, Scottish elites became instrumental in creating a new form of Britishness in the late eighteenth century, one in which they could take part and become global players.

By the turn of the nineteenth century Scotland had become accustomed to this role in Britain; Tom Nairn has influentially argued (1977) that by the early nineteenth century Scotland was ready to give up the chance of the Romantic nationalism taken up by France, Germany and other European nations, for British opportunity, causing a sudden Scottish national cultural amnesia, or a disappearance of Scottish national history. This changed around the time that Scotland created its own Parliament: when asked by Paterson et al. (2001) to describe their nationality, about 60 per cent of people answered 'Scottish', about 30 per cent answered 'Scottish and British', and only about 10 per cent answered 'British'.

It was only in the twentieth century that proposals for the political separation of Scotland became popular again, and only in the last three decades or so that the importance of Scottish history has been raised to its present level. Contradictory as it may seem, calls for

WHAT IS SCOTLAND? 15

Figure 1.3   Princes Street Gardens. (Photograph: Michael Gardiner.)

Scottish independence are not necessarily nationalist; they may stress the need to dissolve the Act of Union in that the union is democratically unsatisfactory for everyone in the UK. The new Scottish Parliament, aiming for example at a 50 per cent proportion of women, representation for smaller parties, a fairer system of voting, constitutional accountability, and a responsibility in law-making towards rural communities, linguistic minorities and the environment, can be seen as a re-vitalising and necessary revision of British politics.

'Nationalism' is in this sense two-sided: it can represent a dangerously ethnocentric chauvinism, but at certain points in space and time, it can also represent a set of progressive democratic demands. Just as in the Introduction I suggested that there are two kinds of national adjective – the concrete and the essential – there are also two types of nationalism. Party-political nationalism in its modern form was born around the time Britain started losing its imperial power, starting with the loss of the Free State of Ireland in 1922. Since the British alliance was intended to prevent a war on two fronts (Scotland and France) so as to consolidate Anglo-Britain's global position, the loss of the empire later brought Britain into question. And we make a serious mistake if we resort to the language of 'race' to describe possible Scottish separation from the rest of Britain, especially since race itself was largely a British invention, helped along by Scottish science and peaking in the imperial fever of the 1880s and 1890s. One of the duties of Scottish Studies is to question the occasional crypto-racial metaphors which are still used.

Whether or not people are aware of it, they invoke a combination of three properties when they judge whether someone is Scottish: one, being born in Scotland; two, being resident in Scotland; and three, having Scottish parents. The last of these is absurd, since for one's parents to be Scottish merely begs the question again, why are *they* Scottish. What would put an end to this ethnocentric slide would be citizenship, the type of status that would properly define Scottishness: while the creation of an independent Scottish state would create a lot of problems, it would also, from this point of view, *reduce* racism, since it would make ethnocentric assumptions about someone's nationality unlawful. (It is moving from the 'spicy Chinese chicken' use of the national epithet to the 'Chinese passport' one.) And Scotland *does* have a problem with racism; it *must* have one, since, without a state, ethnicity always enters into assumptions about who is a Scot. But as I have argued elsewhere, the fact that many members of ethnic minorities are willing to describe themselves as Scottish rather than British – even though 'British' would offer them legal protection against racism – shows that Scotland has an untapped strength of nation-minded people. This sensitivity is one reason why, as Homi Bhabha suggests in a different context, ethnic minorities are actually *more central* to the identity of a nation than those who seem 'naturally' to constitute the nation.

So a vital difference between Scottish and British is one of official state nationality: a person cannot be 'officially' Scottish, since immigration and citizenship are administered by the British state. This means that the status of being Scottish, like that of being English, remains remarkably fluid and forward-looking (as in the distinction between *becoming* and *being*). Certainly, if Scotland became independent, Scottish citizenship would become concrete and protected by law, but as the situation is now, if you (assuming you are not already British) were to settle in Scotland, you could possibly become British by taking up British citizenship, and this status would protect you against racism and give you certain rights. But how would you become Scottish? Or English? Since there is no separate Scottish or English citizenship, these questions are for the time being necessarily cultural ones. And herein lies the importance of studying Scottish, or English, culture.

To recap: all four members of the UK are nations within the UK state, which can no longer really be described as a nation, since its day-to-day cultural cohesiveness is gone. More problematically, each of these members can also be described as *regions* of the British nation-state. Talk of a Scottish region is common, talk of an English region much less so. A regional understanding of Britain usually takes it for granted that England is split up into smaller regions, bypassing the seemingly unthinkable idea of England as a separate nation, and downplaying the importance of Scotland as a nation. The de-regionalisation of England has become more or less automatic: for example in Colin Pilkington's recent interesting and thorough guide to devolution, nowhere is there any mention of (even the absence of) devolution for *England as a region*.

One reason for the lack of talk of English devolution is size: England's population is approximately 85 per cent of that of the UK as a whole, meaning that it might seem strange to describe England as merely one region. A less obvious but equally important reason is that, historically, England has never fully grasped that it is not the same thing as Britain; English society as a whole indeed barely acknowl-edged the term 'Britain' until the early Victorian era, over a century after the Act of Union. Ambitious Scots, on the other hand, saw Britain from the beginning as something to be built anew. England largely assumed that it had 'become' Britain, an assumption borne out by the use of the English constitution. Consequently, much of the world finds it difficult today to distinguish between the terms. And the idea that England can be described as a region of the UK is a difficult one for many people to take in.

The political agenda changed dramatically in 1999, with the enact-ment of the government policy of devolution, which Scotland and Wales had approved by referendums in 1997. A referendum on devolu-tion had been pledged by the New Labour Party (formerly called the Labour Party, until a lurch to the right after 1994) before its election. Some Labour MPs, especially its Scottish ones, welcomed devolution – John Smith, Labour leader before Tony Blair, had pushed for it – though many of the New Labour elite began to regret the promise of a devolution referendum when they came to government. Yet this promise had helped them to get elected in 1997 – the British Labour

Party has a large proportion of Scottish support, and needs Scottish votes – so they were forced to go through with it. In the 1990s Scottish New Labour MPs found themselves in the tricky yet familiar position of having to acknowledge Scottish national cultural 'distinctiveness' via some level of local power, while doing everything they could to keep the UK together. The most obvious strategy was to present Britain as *the* road to success – when Tony Blair became prime minister, the number two and number three in power in his cabinet, the Foreign Secretary and the Chancellor of the Exchequer, Robin Cook and Gordon Brown, were both Scots. When the government in power could present success as being down to Britishness, this strategy worked reasonably well, and certainly there were strongly Unionist periods after the Second World War. The road to London became less attractive however: at the *first* devolution referendum in 1979, the vote for devolution was only lost because of the suggestion of Labour MP George Cunningham that the rules be changed at the last moment, requiring a higher proportion of the vote than had been previously agreed.

During the post-1979 years of Margaret Thatcher's Conservative Party rule, which was increasingly unpopular in Scotland, devolution-ists made an effort to ensure that there would be no repeat of the mis-takes of the 1979 referendum. Thatcher herself, and John Major after her, showed a much remarked-upon lack of interest in Scotland. But the 1980s, a terrible time for Scotland economically, also saw an extraordinary rebirth in confidence in Scottish politics and culture, and a serious rethinking of what kind of thing Scotland was. The 1997 referendum was much more conclusive: 73.4 per cent of voters voted yes to a Scottish Parliament, and 63.5 per cent voted yes to the new Parliament's ability to alter taxes. In 1999 the Parliament was set up (on temporary premises), and Scottish elections took place. Scottish Labour ('Scottish' carefully replacing the epithet 'New', unpopular amongst traditional Scottish socialists) formed a coalition with the smaller Scottish Liberal Democrats, and the nation had a working Parliament again for the first time in almost 300 years. Wales also set up an Assembly at the same time, and Northern Ireland, a special case within the UK, worked along the guidelines of the Good Friday Agreement towards a form of devolution, treading carefully between presentations of devolution-as-national and devolution-as-regional. England has still not seriously discussed plans for a revival of its own Parliament, which had supposedly been given up in 1707, but has rather moved devolution forwards in regional terms under local authorities.

It is vital here to distinguish the Scottish Parliament from 'independence'. Although Murkens et al. (2003) are right to stress that under the present complicated constitutional circumstances, the UK should have to keep its promise to respect 'in principle' any clearly expressed national wish for independence, the Scottish Parliament cannot grant itself independence-like powers, and the British government will not hold a referendum on Scottish independence. In terms of sheer political power, not much has changed: the big issues, such as foreign policy and overall funding, remain British. Having a Parliament is certainly not 'becoming a nation again', as the opportunist press showed banners proclaiming on Edinburgh's Royal Mile in 1999, taking a line from the Scottish national anthem. Besides the fact that devolution did not bring a dramatic change in power, Scotland had never stopped being a nation. One question these banners raise is why awareness of what nationhood means is so low, considering the importance of the question to Scotland. The New Labour government, benefiting from any muddling of terms which helped people believe they were gaining more power, has actually encouraged such slogans, as they seem to celebrate British unity-in-diversity. Scholars such as Tom Nairn have argued therefore that the British government has viewed devolution as another useful means of re-shaping local British government in a way that avoids giving away any real extra powers.

Post-devolution research also tends to support a negative view of the future of the Parliament, by showing that hopes dropped between the high excitement of 1999 and the more realistic views of 2001. It is not yet known whether the British government has really miscalculated in giving Scotland the opportunity of national expression in the Parliament. But however disappointed people become with the actual performance of politicians, the process of devolution has raised questions about nationhood, power and identity, which will not go away easily. Directly after devolution, many Scots – particularly young Scots – believed that the new Parliament would naturally lead to total independence. It is uncertain whether the Scottish Parliament will be able to create for itself the power to leave Britain, or indeed to get around the power of the monarch, who remains the head of state. Even SNP Members of the Scottish Parliament (MSPs) finally have loyalty to the monarch.

To summarise the division of power: the UK Parliament still makes the most important decisions concerning international affairs, immigration and the amount of the overall state budget allotted to healthcare, education, and so on. The UK Parliament is located in Westminster, London, and has lower and upper chambers – the House of Commons and the House of Lords (increasingly 'elected' by the executive rather than a rising by heredity); in addition, laws must receive Royal Assent. The lower chamber's 659 Members of Parliament (MPs) are elected in seats in every part of Britain, including Scotland, though Scotland's number of MPs was set to decline slightly after devolution. Since 1999, these MPs have worked alongside the Scottish Parliament (in Edinburgh) and the Welsh Assembly (in Cardiff), sometimes in a tense co-existence and sometimes to the resentment of Unionists, who ask why particular 'regions' such as Scotland have double political representation. In Scotland, 129 MSPs are elected from seats throughout the country, so that Scots are indeed represented by both MPs and MSPs (as well as Members of the European Parliament, MEPs).

As representatives of a stateless nation, MSPs have no power to intervene into state questions such as foreign policy, though the Scottish Parliament allows them a forum to express opinions on these questions. It is vital to remember that international decisions since 1707 have *all* been British – neither Scotland nor England has had the power to make such decisions. (If you read in textbooks that 'England went to war with Germany' or 'England colonised India', you can regard this as simply wrong.) Many people feel that the most important change in 1999 was the ability to alter taxes – asked as a second question on the 1997 referendum ballot. Since Scotland has generally been a stronger supporter of the welfare state than England, Scottish taxes are liable to be slightly higher to cover the costs of hospitals, education, and so on. Research by both academics and political parties has shown that most Scots are in favour of slightly higher taxes if it means preserving the welfare state.

The law, the church and education, having remained Scottish in principle even after 1707, are still central pillars of identity. Media – broadcasting, newspapers, and so on – exist on both Scottish and British levels. Sports also take place on both Scottish and British levels; usually Scotland and England have separate sports teams, but in the Olympics, there is a unified British team, perhaps because

Olympic thinking is more suited to states than nations. Football (soccer) remains the key sport of Scottish identity; and football matches remain an important meeting place, traditionally for working-class men, though crowds have been much more mixed in recent years. Perhaps even more so than in England, pubs are a meeting-place. The pub – the *public house* – is frequently visible in culture, as the location for a nationality which is constantly having to renegotiate its sense of the *public*, in a nation with no state, *housed* within an increasingly distant state.

SUMMARY

- Scotland, like England, is a nation, but not a state. The state is the United Kingdom. Scotland and England can also be described as regions of the UK, though it is unusual for England to be described as a region.
- In 1707, today's Britain was formed. English elites in general did not take the Act of Union very seriously, while, especially after the mid-eighteenth century, most Scottish elites made a serious effort to create a new form of Britishness, and to partake of Britain's imperial power.
- Today most Scots do not feel British, but see their own Britishness as an historical accident. They are accustomed to a split in their identities between Scottishness and Britishness. If asked, the majority simply use 'Scottish' to describe their nationality.
- In 1999, via devolution, Scotland set up a Parliament and Wales an Assembly, creating locations for political discussion, and in Scotland a forum for a number of other decisions including the ability to alter taxes.
- Devolution in its present form arrived after a strong cultural revival in Scotland.
- The British Parliament still makes Britain's most important decisions; most British MPs tend to view devolution as a regional, rather than a national, process, and frequently fail to understand why Scots see devolution as national.
- Systems of law, education and religion have always been different in Scotland; this did not change in 1707 or in 1999. These civic structures have been particularly strong carriers of Scottish identity.

QUESTIONS FOR FURTHER RESEARCH AND THOUGHT

• Scots rarely confuse their own nation with the United Kingdom, whereas this confusion is quite common in England. Does Scotland's consciousness of nationhood have advantages?
• Around the time of devolution in Scotland and Wales (1999), British newspapers often talked of a growth of 'anti-English racism' in Scotland. Was this accusation fair?
• Would an independent Scottish state make it easier for immigrants to become Scottish, or harder?
• Does the Scottish Parliament reflect the concerns of the Scottish people better than the British Parliament?
• Is *English* national consciousness important to Scotland?

FURTHER READING

Ascherson, Neal, *Stone Voices*, London: Granta, 2003.
A respected voice in the British press as well as a scholar, here Ascherson branches out into a popular investigation of Scottishness.

Ash, Marinell, *The Strange Death of Scottish History*, Edinburgh: Ramsay Head, 1980.
An influential account of how the study of specifically Scottish history disappeared under the study of British history in the nineteenth century; coming a year after the failed first referendum on devolution, this book was prophetic in realising that the recovery of history would be instrumental to the recovery of political representation. To an extent it anticipates the themes of Christopher Whatley and Graeme Morton (see Chapter 3).

Bell, Eleanor, *Questioning Scotland*, London: Palgrave, 2004.
Bell considers the ways in which Scottish culture, especially literature, has often been discussed in parochial, essentialist terms. It begins with the modernist Scottish Renaissance, and goes on to examine the contemporary debates surrounding national identity, taking in postmodern arguments.

Beveridge, Craig and Ronald Turnbull, *The Eclipse of Scottish Culture: Inferiorism and the Intellectuals*, Edinburgh: Polygon, 1989.
Written from a nationalist viewpoint, this describes how Scots have, since the Act of Union, learned to internalise a sense of inadequacy, a habit even reflected in intellectual traditions.

Reid, Donald and Rob Humphreys, *The Rough Guide to Scotland*, 4th edn, London: Rough Guides, 2004.
As do almost all travel guides, this labours under the misapprehension that everything that happens in Edinburgh is more 'historical' than anywhere else; despite this, the book is detailed and entertaining.

Gardiner, Michael, *The Cultural Roots of British Devolution* Edinburgh: Edinburgh University Press, 2004.
This argues that we should see the culture preceding devolution, understood in its unstable and 'political' (as opposed to merely civic) sense, as part of a wider postcolonial process changing the whole nature of representation in the UK.

Keating, Michael, *Nations Against the State: The New Politics of Nationalism in Quebec, Catalonia, and Scotland*, London: Macmillan, 2001, first published 1996.
Although some writers (such as myself) have questioned the comparison of Scotland with Quebec and Catalunya, and the ethics of Keating's accounts of 'post-state' possibilities, this remains an important and provocative account of the rise of nations over states in the post-Cold-War era.

McCrone, David, *The Sociology of Nationalism*, London: Routledge, 1998.
Though not specifically about Scotland, this is strongly informed by the Scottish context; it is a very valuable introduction to nationalism amongst the many books on the subject.

McCrone, David, *Understanding Scotland: the Sociology of a Stateless Nation*, London: Routledge: 2001, first published 1992.
One of the most celebrated books written on Scotland, this has gone on to widespread fame. Accurate and disengaged, it established Scotland's status as stateless nation in the public imagination. It is not often noted that it was preceded by Jacques Leruez's *Ecosse: Un Nation Sans Etat.* Sometimes accused of covert Unionism, for example by Beveridge and Turnbull, McCrone has gone on more recently to see the stateless nation somewhat pragmatically in terms of its efficiency, rather than more ethical concerns.

Morley, David and Kevin Robins (eds), *British Cultural Studies*, Oxford: Oxford University Press, 2001.
This is the best of a series of collections of essays on British culture; there are important essays on Blair's Britishness, the possible recovery of England, the countryside, the English language, and other topics.

Murkens, Eric Jo et al., *Scottish Independence: A Practical Guide*, Edinburgh: Edinburgh University Press, 2003.
This is an interesting and thoroughly researched investigation of *how* Scotland might become independent, and the legal status of the union.

Nairn, Tom, *The Break-Up of Britain: Crisis and Neo-Nationalism*, London: NLB, 1977.
This is a book to be read by anyone interested in Scottish Studies; it is extremely influential, not only in Scotland but around the world. It describes how the Romanticism necessary to build a Scottish nationalism in the nineteenth century was lacking, and the consequences of this.

Nairn, Tom, *After Britain*, London: Granta, 2000.
A key post-referendum account of how devolution seems to imply a slide to independence which New Labour completely misunderstands, it is both readable and incisive. It is made up of a number of essays and the texts of talks.

Paterson, Lindsay, *The Autonomy of Modern Scotland,* **Edinburgh: Edinburgh University Press, 1994.**
Although Paterson is primarily known as an educationalist, this account of Scotland's administration remains a classic. To some extent it can be read in the same frame as David McCrone's interest in how Scots have learned to negotiate 'stateless nation' status. It is perhaps the best guide to Scotland's 'civic' nationalism and the state of its government of Scotland before devolution.

Paterson, Lindsay et al., *New Scotland, New Politics?,* **Edinburgh: Polygon, 2001.**
The first important post-devolution guide to the feelings of Scottish people about key issues of political identification.

Pittock, Murray, *Scottish Nationality,* **Houndmills: Palgrave, 2001.**
Pittock is one of the sharpest and most scholarly analysts of Scotland's situation; here he weaves original research into a general account of how nationalism and national consciousness have related to other historical processes.

Scott, P. H. (ed.), *Scotland: A Concise Cultural History,* **Edinburgh: Mainstream, 1993.**
A collection of essays on Scottish culture. Scott, a former diplomat, was talking about the implications of constitutional change on the Scotland-Britain relationship long before it was fashionable; his often-prophetic journal articles and other books are also worth seeking out.

Scottish Affairs: http://www.scottishaffairs.org/
One Scotland: http://www.onescotland.com/

CHAPTER 2

Cultural History I: Before 1822

When Queen Elizabeth I of England died in 1603, King James VI of Scotland succeeded to the English throne, becoming James I of England, and the first monarch to rule both countries – a Union of Crowns. This was a relief for London politicians; England had been unsuccessfully attempting to exercise control over Scotland for centuries, and had already formally annexed Wales in 1536, without much fuss and using ideas of a shared Tudor heritage. For the preceding few centuries England had been pushing for more influence in Scottish church and government, and there had been frequent wars and almost constant tension between the two states.

The English government's view of Scotland was that it *had* to be annexed: not only did it offend polite society by being dangerous and savage (like Ireland), it also had an outdated system of politics reliant on the clan system, which, if not modernised, could threaten the English system of primogeniture (divine right), in which power derived from God and could only be passed in blood lines from father to son. Justification for wars against the rogue state of Scotland is the main theme of Shakespeare's *Macbeth*, performed in 1606 for the new King James VI/James I, who was already thinking about cultural adjustments for full governmental union between the two states, and who approved of Shakespeare's slightly obsequious unionism. In a pattern that would become familiar, proper history was Anglo-British history: in *Macbeth*, when primogeniture is threatened, so is the *correct passage of time* itself; nothing seems in its right place or *right time*, nature is offended, and fair is foul (but then the Scottish weather is an easy target). Shakespeare realises, in other words, that history after any union or takeover of Scotland will 'naturally' remain English history, otherwise it will not be history at all. *Macbeth* remains an uncanny anticipation of the 'forgetting' of Scottish history which would take place in the nineteenth century. Behind the Shakespearean intellectual package of modernisation, however, there were also more down-to-earth English fears of being surrounded on both sides by enemies – the Gallo-Scottish *auld alliance*.

Within a year or so James had realised that governmental union would be more difficult than he had imagined and he had shelved his plans, but further attempts were pursued in 1667 and 1670, and the English desire for union was accelerated by the 'Glorious Revolution' of 1688, in which the line of William and Mary (the House of Hanover) took over the British throne, making Protestantism – in the form of the Church of England – culturally central to Britishness and its budding empire. From 1688, Catholic Scots of the older Stewart line, or even simply anti-union Scots, were seen as a danger in re-asserting their rights to the throne; ensuring a Protestant-Hanoverian succession for the whole of the kingdom became *the* priority for the new British government.

This is not to say that the Act of Union was forced on Scotland. By the Parliamentary standards of the time, the Act was a fair agreement. After a series of disastrous harvests in the 1690s, and the hugely expensive failure of an attempt to create a colony in Darien in Central America in the mid-1690s – moving Sir John Clerk of Penicuik to compose *Leo Scotiae Irriratatus* (*The Scottish Lion Angered*) – Scotland's government was under severe economic and psychological pressure. Aware of Scotland's difficulties, England blocked its sea ports to Scottish use, preventing import and export via the southern route (as in today's 'economic sanctions'). Tensions further increased in 1701 when the Scottish Act of Security pressed for the right to name a non-Hanoverian successor – an early *Jacobite* move, with the word Jacobite being taken from the Latin word for James, James II of Britain being seen by anti-Hanoverians as the rightful heir in opposition to the Glorious Revolution. The decisive moment came in 1705, when the English Alien Act threatened to remove the rights of Scots resident in England unless Scotland agreed to a political union accepting the Hanoverian succession.

So at the heart of this build-up of tensions leading to union was, on the one hand, England's fear of a non-Hanoverian Catholic monarch occupying the united throne (distasteful enough in itself but also suggesting the strengthening of Scotland's French connections); and on the other hand, Scottish economic desperation, and desire for access to the colonial opportunities opening up in the Americas. And, as T. M. Devine has recently shown, the English navy was also readying itself near the south-west of Scotland, suggesting a possible military strike if Scotland did not agree to union. Decisively, there were also the 'bribes' given to the impoverished nobles who sat in the Scottish Parliament to persuade them to dissolve it. A political union was finally negotiated in 1706, and a depleted and impoverished Scottish Parliament voted itself out of power on 25 March 1707. This was the last time a Scottish Parliament would meet until 1999.

The union of governments brought the following conditions: the Hanoverian Queen Anne would be the next monarch, and her successors would also be Hanoverian; there would be economic convergence, with Scotland having access to English trade but also bearing a part of England's debt; immediate financial aid of £400,000 was given to Scotland; and Scotland was to have forty-five seats in the British

Figure 2.1   Act of Union. (Source: National Archives of Scotland, SP13/210.)

House of Commons (the lower chamber) and sixteen in the House of Lords (the upper chamber). In practice, most of the MPs' constituencies contained few voters, and many would come to be manipulated by Henry Dundas, nicknamed 'Henry the Ninth' because of the political power he held. Scotland's powers to control its own laws, education and religion, were to be respected in principle, though in practice they would be eroded by English constitutional custom.

Although the union was agreed by both Parliaments, only a few ministers took part in the voting procedure. Parliamentary debates on union were poorly attended, and even then mostly by pro-union Scottish members of Parliament, landowning nobles who stood to gain financially. Amongst Scots as a whole, there was in general more hostility. There would be popular anti-union demonstrations in the Scottish cities for the next three decades or so; in the north and west, there was military reaction by Jacobites. Even before the union, after the Glorious Revolution of 1688, a Convention Parliament declared that James II/James VII had illegally given up the throne to William of Orange; at this point embryonic Jacobite movements had begun to form, and these movements would haunt the British union until 1746.

Soon after the union, a Jacobite military rebellion took place in 1708, which recent research has shown to be more popular than once thought (though it was disorganised and unsuccessful). When Queen Anne died in 1714, the Jacobites saw another chance to intervene before the succession of George I; Highland Scottish clans joined and fought at Dunblane, near Stirling, in a campaign today known as 'the '15', but they were suppressed by the new British army. Opposition to the union was not limited to Highland clans; notable examples of popular rebellion include the 1724 Glasgow riots in opposition to a new British salt tax, and the 1736 Edinburgh 'Porteous Riots' in which, at the hanging of two tax evaders, the Town Guard worsened a tense situation by firing into the crowd and killing a number of people, an incident described in Walter Scott's historical novel *Heart of Midlothian* (1818).

One effect of the Porteous Riots was the appointment of the Duke of Argyll to help oversee Scotland's incorporation into Britain, an act of compromise which accustomed Scots to living *as Scots*, but *within Britain*. This would colour the stance of most ambitious Scots from the 1740s to the 1990s: while stressing their Scottishness 'culturally', they used their Britishness practically. We could see this negatively as pragmatic and cynical, but in practice Scots had little choice. Nor was Walter Scott himself free from this 'Unionist Nationalism' (a phrase which will return later); although painting the Jacobite as a *noble savage* of the kind beloved of Romantics, he was also conscious of writing for a British audience centred in London, the capital of a new British state which, as a Tory, he saw in terms of opportunity.

The most serious and famous Jacobite rebellion came in 1745–6, when the young Charles Edward Stewart (Bonnie Prince Charlie), asserting his right to the throne, assembled a Jacobite army and marched from the Highlands to Edinburgh ('triumphantly' according to some accounts; to relative apathy according to others). During the decades of rebellion the British army had taken the opportunity to strengthen military roads to make Jacobite rebellion more controllable. Before General Wade's programme of road building from the 1720s, it had taken ten days to travel from Inverness to Edinburgh. Ironically, the British road system also made it easier for the Jacobite army of 1745 to advance, though their campaign was again unsuccessful. Although Charlie expected to gather popular support in Edinburgh, and to meet with promised French forces, Edinburgh's anger was tempered by the city's relative prosperity after union, and French support failed to appear. Charles Edward Stuart continued to march south, but stopped at Derby, in the English Midlands, largely because English counter-intelligence had made his army believe that a vast English force was ready nearby.

In some confusion, the Jacobite forces were soon pursued back north into Scotland where, exhausted, they were massacred at Culloden on 15–16 April 1746. Many of the most dangerous clans were singled out and eliminated (thus the term *massacre*). This was followed by the 1746 Disarming Act, which attempted to remove any signs of Scottish culture that would imply a desire for independence, outlawing the wearing of tartan and banning the holding of arms. Thereafter, there was a strong British propaganda push against the Jacobites and – somewhat illogically, given the status of the union as partnership – against Scots as such, who were often seen as savage yet calculating. The tendency to see Scotland as a threat is exemplified by the infamous verse added to the British national anthem 'God Save the Queen', a verse that encouraged the British army 'rebellious Scots to crush'. This in itself is a good indication of England's blindspot as to what union entailed.

In unionist accounts, the Jacobites are often described as a disparate bunch of idealists who failed to muster support in the Scottish
capital. Scottish nationalists, on the other hand, tend to see the 1745–6
episode as a near miss, only spoiled by English espionage and French
disorganisation, a rebellion that left a living legacy. What is downplayed by nationalists is the way in which, by the early 1740s, the
Lowlands were feeling the economic benefits of the colonialism made
possible by the British union; Glasgow merchants and Edinburgh
bankers were by 1740 rapidly becoming wealthy from tobacco planta-
tions in the Americas, and Scots were now able to use English ports
without interference. Edinburgh grew rapidly as a financial centre
(and remains one of Europe's most important financial centres today),
and Glasgow flourished as a commercial centre, growing rich on
imperial tobacco. In 1695 an Act of Parliament created the Bank of
Scotland in Edinburgh; in a post-union anti-Jacobite atmosphere,
however, the 'Old Bank' was seen by some Unionists as a quasi-
nationalist institution, and so was created the Royal Bank in 1727.
Today these banks exist side by side and issue their own banknotes,
which *are pounds sterling* (despite what the newsagent at Luton
Airport tells you).

By the time of the Enlightenment, many Scots were travelling
south to England to find their fortunes, and Scottish literary figures
were writing in such tones of praise of the new Britishness that what
English people only gradually accepted as Britain – if they accepted it
at all – largely grew as a popular movement amongst middle-class
Scots; this makes a nonsense of the idea that 'British culture' arose
from an English imposition. This Scottish Enlightenment moment,
ironically, sees the origins of Anglo-British and imperial fields of
study, such as the discipline later known as 'English Literature'. Adam
Smith's *Lectures in Rhetoric* in the 1740s to 1760s were a candid
attempt to rid Scottish students of their provincial accents and speak
'good' English; the first chair in the nascent subject of English
Literature was at Edinburgh University in 1762; and Lord Kames's
Elements of Criticism, also published in 1762, was at one point the best-
selling book in the Anglophone world. Scotland, in other words, is in
large part behind the subject of 'English'.

After 1746 and various subsequent British imperial successes
against France (the Seven Years' War, the Napoleonic Wars), most
Scots came to embrace union and to attempt to better themselves

within it; England kept its default role as the advanced centre, and union stood for opportunity for most people. In 1740, in the musical *The Masque of Alfred*, the Scot James Thomson's song 'Rule, Britannia!' was first performed; it later became an imperial anthem which celebrated the naval power of Britain to 'rule the waves'. In 1742, the Scottish philosopher David Hume was beginning to publish his *Essays Political and Moral*, which, although critical of London politics, praised the 'balance' of the three estates – royal, parliamentary and ecclesiastical – held together by the English constitution (a collection of habits and legal precedents); Hume's *Of National Characters* (1748) notoriously holds up England as the most advanced of all peoples, and his major historical project takes England, not Scotland, as its object.

The point to be made here – one that may be difficult to grasp, but is summed up by the term Unionist Nationalism, recently used as the title of Graeme Morton's influential study – is that there grew up a cultural duality able to retain 'Scottishness' as an everyday lived national identity *within Britain*. Early nineteenth-century literary figures like Walter Scott exemplify this by seeing Britain as the sensible part of a Scottish individual – the 'head' – while the 'heart' is portrayed increasingly nostalgically as a wistful form of memory which can never be realised as a state again. Indeed, the retention of Scottish specificity within Britishness can be seen as a central tenet of the wide-ranging movement known as the Scottish Enlightenment.

During the very wide period that Murray Pittock and others have defined as 'Enlightenment' – a mid-eighteenth century movement spreading well into the late nineteenth (that is, well beyond the previous imagined boundaries of Enlightenment which were placed around the 1790s) – there were an extraordinary number of technological advances in Scotland. John Anderson, who founded what would become Strathclyde University, one of Britain's foremost technological institutions, Joseph Black, the pioneer in latent and specific heat, and James Watt, who developed steam engineering, were all born within a decade of one another – 1726–36. As the Enlightenment (the Pittock projection) continued, James Clark Maxwell discovered electromagnetism, important to the development of the radio; Lord Kelvin was an all-round physics pioneer who helped lay the first transatlantic telegraph cable; John Macintyre pioneered the use of x-rays for medical purposes; Alexander Graham Bell invented the telephone; John Macadam created a road surface; and, later, John Logie Baird pioneered television – in a sense the ultimate Enlightenment instrument since, travelling at the speed of light, it reduces the world to what can be *known* by being *seen*. As I suggested before, it is telling how many of these inventions pertain to communications, as if Scotland is over-sensitive to its remoteness from the British state. With TV the time it takes a picture to travel from Edinburgh to London is zero seconds, and Scots have successfully collapsed the distance to the centre of empire.

Also during the Enlightenment period (Traditional Projection) there were created numerous gentlemen's clubs – perhaps most famously the Select Society – societies which often saw Edinburgh as a miniature version of London. James Craig's plan for Edinburgh New Town, in the shape of a British union flag, is not far from the reality – wide streets spreading out laterally from central gardens and given pro-Hanoverian, pro-British names. Edinburgh had become a centre for all sorts of culture, including publishing. The *People's Journal*, featuring Scottish historical stories, began around the turn of the century, as did the *Edinburgh Review*. The *Edinburgh Monthly* magazine was started in 1817, later becoming known as *Blackwood's*

Figure 2.2   The majority of those involved in creating and maintaining Edinburgh's New Town thought that union was the only way forward. Almost all of the streets have Royalist, British names. (Photograph: Michael Gardiner.)

magazine, one of Victorian Britain's most important vehicles for stories and comment, with its eyes firmly fixed on London. There was also a rapid increase in museum space during this period, again reflecting the desire to *know* and *place* the outside world.

So the Edinburgh of this phase becomes authoritative by retaining its relation to London and promoting its own knowledge-through-vision, and in a sense this tendency has never really gone away. The abiding popularity of Edinburgh in its 'historical' New Town form amongst young Britons is displayed at the outset of the film *Shallow Grave* (1995), which opens with a camera speeding over the 'historical' cobbled streets and moves to its middle-class Anglo-Scottish heroes in proprietorial mood, sizing up potential flatmates over their suitability for this exclusive residence. The candidate for whom they reserve the most abuse even has the name of a Highland clan – Cameron. Yet the New Town is a perfect example of how British individualistic civility tended to consume itself: where philosophical ideas of the role of the individual grew up in an Old Town community which necessitated living in close proximity, ideas of individualism were acted out in the new, large, separated houses of the New Town, destroying the proximity and so the exchange of those very ideas. Such is Britishness: in its beginning is its end.

Here it is important to remember, firstly, that the Scottish Enlightenment's obsession with knowledge not only contributed to individual fields of study (English Literature and so on), but that it also helped create the very categories within which we now think – ideas of democracy and freedom we now take for granted; and secondly, that despite its Europhilia, the Enlightenment was largely about Scots getting to the centre of a new British culture. The way in which the 1746 Disarming Act attempted to destroy the immanent signs of Scottishness is not surprising, given the new British government's keenness to unify and the constant danger of war with France. What is more remarkable is that, by 1782, the ban on tartan had been lifted, suggesting that it had already been incorporated safely into the family of Britishness and had already lost its previous status as a fearful sign of independence. The overall result is a semi-autonomous and 'locally proud' Scotland under the umbrella of Britain: Unionist Nationalism. Visible Scottishness's new incorporation into 'British culture' was confirmed as early as 1822, when Walter Scott organised for King George IV's visit to Edinburgh a strange mock-Highland

Figure 2.3   Scott Monument, Princes Street, Edinburgh. (Photograph: Michael Gardiner.)

spectacle themed on 'tartans' worn by 'clansmen', as he named the British politicians. During the Enlightenment (Traditional Projection), despite much residual antagonism towards the union, official Britishness had been helped by profits from the colonised Americas, and later in 'East India', in both of which imperial situations Scots were extremely active. This made the British family of dodgy tartans seem like a good idea at the time, even though in some rural parts of Scotland itself poverty, and even famine, continued at least into the 1770s.

Edinburgh professionals and Glasgow merchants thus increasingly succeeded to the *haute bourgeoisie* and consolidated their positions with rural and urban property (today, estate agents are equally fulsome about Edinburgh properties). By the 1770s Edinburgh's elegant New Town had become a symbol of the unionist times, as can be seen in the Hanoverian naming of the streets. The city was viewed as a northern London by many Edinburgh professionals, and still is, to an extent, today.

Scots were even more central to the formation of Britain's global empire during the nineteenth century, taking up a disproportionately high number of imperial British positions as engineers, administrators, 'explorers' and diplomats. Although this sometimes had a positive influence, particularly in the *settler colonies* (colonies where white people resettled: for example, Australia and New Zealand together produced twelve leaders with Scottish backgrounds, and Scots were involved in democratic revolts in both the USA and Canada), Scottish imperial soldiers became famous for their ruthlessness. The Scottish soldier/adventurer had by the mid-nineteenth century become a symbol of colonial pride: Scottish military commanders included Ralph Abercrombie, Charles Stuart, David Baird and John Moore; notable 'explorers'/colonists included Mungo Park in West Africa, Alexander Mackenzie in the Arctic Sea, James Bruce of Kinnaird at the source of the Blue Nile, and David Livingstone, who was famously 'found' by H. M. Stanley (in fact Stanley, who was himself lost without his native guides, had a gift for media spin). Yet at the same time as Scots were moving south to London and into the empire, there was significant immigration: from the early nineteenth century, there was an influx of people including Lithuanians, Poles and Asians. Italians arriving later in the century introduced a cafe culture which would still be the focus for young people in the 1950s and would provide Scotland's staple food, the fish supper (fish and chips).

In the late eighteenth century it was common for Scottish unionist writers to describe Scotland as 'North Britain'; indeed *The North Briton* was the name of a literary review of the time (needless to say, England was rarely described as 'South Britain'). Intellectuals like David Hume aimed early at a Britishness centred on English civility – involving, certainly, an ambivalent feeling of resentment, and interfering with Hume's own belief that Scottish literature and philosophy were far ahead of those in England (and the oft-repeated story that Adam Smith was appalled by the low standards at Oxford after his study at Glasgow). In England, meanwhile, Scots' ambitions were met not so much with derision as with lack of interest. Yet Scottish Enlightenment thinking was immensely influential on the revolutionary USA as well as other parts of the English-speaking world. We know, for example, that William Robertson and John Witherspoon were taught on numerous college courses in the States in the 1820s, and the rhetoric of the American Constitution itself, though touched by the contemporary American rhetoric of Thomas Paine, can be linked directly to Scottish Enlightenment writing, as Garry Wills and scholars after him have suggested.

There was thus a paradoxical imperialism *and* liberationism in Scots' taking part in empire, as if Scottish nationalism was exported in British form, or as if the Scottish state had disappeared and gone underground in the US. Yet despite a strong Scottish Enlightenment influence on American revolutionaries, pro–Britain Scottish intellectuals also spoke out during the American war: the poet Allan Ramsay, for example, was one advocate of a strong Anglo-American empire; David Hume's *History of England* (1754–61), unlike Adam Smith's later *Wealth of Nations* (1776), was imperial and Anglocentric not only in its choice of theme but also in promoting England as *the* model of Anglophone civility.

Over-aware of its own newly provincial status (and thus obsessed with travel, science and *speed*), Scotland from the Enlightenment period of adaptation onwards got itself stuck with a 'cultural cringe', in which the local (national) culture is an automatic source of embarrassment in the face of a more polite neighbour. The cultural cringe has now been more or less overcome, at least amongst intellectuals, but only very recently. Sometimes TV programmes like *Rab C. Nesbitt* or writers like Irvine Welsh are still described in terms of a cultural cringe, since they seem to portray the parochial or the pathetic; this may be, however, a disingenuous reading, since it implies that to be really sincere a culture must also be incapable of self-parody. Self-parody, on the contrary, might be described as perfectly healthy in a national culture. Some commentators (typically middle-class academics and journalists) actually *fortify* the cultural cringe by demanding a culture constipated by its own sense of self-worth.

In any case, Enlightenment Anglocentrism led to what Marinell Ash called a 'strange death of Scottish history' at the hands of 'Whig historiography', meaning a reliance on the assumption that a quietly reforming moralism always gradually leads us to more advanced forms of society, and that this pattern should not be broken by any sudden movement, such as that made by France in 1789. Though requiring some generalisation, we can say that Scottish society after Enlightenment gradually came under the sway of Whig historiography. This is not surprising considering the benefits of empire, which were central to how progress was mapped out. If we look during this time for Scottish culture which is politically Nationalist in the sense we understand it today, we are met with a deafening silence. In early to mid-Victorian Scottish literature, there is a blank for which there is no equivalent in the history of literature in England, one that, however Scottish literary scholars struggle to fill it, remains bleak. One of Scotland's most celebrated sons, Thomas Carlyle, even argued mid-century that the images of Scottishness were fit to be used in culture, but that they should be removed from any national historical context so as not to alarm the reader (thus also Carlyle's determination to reduce social history to the actions not of societies but of a few isolated individuals, or 'Great Men'). In essays of the 1820s, Carlyle was describing Scotland as incapable of national patriotism, as later in the 1970s Tom Nairn, from a very different ethical position, would diagnose the loss of Scottish national action. Scottish culture seemed to have been entirely subsumed under the British state.

SUMMARY:

- England and Scotland have shared the same monarch since 1603, when James VI of Scotland became James I of England.
- Before the eighteenth century, England had worried for centuries about the threat of Scotland's alliance with France, and had tried to extend its influence over Scotland.
- James VI/I was a keen unionist; his plans for union failed, but there were many more attempts to join the governments throughout the seventeenth century.
- In 1688, the Glorious Revolution established the British Protestant succession; many Scottish Jacobites, especially Catholics and Highlanders, rose against this.
- As a result of English legal, economic and military pressure, and also as a result of to Scottish poverty, a union of governments was enacted in 1707.
- There were popular riots against the union in 1724 and 1736, and Jacobite rebellions in 1708, 1715, and 1745–6; the last of these ended in the almost total suppression of Jacobite rebels.
- From the early 1740s, Scotland began to feel the union's and empire's economic benefits; culturally, it increasingly adapted to union, especially after legal measures of 1746.
- The Scottish Enlightenment is by far the best known period of the

nation's cultural history. It is usually seen as being based in Edinburgh, but also belonged in Glasgow and Aberdeen. It used to be timed at about the 1740s to 1790s, but recently scholars have extended this timescale both backwards (Broadie, Beveridge and Turnbull), and forwards (Pittock).

• The Enlightenment represented a growth of knowledges ranging very widely through the arts and sciences, and indeed the very dividing-up of these knowledges into academic disciplines.

• As empire expanded, so signs of Scottish identity such as 'tartanry' adapted to a British form.

QUESTIONS FOR FURTHER RESEARCH AND THOUGHT

• How much choice did Scotland have in signing the Act of Union?
• How can we know how ordinary Scottish people felt about union in its first half-century? How about English people?
• Was the Enlightenment a pro-union break from the old Scottish culture, or a continuation of it?
• What kind of record do Scots have on slavery?
• Was Walter Scott's reception of the British monarch in 1822 a kind of parody, a kind of obsequiousness, or a real expression of political Nationalism?

FURTHER READING

Beveridge, Craig and Ronald Turnbull, *The Eclipse of Scottish Culture: Inferiorism and the Intellectuals*, Edinburgh: Polygon, 1989. See Introduction.

Broadie, Alexander, *The Scottish Enlightenment*, Edinburgh: Polygon, 2001.
A highly readable account of the period's intellectual history from a figure who is perhaps the world's foremost expert on it; one could raise questions about Broadie's acceptance of the progressiveness of Enlightenment.

Calder, Angus, *Revolutionary Empire: The Rise of the English-Speaking Empires from the fifteenth Century to the 1780s*, London: Cape, 1981.
An enormous study covering a period up to about the end of the Enlightenment; both informative and narrative.

Campbell, R. H. and Andrew S. Skinner (eds), *The Origins and Nature of the Scottish Enlightenment*, Edinburgh: John Donald, 1982.
A collection of papers by a range of influential writers on Enlightenment and Scottish history; like much writing on the Enlightenment, it tends to be relatively uncritical about the idea of universal development, stressing Reason over revelation.

Colley, Linda, *Britons: Forging the Nation 1707–1837*, London: Pimlico, 2003, first published 1992.
Unloved by nationalists, this account is nevertheless probably the most thorough and important history of the creation of 'British culture', late eighteenth-century British empire, and Scots' place in it.

Devine, T. M., *The Scottish Nation: A History 1700–2000*, London: Penguin, 2000.
This is perhaps the definitive history of modern Scotland so far, and also a bestseller. Devine draws on decades of research and also offers some distinctively new stresses. It is both highly readable and highly popular.

Devine, T. M., *Scotland's Empire 1600–1815*, London: Allen Lane, 2003.
A guide to Scotland's participation in empire (though not *as* Scotland, but as individual Scots); it is written with a tone of authority backed up by immense research. Devine's numerous early books are also worth seeking out.

Fry, Michael, *The Scottish Empire*, Edinburgh: Birlinn, 2001.
A very thoroughly researched account, though it is oddly celebratory of empire, and spends much time relating stories of individual Scottish successes; nevertheless, it is an important unionist addition to the understanding of the 'imperial' origins of Scottish Nationalism.

Harvie, Christopher, *Scotland and Nationalism*, 3rd edn, London: Routledge, 1998, first published 1977.
A classic account of the relationship between nationalism, national thinking, and culture; highly authoritative, insightful, and acidly funny. Start here or with Devine.

Harvie, Christopher, *Scotland: A Short History*, Oxford: Oxford University Press, 2002, pp. 1–142.
A scholarly and entertaining short history. Harvie's more minor publications are also worth finding.

Hook, Andrew and Richard Sher (eds), *The Glasgow Enlightenment*, East Linton: Tuckwell, 1995.
Essays on social history that act as an interesting corrective to the idea that the Enlightenment happened in Edinburgh alone.

Kidd, Colin, *Subverting Scotland's Past: Scottish Whig Historians and the Creation of an Anglo-British Identity, 1689–c. 1830*, Cambridge: Cambridge University Press, 1993.
This influentially follows the growth of Whig histories through the 'forgetting' of Scottish history.

Meikle, Henry W., *Scotland and the French Revolution*, Glasgow: James Maclehose and Sons, 1912.
Not easy to find, but it is illuminating on the effects of 1789 on the Scottish intelligentsia.

Morton, Graeme, *Unionist Nationalism: Governing Urban Scotland, 1830–1860*, East Linton: Tuckwell, 1999.
Highly-acclaimed account of the 'semi-state' thinking of Victorian Scots.

Pittock, Murray G. H., *Jacobitism*, Basingstoke: Macmillan, 1998.
This debates the legitimacy or otherwise of the Jacobite image, who it belonged to, how it was used, and the influence it had.

Pittock, Murray G. H., *Celtic Identity and the British Image*, Manchester: Manchester University Press, 1999.
A thorough cultural analysis of the early union period, involving a wealth of new research, and including perspectives on 'otherness' and gender.

Pittock, Murray G. H., *Scotland: A New History*, Stroud: Sutton, 2003.
A brief history, but one which also takes account of new research in the field; it is readable and very contemporary.

Scott, P. H., *1707: The Union of England and Scotland*, Edinburgh: Saltire, 1979.
One of a number of studies of the period by this leading nationalist.

Smout, T. C., *A History of the Scottish People, 1560–1830*, London: Fontana, 1985, first published 1969.
One of the most influential books of Scottish history, and one that coloured the output of a generation of historians.

Whatley, Christopher, *Scottish Society 1707–1830*, Manchester: Manchester University Press, 2000.
A highly rated and readable account of the period.

Wills, Gary, *The Invention of America*, New York: Doubleday, 1975.
Wills places Hutcheson, Hume and Smith behind the Declaration of Independence; this is a close reading of the document which redefines the Declaration away from assumptions of English Lockean roots.

Wormald, Jenny, *The New History of Scotland Vol. 4: Court, Kirk, and Community, 1470–1625*, London: Edward Arnold, 1981; Rosalind Mitchison, *The New History of Scotland Vol. 5: Lordship to Patronage, 1603–1745*, London; Edward Arnold, 1981; Bruce Lenman, *The New History of Scotland Vol. 6, Integration, Enlightenment, and Industrialization, 1746–1832*, (London: Edward Arnold, 1981.
Highly readable and authoritative narrative histories; they are slightly more detailed than newer, consolidated histories, and more centred on individually important figures.

Historic Scotland: http://www.historic-scotland.gov.uk/

Highland Clearances Stories: http://www.theclearances.org/

BBC Scottish History: http://www.bbc.co.uk/history/scottish history /index.shtml

CHAPTER 3

Cultural History II: After 1822

In the previous chapter I suggested that the way in which the 1746 Disarming Act attempted to remove the signs of Scottishness is less surprising than the fact that, as early as 1782, the ban on tartan had been lifted. The implication is that it had already been confidently incorporated into Britishness, losing its previous status as a fearful sign of independence. Scottish national dress's new Britain-friendliness was confirmed with King George IV's visit to Edinburgh in 1822. This marked a new phase of Scottish culture in the sense that, even were we to read the Enlightenment as strongly 'national', now symbols of nationalism could be paraded in the knowledge that they would not constitute a threat to the British state, and could even add to it. Official love of the apparently pacified Highlands peaked with Queen Victoria's time spent at Balmoral in the 1840s. After the death of her husband Albert in 1848, Victoria settled there for a time, and the pairing of Victoria and her ghillie (manservant) has been dramatised by the film *Mrs Brown* (1997), bringing together the unlikely combination of Dame Judi Dench and the Glasgow comedian Billy Connolly. Despite Connolly's left-leaning politics, the film portrays a typical marriage of English gentility to Scottish roughness, and with the appropriate gender roles – Connolly playing burly masculine to Dench's confounded but slightly charmed noblewoman – a classic expression of the gendered and class-fixed portrayal of Scots' encounter with the English.

Unionist Nationalist culture would occupy the mainstream throughout the Victorian period, as Scotland refined its civic (or cultural) identity in the absence of state government. In early Victorian times there grew up a cult of national heroes centred on William Wallace and Robert Burns, to an extent following Thomas Carlyle's edict to see history as the progress of Great Men, itself an heir of the Enlightenment's emphasis on individual achievement. Wallace, for example, is seen as resisting takeover in the Wars of Independence only in order to pave the way for a better settlement in union, rather than to gain endless independence. The 1860s saw the widespread popularity of a contemporary version of Blin Harry's *Wallace* (1772). T. S. Burnett's 1883 *Rob Roy*, late-Victorian sculpture and painting The ever-expanding 'Burns Cult' was the kind of (typically unionist) exaltation of individual heroes over general cultural movements which would attract the anger of cultural nationalists of the 1920s. Nevertheless, this remains the way many see Scottish cultural history, with the films *Braveheart* and *Rob Roy* being amongst the Hollywood hits of the 1990s, effectively ethnicising and Britishing the Scot all over again in a new global form of Unionist Nationalism. Something of the logic of the great hero tradition can even be seen continuing to the establishment of the Scottish National Portrait Gallery, a canon of individual models, in 1889.

   The Britishness created in the late eighteenth century was increasingly encouraged by colonialism in the Americas, and later in 'East India', where Scots were extremely active, and the imperial Scottish-British soldier in traditional national dress became a sign for imperial terror. Meanwhile, Scottish science was advancing, within the knowing-and-classifying ethic of Enlightenment, which also lent itself readily to racism. The 'bodysnatchers' Burke and Hare, who caused a popular scandal at the time are in a sense a perfect example of Scottish imperialism – colonised Irish settlers digging up bodies to sell to the Edinburgh anatomist Robert Knox – who published his notorious *The Races of Man* in 1850. Scientific racism would later be carried forward in imperialism's second, 1890s phase by another Scot, Alfred Milner, and the 'ethnic' explanation of what makes a Scot, as we have seen, is still largely colloquially accepted. Significantly, Scotland is today still a world leader in genetics research, and Scottish scientists pioneered single-cell cloning, the start of the final stage of the conquering of DNA. A single British craziness links the ideas, thinking that you can 'own' a range of mountains, and thinking that you can 'copyright' a species. Both are symptoms of the same lunatic reading of the 'Free' of Adam Smith's 'Free Trade'.

As Christopher Harvie has pointed out, the figure of the soldier remained respectable in Victorian Scottish families whereas in English families the army was often seen as a social dustbin for the untalented son. From the 1830s Caledonian societies exported a kilted, martial Scottishness mostly to settler colonies; following the pattern of 1822, empire had inherited this imagery from Jabobitism. Scottish 'traditions' would be exaggerated by settlers and, not surprisingly, much of the former British empire now finds it difficult to be sympathetic to Scottish Nationalism, since Victorian Scottish Unionist Nationalism celebrated some of Britain's worst colonial atrocities. Occasionally Scottish colonisers had a reforming influence, particularly in settler colonies: the political ranks of Australia, New Zealand and Canada were packed with Scots. What is less known is that Scotland's reforming influence even stretched to the *exploitation colonies* (colonies ruled by whites but still mostly populated by native people): for example, Allan Hume founded the Indian National Congress, India's eventual organ of independence, in 1885. Ironically, in 1857 the Indian Mutiny had been put down by his countryman Major Clyde, and the cities of Delhi and Lucknow were redesigned for maximum imperial surveillance by Lord Napier (see Chapter 11).

Where American investments in tobacco, sugar and even slaves had made Glasgow prosperous in the mid-eighteenth century, the influx of people from the Highlands and Ireland in the nineteenth century provided a workforce that helped give Glasgow its reputation as an imperial engineering city (as *the* imperial engineering city). Scotland was still relatively wealthy compared to the UK as a whole as late as 1900, so that it is not surprising that nationalism did not really take hold until after the First World War. Glasgow's well-being went together with the advances in science and engineering during and after Enlightenment. James Watt's development of the steam engine had been a key factor in the Industrial Revolution, and resulted in huge leaps forward in communications, and a concentration of workers encouraging a popular culture based on class consciousness – socialism. Glasgow was specifically a centre of shipbuilding, an industry which has only disappeared relatively recently, and has left a rich legacy of music, literature and comedy.

As T. M. Devine says, on the back of Victorian imperialism then, there had grown up a tradition of free trading liberalism, '"respectability", self-improvement, sobriety and education'. Later in the century, prime minister William Gladstone would become a Scottish hero by embodying these principles, especially after his 1879 Midlothian election campaign. Queen Victoria had created the precedent for a respectably British Scotland by drawing the theme-park moment of 1822 into the 1840s, frequently travelling north, and settling for a time at Balmoral after the death of Albert, who had helped design their 'Scotch Baronial' palace. What concerns us here is how Victoria felt 'at home' up north, and the way in which her Scottish vacations, despite her melancholy and her tendency to spend long periods housebound, sparked a trend of holidaying in Scotland which is still popular today – a 'short tour', as opposed to the 'grand tour' of Europe which, after the Napoleonic Wars, seemed a bit scary. To a great extent, this is how Scottish culture is often marketed today; its bleak glens and canny natives are even today stuck in this Victorian moment of rebranding.

Scotland's accessibility from England had been increased by steam railways – ironically developed by the Scot James Watt – and the travel time from London to Scotland had been drastically reduced. In 1842 the Edinburgh and Glasgow line opened, and a link to the English network was completed in 1848, which should be seen as a key moment in defining a unified Britishness (at exactly the time when much of Europe was undergoing *national* redefinition). Today's Forth Rail Bridge was opened in 1890 by the future Edward VII and completed the rail link north of Edinburgh, connecting Edinburgh to Fife (and so to Dundee and Aberdeen in the north-east). With the growth in rail communications to and population in Glasgow came the advent of 'leisure'. There was a huge expansion of working-class *and* middle-class entertainments, including ornate tea rooms, concerts and Clyde cruises, some of which would be wiped out by the economic depression of the 1920s.

The 'short tour', however, developed in tandem with the final emptying of the Highlands, based on dubious interpretations of Adam Smith, whose support for social welfare was pared away in early-nineteenth century readings in favour of enforced 'free trade', as it would be again, globally, in late twentieth-century readings. Landowners rationalised (or 'downsized') inefficient small-time crofting tenants, removing them *en masse* in a process known as the Highland Clearances. Beginning in the 1760s, the Clearances accelerated at the turn of the nineteenth century, and only much later, in the 1870s and

1880s, was there large-scale organised political support for crofters' rights. In the 1882 'Battle of the Braes', crofters in several settlements on the Isle of Skye refused to pay their rents until the landowner gave them back their traditional grazing rights. Attempts to serve eviction notices were often met with violence.

Here there is a significant crossover with the Irish Nationalist movement. The Irish socialist and nationalist James Connolly, for example, emerged from the Edinburgh immigrant community, and Glaswegians provided much of the funding for Irish Republicanism. The late nineteenth century saw a growth of Scottish-Irish cultural associations such as the Gaelic League and Hibernian Football Club, founded in Edinburgh in 1875 (before Glasgow Celtic: in fact Glasgow Celtic were nearly called Glasgow Hibernian). In the work-place, Irish immigrants were often in a no-win situation, being seen as scab (anti-strike) labour by the trade unions and also, contradictorily, as union troublemakers. Irish immigrants split along sectarian lines which corresponded largely to whether they were 'natives' or of 'settler stock', and Ulster Protestant Irish, largely the descendents of settlers, re-introduced a strong seam of British loyalism to the west of Scotland which still exerts a strong 'cultural' influence.

Some crofters dispossessed by the Clearances emigrated to the USA, some to Canada, Australia, or New Zealand; many emigrations (and historians argue about *how* many) were enforced on tenants who lived in virtual serfdom. There was a large-scale move to Canada around the beginning of the nineteenth century, which can be seen in Canadian Scottish cultural associations (which sometimes remain curiously un-modern). Another reason for the large-scale emigration was the 'Irish' potato famine, which was also felt in the Scottish north-west in the 1840s, and was worsened by a cholera outbreak in 1848. In all, there was an emigration of almost 3 million people between 1840 and 1930. However, recent research suggests that the make-up of the emigrant body from Scotland as a whole in the nineteenth century was more skilled than is sometimes assumed, including artisans and pro-fessionals as well as crofters.

With them, the emigrants carried both the culture of the western Highlands (as in Gaelic song) *and* that of the new metropolitan Enlightenment (as in 'English Literature'), leaving pockets of both around the Anglophone world. Meanwhile, Glasgow was massively swollen by internal migration and Irish immigration. Given the British rationale of the Highland Clearances, we might say that wealthy tourists on the short tour created exactly the bleak and breathtaking landscape they were looking for, by removing any residents who were spoiling the view. Even today, the most popular route through Scotland for overseas tourists consists of 'historic' Edinburgh plus the Highlands or Western Isles (for example, Skye), missing out Glasgow and the industrial and farming Lowlands where most Scots now live, and repeating the Victorian 'short tour'. The tourist map of Scotland still looks very different to the demographic map.

Yet the picturesquely bleak Highland region remains one of the most economically challenged areas of the UK. Today crofters support themselves by a wide range of part-time jobs rather than just fishing and small-time farming. (Before we get too caught up in laments over 'authenticity' however, we should bear in mind that, as Murray Pittock has pointed out, flexibility is typical of the crofting tradition, and driving taxis part-time does not necessarily represent a 'dilution' of the crofting lifestyle.) The early Victorian Highland landscape is still marketed as an escape from urban stresses, an idyllic wilderness with low property prices. Poster advertisements by Scottish tourist agencies on the London Underground feature panoramas of empty hillsides, towering over commuters while they wait for their overcrowded train. Some tourists even resettle in the Highlands or buy a second house there, following Victoria's example. Despite reports to the contrary in the tabloid newspapers, English incomers are generally welcomed and contribute to their new communities, though they are occasionally insultingly referred to as 'white settlers'. If there is a real resentment, it is largely down to the way the UK is *economically* skewed: many Londoners can afford a second house in the Highlands, while Highlanders themselves cannot afford a first one. There is little reason to see this resentment as specifically 'anti-English'; it would be much better described in terms of social class.

Why did the Lowlands acquiesce for so long? Politically, until the end of the nineteenth century, Britain was relatively decentralised; Scotland had a quasi-independence within Britain which Lindsay Paterson has described as an 'informal domestic parliament', and T. M. Devine as a 'local state'. But the mid-nineteenth century connection of London to Scotland also sees a *cultural* clearance, since most ambitious individuals saw the move to London as more or less automatic. The 'London diaspora' of writers and artists is still in place today, though recently it has decreased significantly, and an increasing number of London artists are looking north. More generally in the mid-nineteenth century there arose a significant rural/urban division of culture. To an extent this is a normal effect of industrialisation, but rapid urbanisation causes more cultural damage to regions far from government, and stateless Scotland had suddenly been placed far from government. It is perhaps because this kind of internal adaptation came so early to Scots that they are not prone to the image, as is England, of the countryside as the true location of the national heart. Whereas real Englishness was, and is, often viewed via pastoral images of village green/pub/church, since around the turn of the twentieth century, leaving it with problems in appreciating the Englishness of non-white urban cultures today, Scotland has tended to be the object rather than the subject of such cultural re-imaginings, and so lacks the luxury of comfortable rural 'organic' images of the national culture.

Amidst this concentration of the workforce, in Scotland, the labour and reform movements started early. There were pockets of sympathy for the French Revolution of 1789, as in the poetry of Robert Burns; in sympathetic combinations (trade unions) which were viewed with some alarm by the British government and the propertied classes; and in strong support for Chartism (a group demanding fairer voting) before and after the Reform Act of 1832, when campaigners found that although the electorate had increased dramatically, it was still small and property-based, and that universal male suffrage was not on the agenda, far less suffrage for all. There was also strong popular support for the Suffrage Association in the 1840s. Scottish Chartism often also involved Christian participation, and was culturally productive (in the form of, for example, Chartist magazines), merging with the activities of the crafts unions which had peaked in the 1820s. Often the church, then highly influential, would participate in various schemes of non-partisan reform.

From the mid-nineteenth century 'proto-nationalisms', though frequently small and specialised, began to orientate themselves against British centralisation in a way somewhat anticipating devolution. Meanwhile, however, Scots continued to pack the ranks of the British empire; during the period Scottishness can be seen as bound up with its place in empire in various kinds of product packaging and adventure stories which are echoed in the work of John Buchan and J. M. Barrie, in organisations such as the Boys' Brigade (from 1883), and then later in publishers like D. C. Thomson (from 1905). Some of Buchan's work is also heir to an Edinburgh tradition of scientific racism, for example *Prester John* (1910), readable in terms of the British eugenics movement (the attempt to 'rationalise' race). We might argue that this image of energetic loyalist lads o' pairts – the enterprising local boy who finds success – dealing with indolent natives in the colonies was only really killed off about the time of Irvine Welsh's *Marabou Stork Nightmares* (1996), which mercilessly parodies the loyalist-unionist 'explorer' ethic. And as Unionist Nationalism grew, so it gave birth to 'kailyard' culture (the phrase is taken, as are so many phrases used in Scottish cultural studies, from a poem by Robert Burns, and refers to the back garden of small houses or farms where kail, a vegetable like cabbage, is grown). Acknowledged writers of kail-yard stories were S. R. Crockett and Ian Maclaren, whose *Beside the Bonnie Brier Bush* (1894) is generally seen as the archetypical novel of the movement, and which enjoyed a huge readership especially, symptomatically, in the Anglophone settler colonies.

The mid-Victorian period also saw an increase in the nostalgic and popular 'ben and glen' painting, for example those of Horatio McCulloch. The influential view (after Tom Nairn) has thus been that Scotland, lacking political expression and escaping into *British* imperial fantasy, failed to produce a critically national culture in the nineteenth century. This is true to an extent – there is no Scottish Charles Dickens or George Eliot – yet William Donaldson has shown that many stories serialised and popularly read at the end of the nineteenth century do have relatively naturalist thematics of urban poverty, public health and housing. Moreover the 1880s also saw the successes of Robert Louis Stevenson, Margaret Oliphant and George Macdonald, none of whom are reducible to kailyard. The problem of kailyard has been not only the original works' small-minded parochialism, but also that of culturally cringing Scottish readers, searching, at least until the 1980s, for the historiographical apparatus with which to tell any other story after Scottish history's 'strange death'.

Overpopulated late-nineteenth-century Glasgow increasingly became a centre for trade union activity, leading to a socialism for which it is still known. The city's population growth in the nineteenth century is extraordinary: between the 1800s and the 1900s it increased by approximately ten times. As well as creating pockets of socialist community, this explosive population growth inevitably resulted in high rates of slum housing and unemployment, problems that only really began to be addressed after the Second World War, and only then by what turned out to be short-term means, such as out-of-town housing estates. The 1965 Nation Plan for Scotland provided for the creation of Glasgow and Edinburgh satellite New Towns, but these were often system-built, nowhere near the cities whose overflow they were supposed to accommodate and incapable of supporting community – see, for example, Janice Galloway's 1989 novel *The Trick is to Keep Breathing*. A rehousing programme in the 1920s and 1930s was also short-term, though the 'traditionally Scottish' tenement building (three- to five-storey buildings, each apartment having one central sitting room) remained popular, sometimes in a renovated form. This is related to the ethic of *public* housing; the percentage of people living in council housing rather than self-owned housing even today (and even despite rapid growths in property prices in places) is higher in Scotland than in England, despite Margaret Thatcher's attempt to win Conservative voters by selling council houses cheaply to their occupants.

In a way that may seem puzzling to some English and American readers, the connection of socialism and nationalism was, and remains, culturally influential in both Ireland and Scotland. At the end of the nineteenth century this connection was more immediately 'politically' successful in Ireland, still a colony, but it also had a long-running cultural impact in Scotland, although analysts disagree about its extent. Historians disagree, for example, about the significance of the crowds gathered in central Glasgow in 1919 – the Red Clydesiders – which, although its significance may have been exaggerated since then (it is sometimes disingenuously described as a 'myth'), was perhaps the closest Britain has ever come to socialist revolution.

Although the First World War had started with relative British patriotism amongst the Scottish people, the war's atrocities, and the European context of class consciousness given concrete shape by the Russian Revolution of 1917, significantly damaged this state patriotism. The period from 1919 to the mid 1930s would be a newly nationalist and largely socialist one, and might be described as the death-knell of Walter Scott's 1822 tartan circus. The pre-war Home Rule Bill, which suggested a form of devolution for Scotland, was conveniently forgotten during the war by the British government, and by the 1920s unemployment was unusually high north of the border,

Figure 3.1   George Square, in central Glasgow. The significance of the 1919 uprising here is still debated. (Photograph: Michael Gardiner.)

compared to Britain as a whole. In 1926 George Thomson was scathing in his identification of 'a land of second-hand thoughts and second-rate minds'; Edwin Muir's *Scottish Journey* (1935) condemned great stretches of urban wasteland, and the inter-war nation had reached a sense of cultural crisis expressed in post-industrial and post-imperial terms. The Red Clydesiders of 1919 went on to participate in the General Strike of 1926, a moment that caused the British government some panic, and also saw the emergence of the Scottish Renaissance.

The term 'Scottish Renaissance' was probably coined in 1895 by the polymath Patrick Geddes, author of *Cities in Evolution* in 1915 and a figure whose work has recently undergone rediscovery; the phrase was made famous by Alexander McGill in 1921 in an essay describing the group forming around the poet Hugh MacDiarmid. Geddes was a city planner and social scientist who explored a new inter-disciplinary Scottish culture in his 1890s journal *Evergreen*, a publication far ahead of its time. The Renaissance is *the* cultural story of the early twentieth century, and is strongest in its first phase from the mid-1920s to the mid-1930s.

Two things to notice about the Renaissance are, first, that although its literary figures are best remembered (Hugh MacDiarmid, Edwin Muir, Lewis Grassic Gibbon, Neil Gunn), as a cultural movement it crossed a number of media and disciplines; MacDiarmid himself had opinions on everything from education to biology. In its inter-disciplinary attitude, the Renaissance in a sense inherits an ideal of Enlightenment, a great advantage but one that runs the risk of failing to see the imperialist implications of the Enlightenment's singular idea of progress, embodied, for example, in the David Hume of *Of National Characters*.

As with the Welsh Nationalist party Plaid Cymru in 1925, the National Party of Scotland had been established mostly by literary and cultural figures on the left in 1927, including MacDiarmid. In 1934 the National Party of Scotland joined the conservative Scottish Party and smaller splinter parties to form the Scottish National Party (SNP), one of the two main political parties in today's Scottish Parliament. And today's Labour/SNP split in the Scottish Parliament can be seen, to some extent, as a continuation of the division between cultural Unionist Nationalism (*pace* 1822) and independence-driven Nationalism (*pace* 1927), except that the division is not entirely clear; it is complicated by smaller parties which are still determinedly both socialist and nationalist, in particular the Scottish Socialist Party (SSP), which in a sense returns to the labour tradition of the 1910s and 1920s.

The inter-war Renaissance also collapsed the cultural and the polit-ical in a way that would occur again in the 1980s and 1990s. Indeed, the first wave of Renaissance petered out in the mid-1930s in part because of a willingness on the part of some nationalists to accept the compromise solution of societies promoting an apolitical cultural dis-tinctiveness we might describe as 'heritage' rather than culture. The National Trust for Scotland was created in 1931, the Saltire Society in 1936, and both were largely middle-class 'heritage' societies. In 1932 the office of the Secretary of State for Scotland was moved to Edinburgh, and began to grow as a *de facto* regional authority, again mediating outright Nationalism. Today, however (as I have argued elsewhere), cultural difference has become *more than* merely cultural in its innocuous sense, and devolution can take the wheels off British political process irrespective of how well or badly the Scottish Parliament behaves. Voting procedure, for instance: Scotland rejected Westminster's first-past-the-post model in which many votes are wasted or not even cast, and Parliament is merely two main parties locked in perpetual battle over 'management' of a middle ground. The Scottish Parliament now houses the only socialist and green parties in Britain with any national representation.

Conversely, since the 1910s threat of Home Rule, British governments have struggled 1822-style to maintain a sense of Scottish nationality *within* Britain. Since 1913, almost a century before devolution actually happened, the Labour Party was having to use vague promises of constitutional reform, along with perpetual acknowledgement of Scottish 'pride', to keep Nationalism in check, a negotiation that took place in culture. As Tom Nairn has reminded us, the need to keep a sense of union has to come before all other British policy – New Labour would not survive in government without Scotland, since it would not get enough votes – and so in a sense defines *all* policy. Ironically, today's New Labour Party has its roots in the socialist-nationalist movements of the turn of the twentieth century, growing up around Glasgow – and only in the mid-1990s did the party cut its formal links with trade unions and so with the labour movement.

One of the ways in which the Renaissance fails to get beyond the moment of 1822, nevertheless, is in a tendency to continue to support empire, despite notable exceptions (J. M. Barrie's *The Admirable Crichton* (1902) as imperial parody, L. G. Gibbon's *A Scots Quair* (1932–4) as ambivalence over globalisation). And much as they would like to forget it now, mid-century the SNP disingenuously played the anti-Irish immigrant card for popularity. At times and not without reason, the SNP have thus been called 'Tories in kilts'. At any rate, as I suggested before, we must be careful not to confuse growths in nationalism and growths in SNP support. The SNP grew in the 1930s and then again in the 1960s; Winnie Ewing won her famous election victory in Hamilton in 1967, and support for the party topped 30 per cent in 1968. In the 1970s they tried to mobilise Scots' annoyance over the British government's cynical exploitation of oil found in the North Sea off Scotland. Nevertheless, concentrating on North Sea oil relied on the misleading idea that political nationalism amounts to economic independence, whereas economic policy was actually gradually moving towards Europe, which the UK joined at the same time – 1972. (And Britain is not, contrary to popular beliefs fanned by the likes of the *Daily Mail*, still deciding about 'joining Europe': it has been in Europe for decades.) The economic argument for Scottish

Figure 3.2   When oil was discovered in the North Sea, and was somewhat mismanaged by the UK government, the SNP seized on the political capital. (Courtesy of the Scottish National Party.)

independence can even amount to a disingenuously unionist one, being based on the cliché that Scots' constitutional preference is for whatever is most profitable (thus reverting to a popular English eighteenth-century stereotype of Scots). And of course the oil was plainly *not* 'Scotland's oil', contrary to what the SNP pamphlet declared, any more than Lancashire mines produce 'English coal'.

If the First World War had crystallised local/national complaints, arming for the Second World War was a factor in *reviving* the engineering industry of 1930s Clydeside, and there was a relatively unionist period. Scottish culture seemed welded to heavy industry; a 'hard man' image was exemplified by the Glasgow gangs which became the subject of a whole sub-genre of popular fiction and was addressed by the popular English singer Frankie Vaughan who became involved in Glasgow community projects. The Second World War also caused a pulling together of the political parties in a coalition government. And even though the prime minister, Winston Churchill, already had a horrifying record on colonial violence (he supported using chemical weapons in the Middle East, as would the government of Tony Blair), in the public imagination the Second World War was not so directly linked to imperialism. The Scots were drawn back into Britain by a sense of togetherness which found its expression post-war in the welfare state. The welfare state to an extent represents the fulfillment of the wishes of many earlier Scottish Liberals and trade unionists, yet a desire to hang on to the welfare state has drawn Scotland away from Britain, though the prime architect of its destruction, Margaret Thatcher, somehow failed to anticipate this. The period immediately following the *set-up* of the welfare state – the 1950s – saw some of the highest levels of unionism in Scotland in modern times and, briefly, Conservative Party support of 50 per cent, whereas the period following Thatcher's moves towards *dismantling* the welfare state saw some of the lowest levels of support, including the extraordinary 'wipe-out' of *all* Scottish Conservative MPs in 1997. In 1955 the Conservative Party won fifty-five of Scottish MPs' seventy-two seats; in 1997 they won none.

Moreover, constitutional challenges from the Scottish side were increasingly visible after the Second World War. The Covenant for Scottish Home Rule composed in 1949 eventually attracted over 2 million signatures; and John McCormick's 1953 legal challenge to the monarch's right to be called 'Elizabeth the Second' (she was, of course, only Elizabeth the First, the previous Elizabeth having been queen *of England*), though seen in some quarters as a childish wheeze, was successful in getting people to wonder what else was taken for granted in the 'union' of governments. After the publication of the *Claim of Right for Scotland* in 1988, demanding a constitution and more democratic voting, the Scottish Constitutional Convention was set up in 1990 as an inter-party talking shop. Assuming that the Conservative and Unionist Party would at some time be shifted from government, the ingredients for 1997 devolution were largely in place.

In many ways the post-war welfare state, largely engineered by Scottish and Welsh politicians, was highly beneficial. A great deal of housing was built, especially in Glasgow, as an effort to relieve the suffering caused by the city's remaining slum housing. As I hinted above, in Scotland housing often means municipal housing, so that, as Christopher Harvie has noted, Scotland by the 1970s had 'probably the largest share of council housing of any advanced economy outside the communist bloc'. This can still be seen as characterising the national culture: the fact that growing up on a council estate has been a common experience north of the border has important implications for how people think through their own class identity and their ideas of community.

Not that the new housing was without problems: planners were so keen to get people out of the old houses and into new ones, that they often forgot about infrastructure and location. The Clyde Valley Plan was sweeping in its creation of New Towns and out-of-town settlements, often meaning multi-storey blocks. Some Glaswegians were bemused and resentful about being rehoused vertically: the comedian Billy Connolly has often lamented the loss of the tenement communities in his stand-up comedy; Stephen Mulrine's famous 'Jeely Piece Song' describes a 'skyscraper wean' waiting for a sandwich to land from a multi-storey verandah, reflecting how tenement customs had disappeared. On the other hand, there is a tendency to overstate the problems of the multi-storey boom. Some people still talk as if height above sea level is proportionate to crime (maybe this is why Colombia is so dangerous). But there is no reason why a high-rise flat cannot be a perfectly good solution to slum housing, as long as it has proper infrastructure, amenities and a lift that works. Another possible interpretation is that those rehoused in multi-storey blocks have been punished by later administrations for the post-war socialist dream of decent housing for everyone, with the estates being turned into dustbins for the 'deserving poor'.

Meanwhile, the 1960s saw a simultaneous revival and modification of Renaissance ideas, as a new generation of poets rediscovered MacDiarmid, and then the influences of European Sartrean humanism and New Left modernism were absorbed by writers as various as Edwin Morgan and R. D. Laing. The Association for Scottish Literary Studies was set up in 1971, and the publisher Polygon, formerly run by Edinburgh students, went independent with great success; Polygon's 'Determinations' series from the end of the 1980s is a good example of the range of cultural questions which were now being asked. The publisher Canongate was revived in 1994, and went on to occupy a central place in literary production, and also to dig up a number of out-of-print Scottish classics. In the 1990s, that most British canon of Eng. Lit. was already bent out of shape under the weight of theory, and scholars of Scottish Studies became less keen to be included simply under 'English'; some university departments prudently rethought their names.

Where in 1979 a devolution referendum failed, in part as a result of a piece of political chicanery which changed the absolute rate of votes required, the ''79 group' that emerged, sickened by the failure, though subsequently unsuccessful in their stated aims, captured the mood of many people and encouraged another cultural renaissance in the 1980s. So too did the journals *Chapman* and *Cencrastus*, the latter named after a MacDiarmid poem. Throughout the 1980s the Scottish press distanced itself from the British press by becoming strongly anti-Tory, and building up a new national identity, albeit at times a 'negative' one. Resistance to the Poll Tax in 1989–93 also united the people against the government, in what was probably the biggest non-payment protest Britain has ever seen, when prime minister Margaret Thatcher decided, unfathomably, to 'test' the policy on Scotland. Non-payment was so common that bailiffs couldn't deal with the arrears, the policy had to be scrapped and, later, Conservative leader Michael Howard 'apologised' for the tax. (Those who paid it were not reimbursed.)

In the 1980s Scotland became more vulnerable to problems like unemployment, as it had in the 1920s. The Conservative government was significantly 'Englished' (this is the puzzle: self-professed Unionists failed to see how vital Scotland was to the union), and Scottish people felt increasingly disenfranchised from British politics and culture. The elevation of vaguely stated Anglo-British 'nation' over

Figure 3.3   'Yes' campaign poster for the 1979 Devolution vote, invoking Russian constructivism. (Courtesy of Christopher Harvie.)

British state by 1979–97 governments could have worked, had there been a core of brilliant party ideologues able to sell Anglo-Britain to another generation of Scots. But instead there were multi-chinned right-wingers like Norman Lamont and Nigel Lawson, who were incomprehensible to most Scottish people. While Scotland underwent cultural revival, Margaret Thatcher and then John Major grasped a disingenuously *English* thread of anti-intellectualism, she using the word 'heritage' instead of culture, and he telling us his favourite book was *Vanity Fair* (which is a bit like signing your name 'John Smith' at a country hotel where you're having an affair).

Nor did Scotland's economic restructuring come off as Scots were led to expect: the celebrated 'Silicon Glen' of electronics factories departed from Scotland's scientific tradition in its reliance on semi-skilled labour outsourced by foreign companies, which sometimes put Scotland on the wrong side of the international division of labour. In 1993 Ravenscraig steel works, one of the last major symbols of Scottish industrial power, closed (see Christopher Harvie, from Motherwell himself). The stage of the Scottish working-class narrative had more or less been entirely transformed – as Cairns Craig has noted in terms of the novel – from tenement-factory/ship-yard/working men's club to deserted estate/dole queue/drink and drug culture. In 1993 the title of Irvine Welsh's *Trainspotting* made a grim joke on industrial decline, describing the spotting of spectral trains by alcoholics at the disused Leith Central Station. Not kailyard, but dark comedy; really dark, the kind that is sharpened by economic depression and being ruled seemingly *ad infinitum* by incomprehensible politicians in another nation.

By the mid-1990s the Conservative Party had realised that 'regions' like Scotland were liable to vote it out, and they really did become – as was snidely said of the SNP – Tories in kilts. As the prospect of devolution loomed, all the major political parties in Scotland brazenly stuck 'Scottish' at the front of their names, most brazenly of all the 'Scottish Conservatives' who opposed the Parliament right up until it became a reality and its proportional representation system gave them some national power. In a perfectly neo-1822 moment, Michael Forsyth, Conservative Secretary of State for Scotland and a Walter Scott for the 1990s, who appeared at the premiere of the film *Braveheart* in Highland dress, 'returned' to Scotland the Stone of Destiny (an ancient symbol of the coronation of monarchs).

Mercifully, unlike in 1822, Forsyth's cheesy move met with the derision it deserved. One episode of the TV series *Hamish Macbeth*, a
mine of myths dressed in post-kailyard kitsch, suggests that the real
stone – the real spirit of sovereignty – was actually hidden elsewhere
in Scotland anyway, and was never Forsyth's to give back.

Since 1993 some Scottish cultural organisations have begun to
benefit from funding by the National Lottery, which is automatically
'devolved' (though the National Lottery can be viewed as the most
insidious form of taxation, sapping the hope of the poor to pay for elite
cultures, and avoiding the need for unpopular direct taxation). In the
Scottish Parliament, in tandem with the first New Labour administration in the UK, there has been a 'modernising' move towards stressing Scotland's potential for tourism, sport and (in Thatcherite vein)
'heritage'. In 2000 the National Cultural Strategy *Creating our Future:
Minding our Past* insisted that a new, less 'political' definition of
culture 'play[s] an important role in bringing people together and promoting social inclusion'. But while the late-1990s 'New Britain' did
re-enliven Scotland in some ways, the years before devolution (see
Chapter 8) also gave rise to the cultural sense that Britain had less than
ever to say to Scotland. Enthusiasm for a Scottish Parliament dipped
rapidly in the early 2000s, a fact often repeated by unionists. We might
also note, however, that the Scottish people's only mistake was in forgetting that all parliaments are run by politicians; this is an easy
mistake to make, and does not diminish the achievement of denting
British Parliamentary 'tradition'. It may be that the Scottish
Parliament, with all its problems, is a *symptom* of a larger movement,
rather than the end-point of a shorter one.

SUMMARY

- By the mid-nineteenth century the motifs of Scottishness had come
  to be seen as part of an Anglocentric British imperial family.
- The Highland Clearances decimated the largely Gaelic culture of
  the Highlands and Islands from around the time of the late
  Enlightenment, and especially in the early nineteenth century.
- Scots participated enthusiastically in British colonialism in the
  nineteenth century.
- The population of Glasgow swelled hugely in the nineteenth

century, and the city became world-famous for engineering, science and shipbuilding.

- Modern Scottish party-political Nationalism took shape in the 1920s, and was originally, but briefly, a strongly socialist movement. At times it has been anti-Catholic.
- After 1945, many Scots worked to build and maintain the welfare state. The desire to hang on to aspects of the welfare state can be seen as one of the cultural particularities leading to devolution.

QUESTIONS FOR FURTHER RESEARCH AND THOUGHT

- Approximately how many people spoke Gaelic as a first language in 1800, 1900 and 2000.
- Why (in addition to the obvious answer – shipbuilding) was Glasgow known in the nineteenth century as 'the second city of empire'?
- Give some concrete examples of Glasgow's 'leisure boom' at the end of the nineteenth century.
- How did the First World War affect Britons' image of Britain?
- What was the attitude of the writers of the Scottish Renaissance (c. 1922–35) to empire?
- Why was the mid-twentieth century Scottish National Party so keen to present itself as a Protestant party?
- Does the mismanagement of North Sea oil by the British government make it a Scottish nationalist issue?
- How did prime minister Tony Blair's vision of Scotland-in-Britain differ from that of Margaret Thatcher?

FURTHER READING

Ash, Marinell, *The Strange Death of Scottish History*, Edinburgh: Ramsay Head Press, 1980.
See ch. 1.

Checkland, Sydney and Olive Checkland, *The New History of Scotland Vol. 7 Industry and Ethos 1832–1914*, London: Edward Arnold, 1981.
See ch. 1.

Craig, Cairns, *The Modern Scottish Novel*, Edinburgh: Edinburgh University Press, 1999.
As the title suggests, this is a (much needed and persuasive) history of the twentieth-century Scottish novel, its historical contexts and linguistic strategies.

Devine, T. M., *The Scottish Nation*, London: Penguin, 1999.
See pp. 105–617, and ch. 1.

Devine, T. M. and R. J. Finlay (eds), *Scotland in the Twentieth Century*, Edinburgh: Edinburgh University Press, 1996.
An authoritative guide to twentieth-century cultural history, with contributions from leading scholars in their fields.

Harvie, Christopher, *Scotland and Nationalism*, London: Routledge, 1997.
See ch. 1.

Harvie, Christopher, *Scotland: A Short History*, Oxford: Oxford University Press, 2002.
See pp. 144–245, and ch. 1.

Hutchinson, I.G.C., *A Political History of Scotland, 1832–1924: Parties, Elections, and Issues*, Edinburgh: John Donald, 1986.
This is perhaps more detailed than the beginner needs, but it is invaluable in understanding the transition from Victorian loyalism to the beginnings of modern nationalism.

Kendle, Martin, *Federal Britain*, London: Routledge, 1997.
This does not directly concern Scotland (indeed this is one of its problems), but it is a useful guide to the interplay of 'region' and state throughout British history; it is particularly valuable on the later nineteenth century.

MacDonald, Catriona (ed.), *Unionist Scotland 1800–1997*, Edinburgh: John Donald, 1998.
Essays by a range of writers based in Scotland and Northern Ireland forming an interesting history of unionism, and covering the whole period up to devolution from a devolutionary perspective

Marr, Andrew, *The Battle for Scotland*, London: Penguin, 1992.
Semi-journalistic account of the negotiations between Westminster and Edinburgh leading up to devolution, by a highly respected political journalist.

Morton, Graeme, *Unionist Nationalism: Governing Urban Scotland 1830–1860*, Phantassie: Tuckwell, 1999.
See ch. 1.

Scottish Executive, *Creating our Future: Minding our Past*, Edinburgh: Scottish Executive, 2000.
Jargon-laden description of a joint cultural and tourism strategy; interesting as a post-devolution description of how Scotland is to be marketed.

Smout, T. C., *A Century of the Scottish People, 1830–1950*, London: Fontana, 1987, first published 1986.
Follow-up to Smout's *A History of the Scottish People, 1560–1830*, see ch. 1.

Scottish Arts Council: http://www.scottisharts.org.uk/

SAC list of venues: http://www.scottisharts.org.uk/1/resources/links/capital.aspx

Scotland Internet (directory of websites): http://scotlandinter.net/

CHAPTER 4

Modern Scottish Philosophy

How can we talk of a philosophy belonging to a nation, bounded by national borders? How can philosophy be *national*?

Yet the passage through time of modern Scottish philosophy is very like that of modern Scotland itself: in the eighteenth century and at the start of the nineteenth century it embraces a British and 'global' standard and struggles to get to its centre; in the Victorian period it upholds this standard via an Anglocentric *laissez-faire*; in the twentieth century these standards begin to be corroded, again approaching the continental-European and moving away from the British. During this arc of Britishing and de-Britishing, Scottish intellectuals struggled to maintain philosophy's place *in general* at the centre of the educational syllabus, whereas in England, philosophy was often seen as a support for more specific disciplines. Scottish philosophy is tied to Scottish culture, and the story of modern Scottish philosophy is, in a sense, the story of the nation.

Philosophy has always been a field of study central to Scottish education. Undoubtedly, its most celebrated phase is the Enlightenment, which lasted, depending on whose account you buy into, for about half a century from the 1740s, or over a century well into the mid-nineteenth. Thus, although a number of writers (for example, Beveridge and Turnbull 1997; Broadie 2001) have linked Enlightenment philosophy back to earlier seventeenth-century models, and others (for example, Pittock 2003, perhaps taking up the call from Devine (2000)) have made a case that the Enlightenment is to be seen coming to fruition in the nineteenth century, what we must stress is the Enlightenment strengthening *as philosophy*. In the nineteenth century, Scottish common sense notwithstanding, the Enlightenment becomes lost under Anglo-British practicalism; the J. S. Mill who is ironically invoked by Muriel Spark in *The Prime of Miss Jean Brodie* as the apex of an Edinburgh education is also someone who is primarily concerned with getting things done (usually in empire). In the 1910s David Hume became an inspiration for the Anglo-British school of logical positivism, whose concerns focused on sceptical problem-solving of individual propositions, a method fairly unfriendly to philosophy as such, if philosophy is to investigate the intellectual contexts of historical situations.

As suggested above, the Enlightenment coincided with the expansion of, and moral justification for, the British union. What the Enlightenment did, in positive terms (Adam Smith, in particular), was to tie rationality to ideas of social improvement. Some recent analysts have thus connected Enlightenment to an earlier phase of indigenous Scottish philosophy of sympathy and justice not reliant on the conditions of union. This argument stresses that Enlightenment was not simply a form of modernisation enabled by joining with a more 'advanced' nation, but that it was a continuation of Scottish philosophical, scientific and theological advances from the seventeenth century and before. This interpretation, however, has the disadvantage of assuming that as well as being native to Scotland, the Enlightenment was primarily philanthropic. But despite the talk of society and equality, this is not how most of the world felt the effects of the Scottish Enlightenment – especially those colonised peoples who had the civility of the Enlightenment imposed on them, as their own cultures were assigned to an earlier phase of what the Enlightenment saw as universal progress.

So not only did Scotland recognise itself as a 'developing country'; it invented the very ideas of development that underpin the way in which today we divide the world's countries into mature and immature. (Get out a popular travel guide such as a *Rough Guide* or *Lonely Planet* book, read about how when you go to parts of Thailand/Turkey/Peru you are 'leaving the twenty-first century', and take a minute to think about how nonsensical and *violent* this statement is.) Adam Ferguson's *Essay on the History of Civil Society* (1767) does have an ear open for other kinds of experience and other possibilities for progress, and recognises the dangers of the division of social classes for economic efficiency. But in general the progress of reason is, in the Enlightenment, one-way – as in Smith's 'stadial theory' of history, which sees all society going through the same stages (with 'us' in the lead). The stress of the likes of Smith and William Robertson on universal narratives of progress – 'teleological' explanations for events – can also be seen leading into the work of the Scottish anthropologist James Frazer, especially in *The Golden Bough* (1890–1915), from which it passes to Eng. Lit., especially T. S. Eliot's and Anglo-American modernists' anxieties over imperial decay. Anthropology indeed was another of the Enlightenment's new knowledges, and in many ways the whole movement of Enlightenment is a 'science of man'. Where it brings progress, it also brings surveillance and the demand that people behave as discrete individuals. And some neo-Enlightenment Utilitarian thought saw colonial administration as an exercise in Reason *par excellence*, as did Jeremy Bentham and other English liberals after him.

So the thought of the Enlightenment was in some ways libertarian, as well as being both pro-European and, in a qualified but enthusiastic sense, pro-British, though for the more nationalist Adam Ferguson civic duty saved a nation from self destruction. Largely from the position of lowland Edinburgh, Enlightenment thinking ignored much of Scotland's Gaelic culture, which withered almost to extinction as 'good English' became a key to empire, and then as the Highland Clearances began. David Hume's *Essays, Moral and Political* started to appear in 1742, arguing on behalf of the English constitution (albeit in a qualified and sarcastic sense) even before the 1746 Disarming Act had begun to illegalise the signs of a Scottish state.

Hume is more remembered though for the sceptical philosophy of his *Enquiry Concerning Human Understanding* (1748), which stands at the heart of European Enlightenment thought as a whole. Here he argues that we cannot *assume* conclusions from the evidence of our senses, since the mind is always involved in creating conclusions. Objects in the world have their basis in perception, and are always processed by the individual mind. This means also that we cannot take belief for granted, and that events are always open to our own determination. This replacement of belief by individual determination had a great influence on the emerging states of America, which were seeking to control their own fate and free themselves from Britain. In his own time Hume, because of what was seen as his demeaning of Christian destiny, was at times bordering on the heretical, and on these grounds he was refused a position as professor in 1745 at Glasgow University. His celebrated shift from authority to Reason can, however, as more recent Scottish thought has stressed, be seen as another form of authority: in Hume's thinking, although we may have lost religious *certainty*, through experience – a combination of Reason and our senses – we can make certain *predictions* about the world, and cultivating these predictions should be the role of education. Even Francis Hutcheson, who blocked Hume's academic career, understood that Enlightenment was bound up with some kind of change in the nature of belief.

For Hume, knowledge itself was improvement. Hume's universalism was in part motivated by the 'universal' physics of Isaac Newton, whose ideas spread more quickly through Scottish universities than English ones. But universalism is not so universal: the population of the US is only about a quarter that of India, but can you name India's president? And that most Enlightenment nation itself, the US, which famously declared – following Scots like Francis Hutcheson and John Witherspoon as well as the American Tom Paine – that all men are born equal, has since the Second World War seen constant war as a necessary accompaniment to economic development (the military-industrial complex). Oceania has *always* been at war with Iraq/Iran/Afghanistan: the Orwellian warning is really an extension of Enlightenment logistics, which projects an eternal enemy/object of fear, leaving out the fact that 'free trade' means that we sold them the arms they now attack our youth with. This also makes our humble wee city of Edinburgh one of the great world capitals of Eurocentrism.

Even prior to the 'global division of labour' described by Marx, caught up as he was in the highly visible exploitation of the Industrial Revolution, there was a global division of knowledge – and indeed Marxism, closer to Enlightenment than many would like to admit, helped to contribute to this, with its emphasis on the need to develop through exploitative capitalist stages. And what else is the 'digital divide' but a hierarchy depending on the ability to arrange certain types of officially sanctioned knowledge? If today's Europe and the US are not explicitly racist, it is because they can export their racism to their client states – just as Scotland after Enlightenment turned its population into a highly 'distinct' people trying to play an ethnic part in imperial globalisation, so today non-Western nations are led increasingly to see themselves as 'distinct' rather than global.

So Hume's philosophy, though liberating in returning determination to the individual, raises certain problems which are also general problems of the Enlightenment. The 'predictions' arising from experience are assumed to belong to a form of civility which is the same for everyone: one single pathway of civilisation for every human. Where 'we' are advanced along this single path, others may be lagging behind; and 'ancient civilisations' may have had their day but failed to modernise. This type of thinking is, of course, handy for imperial domination. Alexander Broadie famously describes the Enlightenment as 'the historical age of an historical nation'; however a counter-argument could be made that the Enlightenment was Scotland's *least* historical period. Firstly, its universalism, its concern about how every society and every individual undergoes processes that are patterned and can be generalised, tends to flatten out the otherwise uneven inter-personal experience that makes up history. Secondly, the object separated via sceptical method demands an isolated observing individual, a *subject*, which is highly specific (European, male, white). The subject also provides a model for British imperialism, encouraging each member of the British empire to identify with the ideal individual, and preventing communal thought. Thirdly, Hume's stress on individual betterment in the world came at the worst possible time for Scotland, a nation coming to terms with the loss of its statehood in the 1740s. Despite his frequently voiced suspicion of London politicians, Hume can be seen as a pro-British philosopher assuming the need for each individual to adapt to union. The conflict between individual and community is still there in today's arguments over devolution, presented by the British government as a process empowering individuals within union, whereas many Scots tend to view devolution as national and shared.

Adam Smith was probably the second-most influential philosopher of the Scottish Enlightenment. Here, we are concerned with two main works. Firstly, in *The Wealth of Nations* (1776) he argued for a form of free trade that allows for the welfare of all, yet makes economic profit central to human relations. (As an overall scheme of economics, it does have one close antecedent: James Steuart's *Inquiry into the Principles of Political Oeconomy* (1767)). Again, as we might imagine, this book also had a great influence on the emerging states of America, ready to declare themselves independent from Britain. Smith indeed argues here that the American colonies should be freed, since they form part of a British monopoly which chokes healthy trade. The thinkers of the

Enlightenment were certainly anti-slavery, and their influence lived on to mid-nineteenth-century English liberalism. Yet their prosperous surroundings, the Glasgow and Edinburgh from which they wrote, were dependent on colonial money, which was in turn reliant on slavery, putting them in a similar position to the US as it has developed from Enlightenment principles to today's 'multiculturalism', built on investments reliant on an international division of labour, the outsourcing of labour to Mexico via NAFTA and so on.

The Wealth of Nations appeared in 1776, the year that the American separatists produced the Declaration of Independence. American events were watched closely and sympathetically by Scottish Enlightenment intellectuals like Smith, perhaps in part because they had given up their own chance of an independent republic. Smith is also known for his earlier Lectures of Rhetoric and Belles Lettres, not authored but collected by his students, and not properly published until the twentieth century. Smith's lectures were first delivered to law students at Edinburgh University in 1748–51, and to students of 'Rhetoric and Belles Lettres' (an antecedent of 'English Literature') at Glasgow University in 1751–63. We have seen how important the period of the 1740s to 1760s was in terms of Scottish acceptance of the new British union; to modern readers, Smith's Lectures can be seen as speeding up Scotland's Anglicisation by helping ambitious individuals adapt to the new union. Smith's stated aim here is to remove 'Scotticisms' from his students' speech, calling 'the dialect of this country most imperfect'. He offers a mixture of ancient Greek and Latin and contemporary English sources to 'improve' his Scottish students' English. The Lectures are typical of Enlightenment thought's aspirations and pitfalls, aiming at an ideal communication which actually makes communication more difficult.

Since decolonisation, philosophers throughout Europe have become much more aware of the dangers of assuming that people are all moving as individuals towards a form of civilisation imagined to be the same for everyone. These dangers have in particular been described by deconstruction and postcolonial studies, closely allied bodies of thought which used to go under the general rubric of 'theory'. Late twentieth-century Scotland was assumed to be far from such fashionable philosophical criticisms of Enlightenment, but twentieth-century Scottish philosophy, in hindsight, is itself very post-Enlightenment. Indeed, in Scotland, one response to Enlightenment came almost immediately, in the form of Thomas Reid's 'Common Sense' philosophy. Reid was a contemporary of Hume's, but he rejected Hume's scepticism about communal beliefs since, he thought, this scepticism placed too much emphasis on sensory experience. For Reid, especially in his *Inquiry into the Human Mind on the Principles of Common Sense* (1764), there existed types of experience related to the 'before' and 'after' of present perception which constituted a continuity, and allowed for social beliefs beyond Hume's sceptical approach. Reid was also particularly ahead of his time in stressing that vision is really an image *made by* the eye. The criticism of 'natural' vision as central to civility is a strong one: in post-Enlightenment times, we understand that basing all knowledge on vision allows for scientific advances (examining objects), but also risks racism and mass surveillance – controlling by seeing and placing.

For Reid, perception involved sensation *and* intuition, and there existed a natural justice based on a commonly believed connection between will and effect (precisely the connection Hume denied): 'Common Sense'. Common Sense philosophy, rejecting individualist scepticism, exerted a huge influence in the US and Europe as well as on later American pragmatist philosophers such as John Dewey and William James. Reid's Common Sense philosophy maintained its influence into the nineteenth century, and in the twentieth century Reid's mistrust of scepticism became quite common, despite Hume's stature. Alexander Broadie, who now holds the Edinburgh chair in Moral Philosophy and Rhetoric once occupied by Adam Smith, has been a major exponent of Reid's ideas. Reid's arguments were carried forward by James Beattie, Dugald Stewart and George Oswald, via whom Scottish Common Sense philosophy became almost an orthodoxy for, amongst others, some English philosophers in the early nineteenth century.

There was certainly also a measure of republicanism in the later Enlightenment, reflected in reactions to the French Revolution, in popular journals of the time, and then in literature, most famously in the poetry of Robert Burns, whose egalitarianism was to exert a strong, if not always acknowledged, influence on English Romanticism. The influence of Adam Smith was also carried on into the nineteenth century via his students and disciples, such as, again, Dugald Stewart, who produced an authoritative edition of Smith in the 1810s. John Ramsay McCulloch was editor of *The Scotsman* and then the *Edinburgh*

Prof' Thomas Reid D.D.

Figure 4.1   Henry Raeburn's portrait of Thomas Reid, 1796. (Courtesy of the
National Trust for Scotland.)

Review, a journal revived in 1802 in part to argue for a Smith-
influenced liberal form of French and American anti-colonial free
trade. It is important to remember that many of these early nineteenth-
century followers of Smith were still very concerned with provision for
welfare for the less fortunate, much more so than is suggested by
today's use of the term 'free trade' (or indeed the right-wing think-
tank 'The Adam Smith Institute').

   Around the turn of the nineteenth century, James Mill established himself a utilitarian influenced by Jeremy Bentham. His utilitarian beliefs were carried on by his son John Stuart Mill, who attempted to create a kind of science of linking personal desire to the maximisation of human welfare. J. S. Mill attacked simple intuitionism on the grounds that self-evidence could be a justification for self-interest. Following a somewhat different track but around the same time, J. F. Ferrier was reckoned by some to be the most influential philosopher in Europe; he was afterwards neglected somewhat in Scotland, though G. E. Davie revives him in *The Crisis of the Democratic Intellect* (1986). What is notable for Ferrier, for example in his *Scottish Philosophy, the Old and the New* (1854), is his assertion that there could be a Scottish philosophy not beholden to all of the tenets of Common Sense, but also able to incorporate a kind of Hegelianism. In a sense this anticipated later socialism, while maintaining a Reidian stress on metaphysics.

In the later nineteenth century in general, philosophy in Scotland was increasingly having to fight for its own centrality to the educational curriculum (which demanded that it become more 'practical' – early twentieth-century British logical positivism would see its function as serving other fields). While Scottish education battled to maintain philosophy's position in universities, some of the loudest Scottish voices of mid-nineteenth-century philosophy were pro-British, often even arguing for an imperialist liberalism, as in the individualism of Thomas Carlyle, or the utilitarianism of J. S. Mill, which tried to make overall calculations about ethics broadly incorporating Enlightenment assumptions about goodness and civility. Mill himself, not surprisingly, had a long and successful colonial career. His thinking is typical of the figure of the great liberal imperialist Victorian reformer. Smith's free tradeism was carried on in a reformist vein in Mill; then, in a similar Anglo-Scottish practicalist crossover, Hume's scepticism was championed as the light of the liberal West by Bertrand Russell in the early twentieth century. In an age where science was increasingly seen as the solution to social problems, for Russell, Hume had (again, following Newton) taken up philosophy as a branch of science. (This, of course, is really a reversal of Scottish philosophical tradition, in that Scottish education had tended to see science as dependent on philosophy, rather than vice-versa.)

Also however, the large working populations of the cities in the later nineteenth century, especially Glasgow, and the increase in suffrage at the turn of the twentieth century, helped lead to a growth of philosophical Marxism. Trade union leaders increasingly stressed social and economic explanations for inequalities – a tradition that we could easily tie to the split between owner and worker during the Industrial Revolution, but which has (as E. P. Thompson has shown has shown in his classic *The Making of the English Working Class* (1963)) much deeper local roots in small unions and 'combinations'. As noted in the previous chapter, one apparently odd characteristic of Scottish politics is that many Marxist and socialist movements from the nineteenth to the twenty-first century have also been nationalist in character. The Scottish Home Rule Association and the Scottish Labour Party were founded in the 1880s, and both broadly fit the 'red and black' model. The 1919 attempt at Marxist revolution in Glasgow, albeit ill-organised and over-hyped, led to Scottish philosophy being drawn into more serious political engagement, and modern party-political Nationalism rose in the 1920s. This is not to say that political Nationalists were all intellectuals, but around this time Scottish philosophy departments tended to turn Hegelian (Hegel being the figure from whom Marx had derived much of his thinking on history).

By the mid-twentieth century a post-Enlightenment, critical, more 'European' stress was becoming apparent in Scotland. In the mid-twentieth century, some Scottish philosophers began to break away from Anglo-British thought, setting themselves against the movement of logical positivism still dominant in England and associated with Bertrand Russell, Ludwig Wittgenstein and A. J. Ayer – Oxbridge philosophers whose aim was to make absolutely true statements about the world, restricting philosophy as far as possible to 'language problems'. (Ironically, this is an accusation that was often hurled at Eng. Lit.'s 'theory' in the 1980s, a body of thought far removed from logical positivism.) Alistair MacIntyre's *After Virtue* (1981) argues that the Enlightenment's creation of atomistic individuals entailed a denial of a common nature; MacIntyre turns against the Enlightenment link between personal desire and sympathy with others (as in utilitarianism), and returns to Aristotelean virtue as an alternative basis for ethics less prone to abuses of power. He explores similar post-Enlightenment (or, as in the artist Ian Hamilton Finlay's phrase, 'neopresocratic') themes in *Whose Justice? Whose Rationality?* (1988), and in the recently fashionable *Three Rival Versions of Moral Inquiry* (1990).

Another Scottish response to the solipsistic and Humean bias of logical positivism was the 'European' movement of phenomenology and existentialism, sets of ideas questioning the nature of the person's relationship to the world, from around the 1950s. The Scottish psychiatrist R. D. Laing attempted to overturn the world of mental categorisation from an existentialist angle in the 1960s, *socially* redefining the position of the schizophrenic in a way comparable to later French thought, in particular the work of Michel Foucault and Gilles Deleuze and Felix Guattari. Particularly in *The Divided Self* (1960), Laing insisted on the primacy of the fact of humans' difficulty in connecting with other humans, a thinking already influenced by Karl Jaspers and other European existentialists. Britain's best-known philosophical existentialist, the Scot John Macquarrie, produced in 1973 perhaps the single most important guide to the field available in English, simply titled *Existentialism*.

A middle ground between existentialism and marxism was a 'personalist' tradition represented by John Macmurray, in part indebted to the tradition of Reid and strongly aligned against logical positivism. 'Personalism' still exerts a significant influence; John Macmurray, particularly his later work, is currently being rediscovered in philosophical, cultural and literary studies. For Macmurray, *contra* Enlightenment assumptions, we should not assume that Reason is primary, coming before personal feelings and beliefs. Rather, belief and emotion shape the form of Reason itself. Here the description of the Enlightenment's becoming historically 'self-aware' is exemplified by Immanuel Kant's 1784 'Was ist Aufklarung?' ('What is Enlightenment?'). From Macmurray's standpoint though we would also stress the *material* conditions behind the making of the 'conscious' idea of 'self', the ways in which the individual person is singled out by various types of interested knowledge (or is 'interpellated' by discourse) as *the* unit via which experience should be understood. These individuating processes frequently turn out to be highly British and imperialist. In this sense, 'self-awareness' has not been the solution, but the problem.

For Macmurray, recognition (in the Hegelian sense) between persons should be seen as the basic unit of thought, whereas mere individual reflection shows a disappearance from the world. Moreover, Macmurray stressed the distinction between *subjects*, who remain individual (and sceptical/Humean), and *agents*, who recognise

Figure 4.2   John Macmurray. (Courtesy of Floris Books.)

one another's humanity and are thus able to act in the social sphere and create humanity. For Macmurray, persons are always *both* subject and agent and cannot *act* simply as subjects, but merely undergo *activity*. This can readily be compared to the way in which Scots are both British – as in the activity-laden Humean subject – and Scottish – as in the acting person. For personalist thought, the self becomes subject at times, while trying to act as the agent, and wavers between the two poles. Macmurray and other personalist philosophers like him are in this sense much closer to a continental European tradition of describing post-Enlightenment action, than is any movement in England. Recent writing on Englishness, moreover, has stressed that philosophy has not really been central to English identity. In this sense, the 'auld alliance' between Scotland and France remains as intellectually solid as it was in the Middle Ages.

SUMMARY

• David Hume is perhaps Scotland's best known philosopher. His work is libertarian in the sense of taking will away from the Christian God and pushing it underground as individual civility; this form of individualism, however, also made it easier to pull Scots away from local/national community and towards a new British identification.
• Adam Smith is perhaps best known for his economic theory, an enormously important mix of free trade and care for others. He also championed a form of rhetoric that was extremely Anglocentric.
• Both David Hume and Adam Smith, as well as their followers, had a huge influence on the polity of the emerging United States.
• Thomas Reid moved away from Hume's scepticism, believing in a continuity of social belief, or Common Sense.
• Reid's Common Sense prevailed, along with a socially-minded version of free trade, and occasionally a Francophile republican Jacobinism, in the earlier part of the nineteenth century; in the latter part of the century, philosophy's central place in Scottish education came under attack.
• At the end of the nineteenth century, Scotland developed strong socialist and Marxist traditions, which remain to an extent in place today, especially in Glasgow and its environs.
• Modern Scottish philosophy has built on Common Sense and socially shared action; it has also more recently taken a decisively post-Enlightenment turn in questioning the solidity of the individual over community, and universal moral standards.
• In the mid-twentieth century, the most important exponent of a 'personalist' tradition was John Macmurray; Alisdair MacIntyre's Nietzschean-Aristotelean destruction of universalism has also been influential.
• Existentialist and Sartrean concerns have remained strong in Scottish thought since the 1960s.

QUESTIONS FOR FURTHER RESEARCH AND THOUGHT

• How has David Hume influenced Scottish culture?
• Should Common Sense be seen as within Enlightenment tradition or as pulling away from Enlightenment tradition?

- Does Scotland's Reidian Common Sense have similarities with Thomas Paine's American revolutionary book *Common Sense?*
- Why has socialism been stronger in Scotland than in England?
- What is mid-twentieth century English philosophy's (specifically, logical positivism's) relation to Scottish thought?
- Does late-twentieth-century 'theory' (deconstruction, postcolonialism, poststructuralism, Lacanian psychoanalysis) seem closer to Scottish, English or British thought?

FURTHER READING

Allen, David, *Virtue, Learning, and the Scottish Enlightenment*, Edinburgh: Edinburgh University Press, 1993.
A huge and very thorough study of the period.

Beveridge, Ronald and Craig Turnbull, *Scotland After Enlightenment: Image and Tradition in Modern Scottish Culture*, Edinburgh: Polygon, 1997.
A follow-up to their well-known study *The Eclipse of Scottish Culture*; it is useful in documenting the ways in which images of Scottish culture were for a long time associated with darkness and backwardness.

Broadie, Alexander, *Why Scottish Philosophy Matters*, Edinburgh: Saltire, 2000.
A short but important introduction to three Scottish thinkers – Scotus, Hume and Reid – attempting to link them to a single Scottish tradition.

Broadie, Alexander (ed.), *The Scottish Enlightenment: An Anthology*, Edinburgh: Canongate, 2000.
A weighty and wide-ranging compendium of classic Enlightenment thinking. See also Broadie's *Cambridge Companion to the Scottish Enlightenment* (2003).

Broadie, Alexander, *The Scottish Enlightenment: The Historical Age of the Historical Nation*, Edinburgh: Birlinn, 2001.
An important and celebrated overview of the period. It convincingly ties the period to earlier traditions, carefully distancing himself from the idea that Enlightenment was pure benefit brought

by Britishness. One problem might be that the Enlightenment is for Broadie purely beneficial, bypassing problems of Eurocentrism and 'race'.

Docherty, Thomas, *Criticism and Modernity: Aesthetics, Literature, and Nations in Europe and its Academies*, Oxford: Oxford University Press, 1999.
A scholarly account of the Enlightenment, and Scottish culture's interaction with Europe during it.

Ferguson, Adam, ed. Fania Oz-Salzberger, *Essay on the History of Civil Society*, Cambridge: Cambridge University Press, 1996, originally published 1767.
Ferguson argues for a 'natural' history of mankind, sensitive to the diversity of societies but economically highly pragmatic.

Hume, David, ed. Knud Haakonssen, *Political Essays*, Cambridge: Cambridge University Press, 1994, originally published early 1740s.
A collection of Hume's political works.

Hume, David, ed. Tom L. Beauchamp, *An Enquiry Concerning the Principles of Morals*, Oxford: Clarendon, 2003, originally published 1739.
A description of Hume's idea of a 'science of nature', placing high importance on passions and inspiration, a stress that would resound in utilitarianism.

Hume, David, ed. Tom L. Beauchamp, *An Enquiry Concerning Human Understanding*, Oxford: Oxford University Press, 1999, originally published 1748.
The classic account of scepticism and the problems of causality.

Laing, R. D., *The Divided Self*, London: Penguin, 1960.
Ground-breaking account of the doubleness of the individual in modern capitalist societies, moving towards Laing's late-1960s work, which would further stretch Sartrean anti-capitalism to show how schizophrenia was to an extent a defence against economic demands – and would thus exert an important influence on Deleuze and Guattari. It can be compared to other early 1960s classics of the New Left, such as Herbert Marcuse's *One Dimensional Man*.

MacIntyre, Alistair, *After Virtue*, Notre Dame: University of Notre Dame Press, 1984.
MacIntyre strikingly returns to Aristotle for ethical guidance, bypassing the 'Western tradition' as it is understood from Plato to Hume.

Macmurray, John, *The Self as Agent*, London: Faber and Faber, 1969; John Macmurray, *Persons in Relation*, London: Faber and Faber, 1969.
These two books, based on Gifford Lectures at Glasgow University in 1953–4, are the classic account of the Scottish attack on logical positivism; comparable to postcolonialism (as I have argued) and postmodernism (as Cairns Craig has argued), Macmurray's work as a whole is currently being rediscovered.

Macquarrie, John, *Existentialism*, Harmondsworth: Penguin, 1973.
Perhaps the best-known overview of existentialism in any language. Scrupulously impartial but it does indicate how important existentialism was in Scotland; the Sartrean context links R. D. Laing in the 1960s to James Kelman in the 1990s.

Mill, J. S., *Utilitarianism*, Oxford: Oxford University Press, 1998, first published 1863.
Perhaps the defining book of nineteenth-century liberalism by this Scottish-raised and educated figure; it sets out the famous argument that good should be defined as the greatest benefit to the most people. This Kantian ethical stress is problematic and depends on how we identify persons and benefit; it is open, for example, to accusations of Eurocentrism. Mill was himself with the East India Company for thirty years.

Paton, H. J., *The Modern Predicament: A Study in the Philosophy of Religion*, London: George Allen and Unwin, 1955.
An under-rated (and difficult to find) study, like John Macmurray primarily questioning logical positivism and its tendency to isolate specific knowledges (again, to an extent, the legacy of Hume and the Scottish Enlightenment). Paton is more explicitly Christian than Macmurray in seeing religious spirit as the missing unifying element.

Reid, Thomas, *An Inquiry into the Human Mind, on the principles of Common Sense*, Edinburgh: Edinburgh University Press, 1997, first published 1764.
This is now recognised as a classic, yet also as problematising the Enlightenment project as a whole. Against Hume's dissociated sensory impressions, it sets up a model of perception as a historical process, thus pointing away from civility as awakened in the individual, towards a more communitarian understanding

Smith, Adam, *The Wealth of Nations*, New York: Modern Library, 2000, first published 1776.
Frequently cited as the most important book ever written on economics. A right-wing British tank has taken Smith's name, yet even a cursory reading of the text shows that Smith argues for (in more modern terms) a 'mixed economy' in which people can realise their full social potential. Contrary to late twentieth-century popular belief, he argues for checks on the worst excesses of *laissez faire*.

Smith, Adam, *Theory of Moral Sentiments*, Cambridge: Cambridge University Press, 2002, first published 1759.
This puts forward the then-sensational argument that people are born with an innate sense of good and evil, rather than good and evil being products of Reason or law, and that mutual benefit rather arises from 'sympathy' with others.

CHAPTER 5

Education in Scotland

In Scotland there remains a common feeling – sometimes quite a vague one – that the Scottish education system is more prestigious and just than its English equivalent, with which it has never been unified, and from which it takes care to distinguish itself. Educationalists have offered two different interpretations of this belief: firstly, that it is a mistake arising from the need to stress whatever is different and unique about Scottish society, leading people to over-estimate the chances ordinary people have had to enter university; secondly, that Scottish education is based on entirely alternative precepts and an un-British relation to other civic bodies, based on an ideal described – after the phrase made popular by G. E. Davie – as a 'democratic intellect'.

Elements of both of these conflicting arguments are relevant: the Scottish education system is generally more ancient, more comprehensive and has more pride in its open access than the English one, but this is not to say that young Scots have always had easy access to the education they have wanted, or that their choice of subject-matter is wider than that of their English counterparts. Certainly, however, *generalism* in education remains important in Scotland *as an ideal*, and this ideal itself creates a certain social unity.

Davie's generalism makes him, to an extent, an heir of Adam Smith in placing importance on an all-round education, which he sees being attacked in particular in the 'Britishing' Education Act of 1872, and Smith's Enlightenment was inter-disciplinary in a way to which Davie's general education wanted to return. Christopher Harvie reminds us that Enlightenment thinkers were not just 'in favour of' inter-disciplinarity, but *in need of* it, in an environment requiring extreme academic flexibility – one that saw Smith writing on linguistics, aesthetics and economics, and teaching physics.

What is certain is that, as a popular institution, the Scottish university is generally older than the English one: in the Middle Ages there arose a tradition of Scots travelling to Paris and other European centres of learning (not often to Oxford and Cambridge), and bringing their expertise back to Scotland. Eventually the pressure of knowledge led to the set-up of St Andrews University in 1411, and students of the university continued the tradition of studying abroad and bringing back their academic skills. Some stayed in Europe for considerable periods of time, and the University of Paris in particular had a huge proportion of Scottish professors.

Glasgow University was established by Papal Bull in 1451, Aberdeen in 1495, and, last among Scotland's four 'ancient' universities, Edinburgh in 1582. This means that, for the long period between 1582 and the establishment of Durham University in 1832 and London University, in its current form, in 1836, Scotland had four universities compared to England's two. This fact in itself is not that striking; what is more significant is that whereas the ancient

Figure 5.1   St Mary's College, St Andrews. (Source: University of St Andrews.)

English universities, Oxford and Cambridge, have a long history of conflict and boundary disputes with their host towns, the Scottish ones have been more successful at maintaining close relationships with their communities. The 'town and gown' basis is also reflected at a local level by the wide system of parish schools established according to the recommendations of John Knox's *First Book of Discipline*, published in 1560. The broad-based university feeding system meant that a number of boys (for, until the late nineteenth century, 'boys' they always were) from poor backgrounds were able to reach university (often returning to their old schools as teachers), leading to the tradition of the 'lad o' pairts', or 'boy of means', the occasional lucky boy for whom education was a gateway to a better life. How common the story of the lad o' pairts was – how many independent-minded working-class boys really made it to university during any one period – is an ongoing debate in Scottish Studies.

So there are two elements to the 'democratic intellect' ideal described by Davie: the first is *inclusiveness*: how many common lads made it all the way. The second element is *generalism*: the ideal of an education that ranges across a large area of connected subjects, rather than specialising in any one subject. For Davie and most subsequent commentators, at the centre of the generalist approach has been philosophy, seen in Scotland as a practical subject from which other subjects have grown (see Chapter 4). Indeed, until the mid-nineteenth century a wide range of subjects from geometry to physics were studied *as* philosophy – from first principles, and with the question *why* never far off. And, according to Davie, in Scotland topics were much more often discussed in class than simply passed as knowledge from teacher to pupils, and achievement was more often measured by peers rather than by superiors.

Tellingly, during the 1980s, when Scotland was least well represented politically, and even though Thatcherite policy was stressing economic practicality, there was something of a revival of 'generalist' philosophical and social thought in Scotland, as typified by the Polygon 'Determinations' series of books, of which Davie's *The Crisis of the Democratic Intellect* was one important volume. Put another way, questions arising in seemingly disparate subjects all became *ethical* questions – in part as a defence against the dismantling of Scottish infrastructure – and generalism was back in place. The 'democratic intellect' stands for more than merely a way of managing universities

– it implies a commitment to a public ethics in which as many people as possible should be active, well read and critical. Today, almost one and a half times more people in Scotland are involved in higher education at the age of twenty-one than in England. And although not all of these students are majoring in Moral Philosophy, there may again be a mood in the country that sees education as something to be protected from the bare aims of corporate sponsors demanding specifics, and tuned to the personal development of each student.

Despite being eroded by British standardisations of the late nineteenth and early twentieth century, the 'democratic intellect' ideal retains a great deal of currency. As in the ideal, people educated in Scotland today tend to enter the critical community of the university at a slightly younger age – typically seventeen or eighteen instead of eighteen or nineteen – and secondary education is structured accordingly, the Scottish Higher being an exam usually following a one-year course as opposed to the two-year A-level in England. Entry to university in Scotland is based on the results of these exams – an extension of the ideal of universal and fair access – where English universities often also require interviews or recommendations (however, the process of entry itself is administered in both England

Figure 5.2 Typical comprehensive school today. (Photograph: thanks to Mainholm Academy.)

and Scotland by a common British system). More importantly, specialisation is still often postponed as long as possible in the Scottish system, and secondary school students tend to take a maximum of five or six Highers, where most students in England take a maximum of three or four A-levels. Even after entering university, the generalist emphasis continues, with most first and second-year university students in Scotland choosing from a range of three, four, five, or more subjects, rather than specialising immediately, as is common in England. It is also much easier for Scottish students to 'switch' courses after a year, or not to specify their major subject until their second, or even third, year. Correspondingly, the Scottish degree usually lasts four years as opposed to the typical English three years, though it is possible to take a three-year 'General', non-Honours BA in Scotland, an option defended by Davie as increasing inclusiveness (though the non-Honours degree is much less popular than it once was). The perceived difference in levels is hammered home by the fact that, at the four ancient Scottish universities, the first degree awarded is a Master's, rather than a Bachelor's, degree.

Davie caught the question of general, open-access education just as it was becoming topical. As recently as the 1960s, Scots supported 'comprehensivisation' – the creation of inclusive and non-examined comprehensive schools catering for most twelve to sixteen year olds – much more enthusiastically than did the English. Even more recently, the first real arguments between the Edinburgh and Westminster Parliaments involved the Scottish Parliament's determination to keep university education free despite the British trend (inherited by Tony Blair from Margaret Thatcher) to gradually privatise education, and require students to pay part of their own fees. This argument led to the set-up of the Independent Committee of Inquiry into Student Finance in 1999, and indicated Scots' feelings on free education.

It is highly significant that the first major threats from Edinburgh to test its Parliamentary powers should relate to education. Research has shown that the issue of education is still closely associated in Scots' minds with the Parliament, and even with their Scottishness as such. Many of the people who campaigned for devolution in the 1980s and 1990s were educationalists – teachers, lecturers and students – as at the birth of modern Scottish Party Nationalism in the 1920s. And in 1999, 60 per cent of Scottish people believed that the mere fact of having a Parliament would increase the quality of education. Education is tied to Scotland's sense of community: many Scots remain committed to free education even in the face of creeping privatisation, and Westminster has to tread lightly when dismantling this particular pillar of the welfare state. There are still remarkably few private schools (or 'opt-out' schools, which have left their local education authority) in Scotland as compared with England. In Scotland, boarding-school culture is a rarity. Most parents send their children to the school nearest to their homes, and expect a decent level of education there. (It should be noted also that there is a kind of religious 'opt-out': in 1918 the Education (Scotland) Act relieved Catholics of paying double school fees – a boon for Catholic children, though they still faced pockets of sectarianism in employment in the mid-twentieth century.)

Significantly, a number of English figures in major positions of power have been educated in Scotland or chosen to send their children to Scottish institutions, at either secondary or university level. Prime minister Tony Blair was educated at Fettes College in Edinburgh (where Sean Connery, famously, delivered milk) before going on to Oxford University; the heir to the British throne, Prince Charles, attended school at Gordonstoun, and his son William, second in line to the throne, attended Scotland's oldest university, St Andrews. And while we are only talking about elite cases here, it is a good indication of how the distinctiveness of Scottish education is well known and carefully protected; it is fair to say that Scottish education has long been thought of as a marker of academic excellence.

Following the ancient and already prestigious universities, Anderson's College in Glasgow became Strathclyde University in 1964, and Heriot-Watt near Edinburgh also achieved university status in 1966. In 1967 Stirling University was built, and in the same year Dundee University split from St Andrews. More sweepingly, in the 1990s the 'new universities' were created from old further education colleges, among them Glasgow Caledonian University, and Napier University in Edinburgh.

The creation of new universities in Scotland is part of a general trend: number of universities across the UK has increased rapidly, for better or worse (and worse is not unthinkable: some argue that more full-time students merely means lower unemployment figures). More ominously, the Research Assessment Exercise (RAE), which 'rates' academics on a point scale according to how many blind-refereed articles they have published, has begun to be used to create 'league tables' of university research (the term seemed more apt, perhaps, during the 1990s soccer boom when every politician suddenly became a lifelong supporter of a Premiership team). The RAE, viewed from the stance of generalism, causes all sorts of problems: it limits the kind of publications academics, especially young academics, want to produce, so that instead of the university taking its place in the public sphere and sparking debates (a role traditionally fulfilled by 'semi-academic' journals like *Blackwell's*, *Cencrastus* and the *Edinburgh Review*), it is increasingly talking to itself. You may still find the *Edinburgh Review* on the bookshelves of a good bookshop; you are extremely unlikely to find the kind of high-prestige academic journal in which most young academics have to publish to get 'RAE points'. This removal of the university from the public sphere goes against the Scottish tradition of generalist criticism – it creates a community of academics with no outlet. If the anxiety of 1872 was of Scotland's civic educational traditions being swamped by a Anglo-British insularity and atomisation, then the change that took place at the end of the 1990s, with 'league tables' of academic performance, was perhaps even more significant.

SUMMARY

- The Scottish and English educational systems have never been unified; their separateness was guaranteed by the Act of Union (1706).
- Scotland has four ancient universities, England only two; the Scottish universities took some of their students from 'parish schools' established along the guidelines laid down by John Knox.
- The Scottish educational tradition of the 'democratic intellect', a phrase coined by G. E. Davie, incorporates both ideals of social inclusion and general education, in which a range of subjects are studied, typically centred on philosophical and critical thought.
- Scots' ideas about education are closely tied up with their ideas about their political representation and the Scottish Parliament.
- In Scotland, although students tend to go to university slightly younger, they specialise in a single subject slightly later.
- A Scottish Honours degree lasts four years, not three, as is usual in

England. At the four ancient Scottish universities, the first degree is a Master's, rather than a Bachelor's.

* Scottish education is generally thought of as highly prestigious.

QUESTIONS FOR FURTHER RESEARCH AND THOUGHT

* Is Scottish education really as 'generalist' as it likes to think?
* What was the relationship between the form of Scottish education and the way Scottish ideas were disseminated up to 1872?
* Education is a common subject of Scottish fiction. What were some of the attitudes of twentieth-century novels to secondary education in Scotland?
* Is the impact of the British Research Assessment Exercise comparable (RAE) to the impact of 1872?
* How do Scots view 'opt-out' schools (schools which have left their education authorities to go private)?

FURTHER READING

Anderson, John, *Education and Inquiry*, Oxford: Blackwell, 1980.
With retrospect, this can be seen as a classic of pro-generalist, pro-philosophical educational thinking; Anderson's influence is perhaps now better understood than it was in the 1980s.

Anderson, R. D., *Education and Opportunity in Victorian Scotland*, Oxford: Clarendon, 1983.
This tackles the thorny question of the viability of the story of the 'lad o' pairts', and access to education on the part of common people.

Anderson, R. D., *Education and the Scottish People*, Oxford: Clarendon, 1995.
Similar to the above, but rethought and expanded.

Davie, G. E., *The Democratic Intellect: Scotland and Her Universities in the Nineteenth Century*, Edinburgh: Edinburgh University Press, 1981.
Originally published in 1963, this book changed the way Scots saw their education, and eventually also led to some concrete institutional changes.

Davie, G. E., *The Crisis of the Democratic Intellect: The Problem of Generalization and Specialization in Twentieth-Century Scotland*, Edinburgh: Polygon, 1986.
A follow-up to the above, intended to update the original thesis; part of the important 'Determinations' series.

Paterson, Lindsay, *Education and the Scottish Parliament*, Edinburgh: Dunedin, 2000.
This is hard to find and written in slightly technical language, but it is an important and thorough speculation on the place of education in Scottish politics.

Paterson, Lindsay, *Scottish Education in the Twentieth Century*, Edinburgh: Edinburgh University Press, 2003.
At the time of writing, this highly readable account is the only recent and comprehensive history of modern education in Scotland, starting around 1872 and moving through to devolutionary times.

Scotland, James, *The History of Scottish Education*, London: University of London Press, 1969, 2 vols.
The only complete modern history before Paterson; although weighty and authoritative, it has been partly overtaken by political and structural changes.

Walker, Andrew Lockhart, *The Revival of the Democratic Intellect: Scotland's University Traditions and the Crisis in Modern Thought*, Edinburgh: Polygon, 1994.
Another of the 'Determinations' series this argues,with a somewhat anti-Oxbridge tone, that the time for a distinctively Scottish education is returning.

CHAPTER 6

Religion in Scotland

L eaving aside education, which was discussed in Chapter 5, law
and religion have been the main props of Scottish civic society
left since 1707 – at least on paper – and much of Scotland's nationhood within union has been negotiated via these two other institutions. Chapter 7 will look at law; here I sketch out some of the
parameters of religion as it affects culture.

Religion is a notoriously unreliable way to describe a national
culture: reading contemporary Scottish literature for Calvinist
themes is like looking for signs of Buddhism in Tokyo department
stores. This is not to say there is no relation to Calvinism (or
Buddhism) at all, but that religion's 'culture' is usually buried, and
tends to have only dubiously 'national' characteristics. In any case,
while the UK is usually seen from abroad as a Christian country,
numbers of Christian worshippers have been in sharp decline for the
past half-century or so.

But religion certainly tells us something about a nation's mythscape, about how that nation conceives of its own sense of community. And at least until the mid-twentieth century, Christianity
determined everyday behaviour to a large extent. We should be
careful here, however. Firstly, Christianity no longer has the cultural
stronghold it once did. This is not to say that people feel less spiritual, but that their spirituality can less easily be placed relative to specific institutions. Secondly and similarly, linking 'a religion' and 'a
culture' risks simple old-fashioned racism, since it implies an unbroken and ongoing community. As I hope I have made clear by now,

unbroken lineages are not what makes a nation: nations are made of both continuities *and* discontinuities.

Modern Scotland, moreover, is not only a secular nation, it is also to a large extent behind the *invention* of the modern secular nation itself. Enlightenment thinkers like David Hume tried to *rationalise* religion, to make it answerable and useful, rather than merely reject it – though they were still sometimes seen as bordering on heresy. One change that occurred around the 1740s and as part of the general movement of Enlightenment, was that moderates came to control the kirk (church). If Scottish Christianity has a distinct character, it comes not merely from the Reformation, but also from the Enlightenment, and rationality and applicability are bound up with it. Even during the high point of Christian socialism – at the end of the nineteenth century and the beginning of the twentieth – Scottish religion had a 'secular' feel, being associated with specific uses in various kinds of community. Even the missionary movement in which Scots played such a promi-nent part, for all its faults, was trying to bring specific benefits to spe-cific communities. Religion and reform continued to be linked within Scottish Christianity through to the time of the early BBC, whose first director general, the Scot John Reith, insisted that it carry pro-grammes with some religious (that is, Christian) content.

Before union, the convergence of Scottish and English religion had already been a touchy issue for centuries. Charles I and other English monarchs had been trying to conglomerate the two nations' churches, insisting on the Book of Common Prayer in church services. Opposing Scots drew up a National Covenant demanding religious separateness and protesting against Charles II's restoration of bishops and royal control over the church. The issue persisted until the crises which led to 1706 and the guarantee of a Hanoverian succession.

In Protestant/Reformation tradition, the individual's relationship with God takes priority, and Catholic symbolism is viewed as heret-ical. Protestantism also tends to be fatalist, relying on concrete forms of good, evil and destiny. The role of Providence is well illustrated immediately post-union by *Robinson Crusoe* (1719), an adaptation of the misadventures of the Scot Alexander Selkirk written by the English Protestant unionist pamphleteer Daniel Defoe.

As against a Scottish habit of thought which I am calling a 'secular religion', the UK, like a handful of other states including Saudi Arabia, Yemen and Israel, has an *established* church – a church tied to the state

– which is, symptomatically, not British at all: the Church of England. And the loss of interest in the Church of England is perhaps more traumatic for England than the loss of interest in the Church of Scotland is for Scotland: the idea of the English church, maybe because it lacks the utilitarian character I have been talking about, has remained welded to the idea of a peaceful, live-and-let-live 'organic' country life that Anglo-Britain persisted with as a 'national' image throughout the entire twentieth century. Thus, Margaret Thatcher's 1988 'Sermon on the Mound' address to the General Assembly of the Church of Scotland upset many believers by equating Christianity and her own interpretation of conservative values; it produced the opposite of the desired effect, and confirmed many Christians' devolutionary views. This arises from a real Anglo-Scottish misunderstanding: in English culture, the pastoral vicar still has real imaginative currency; in Scotland the image of the nation as spiritually united around small churches is usually met with irony when it still appears, for example via the neo-kailyard output of publishers D. C. Thomson.

After the Enlightenment the kirk lost its monopoly on the spirit. As well as noting the move to 'reason', it could be argued that this secularisation was a result of an early form of class consciousness caused by industrial reorganisation. However, T. M. Devine points out that the idea that Europe simply became secular on industrialisation is problematic: in fact the churches had an *increasing* influence throughout the nineteenth century, frequently speaking authoritatively on public issues. Thomas Chalmers, for example, was a focus for evangelism in the early nineteenth century, and used this position to exert influence over welfare policy and foster a culture of evangelical philanthropy. And churches' membership significantly *grew* in the Victorian era; their decline is much more recent than the 'industrialisation' argument implies. The 1845 Poor Law and the 1872 Education Act, and later the removal of parish councils in 1929, did erode some of the power of the church, but religion remained important to public life, in what Devine calls a 'fusion between Christian ethos and civic policy'. The General Assembly of the Church of Scotland has at times acted almost as a *de facto* Scottish Parliament (and this is doubtless another reason – as well as empire – why there was so little interest in a Scottish Parliament in the nineteenth century). From the 1870s the church became more willing to explicitly criticise social policy, and continued to do so well into the twentieth century. Until relatively recently, for example, the closing of shops on the holy day of Sunday was taken for granted.

Late nineteenth-century Scottish socialism was also at times allied to Christian beliefs – the Scottish Labour Party leader Kier Hardie, who entered Parliament in 1892, was a committed Christian; in the twentieth century, the Labour Party leader before Tony Blair, the Scot John Smith, was a committed devolutionist as well as a Christian. Nevertheless, many Scottish socialists have been broadly hostile to Christianity and, during the period from the 1880s to the 1930s, the Church faced a number of doctrinal problems posed by science and socialism – such as the debate between creationism and Darwinism – to which it struggled to find clear answers. A. C. Cheyne has also described how the late nineteenth century and early twentieth century saw a growth in popular culture which seriously dented religious participation – but at least one sector of the church responded with sub-organisations such as the Boys' Brigade, the Band of Hope and Sunday schools, matching wholesome group activities with a strongly Protestant and imperial agenda.

Although the missionary movement was originally blocked by the moderates in the Church of Scotland, from the 1830s Scots were active in what was viewed by all sections of the church as a social improving mission, encouraged by the terminology of race (which placed the unfortunate natives 'behind' us). By the 1890s Scots also had huge bases in central Africa, for example Nyasaland, 'a sort of Scots colony', following the work of David Livingstone. And to the embarrassment of today's church, during this period the *domestic* Christianising mission was seen as running in tandem with the *overseas* Christianising mission: the Highlands were at times viewed as an imperial hinterland comparable with deepest Africa.

The people of the West Highlands began to be converted to evangelical Christianity (that is, away from the Church of Scotland) in significant numbers between the 1820s and 1840s, when the Clearances and the famine were doing their worst. The Free Church supported crofters in their political struggles of the 1880s, when they organised against the Clearances with some political success. The picture usually painted of the Free Church is austere, but the 'revival service' was not entirely puritan, and some have noted its enthusiastic use of music. The breaking point that defines much of early Victorian Scottish culture came in 1843, when the Free Church demanded independence (in the end this was only guaranteed as late as 1921, by the Declamatory Articles). The 'Ten Years' War' of 1833–43 had seen the evangelicals' anger rise against what they saw as the established church's casual, and apparently corrupt, attitude to patronage. The Disruption was finally provoked by a walk-out in Edinburgh in May 1843. Secession – that is, churches leaving the established kirk – had been popular since the early eighteenth century, but had now turned into a national cultural rift as the church split, in a bid for separation that some scholars have seen as a kind of proto-nationalism. After 1916 there was an attempt to rejoin the churches, but this failed, in part as a result of a growing popular disillusion over the war.

It was perhaps only in the 1920s that the Church of Scotland reverted to an anti-Catholic stance for which it became known. Mid-century, Catholics, largely Irish immigrants, became scapegoats for social ills, being seen as encouraging indolence, intemperance and, especially during the depression, union agitation (the Church of Scotland was strongly opposed to the General Strike of 1926). Church of Scotland leaders, and often political Nationalist leaders, were keen to finger the 'alien' population as a cause for economic ills, so that to an extent the Church and the SNP do deserve the vaguely racist reputation which they retain from this time.

So from 1688 (the 'Glorious Revolution') and 1706 (the signing of the Act of Union), Scoto-*British* religious identity has been strongly Protestant, and Protestantism and imperialism have tended to develop together. As Linda Colley and others have pointed out, Britain's margins – Scotland and the Northern Irish settlers – *exaggerated* the Protestant identity integral to the British empire. Thus, until surprisingly recently, Scotland bought into (indeed, in figures like the anatomist/race theorist Robert Knox, helped to *create*) the pseudo-scientific image of Irish Catholics as dirty and indolent.

Most Scottish Catholics are descendants of the Irish who came to Scotland in the late nineteenth century or after, meaning that their families were relatively recent immigrants. Some of the considerable inequalities Catholics faced in the early to mid-twentieth century, in the workplace, in housing and in other sectors, can thus be explained by anti-immigrant prejudice as well as by religious prejudice. Catholics often had to set up alternative support communities within Scotland, Celtic Football Club being an obvious example. After 1918 separate Catholic schools were established with a curriculum including, for example, more religious study, meaning that the image of Catholics being 'more devout' is in a sense true, since religion is built into the curriculum. The writers of the Scottish Renaissance – the 1920s and 1930s boom in Scottish culture – also downplayed any Protestant Calvinist inheritance, this time in favour of an atheist socialist internationalism. It is notable that many Lowland Labour politicians have been Catholic, suggesting that their families were traditionally disenfranchised from British-imperial society. Scottish Catholics still tend to support Labour, and research by Steve Bruce and Tony Glendinning suggests that there are virtually no Catholic Tories *at all* in Scotland.

As suggested above, within the Church of Scotland there have been pockets of serious sectarianism. As early as the start of the 1850s the Scottish Reformation Society was producing anti-Irish-Catholic magazines. Irish and pan-Celtic political activity were used to demonise the Catholic community in the late nineteenth and early twentieth century. In 1923, a year after the agreement of Irish semi-independence, the Church of Scotland published *The Menace of the Irish Race to our Scottish Nationality*, and anti-Catholicism grew to a peak in 1935, when it became quasi-official policy. The Orange Order, named after the 'Glorious Revolution' and celebrating Protestant values with varying degrees of aggression, was boosted in the early nineteenth century by *Protestant* Irish immigration; today an Orange Walk still takes place annually on 12 July in Glasgow, with smaller walks in other, mostly western, towns. Orangeism remains a strong part of west of Scotland 'culture', exerting various kinds of loyalist influence from the pub to the football terrace to the Boys' Brigade. Visitors to Scotland, especially Glasgow, are sometimes surprised to see crowds of all ages walking *en masse* through the streets waving union flags, wearing Rangers FC shirts and playing flutes, in an odd combination of celebration and hatred. The Orange Walk is a kind of anti-carnival, one that supports empire instead of opposing it. The problem, of course, is the lack of empire (or technically, colonial empire). The fact that most marchers do not know what their union flags are celebrating is backed up by research which shows that there is little difference between Catholics and Protestants in terms of their attitudes to devolution, or even independence from the union.

In both Scotland and Northern Ireland, areas joined by cross-migration, British imperialism has thus historically created a sense of

Protestant defensiveness. From the Reformation to the Napoleonic Wars, Catholics were often an object of fear; in the early twentieth century discrimination continued even when both sides were experiencing poverty. The situation recalls that of the colonised Antillean described by the anti-colonial writer Frantz Fanon, the Caribbean who thinks he is a cut above the Senegalese because his skin is lighter, missing the obvious fact that both are equally colonised. Mercifully, evidence shows that sectarian 'culture' has largely disappeared among the young, but then organised religion as a whole has declined. Figures show that while some people are choosing to remain Christian, few are *becoming* Christian. And those who still are Christian don't go to church that often: while a reasonable proportion of people are sympathetic to Christianity, regular church (or place of worship) attendance has fallen to about 15 per cent. Perhaps surprisingly, this is not to say that people no longer believe in God: the proportion of people who think that there is no deity is actually much higher in England than it is in Scotland. In other words, Scotland still has a strong *spiritual* feeling, one much more pronounced than any specific *religious* feeling. This would also fit in with my previous suggestions that modern Scottish religion has tended to manifest as context-specific acts of good.

If any organised religion is growing in Scotland, it is not Christianity. A conservative census finds that around 1 per cent of Scotland's population are Islamic – a small proportion, but by far the largest non-Christian religion, and one that is growing, and is almost by definition more religiously devout than those who see themselves as Christian by social default. Mosques are springing up across Scotland, one of the best known being visible from this publisher's office (or outside it, anyway). The Tharpaland Kadampa Buddhist Retreat Centre is also well known, and patronised by celebrities. But an influx of apparently exotic religions is, as T. M. Devine reminds us, hardly new: the Gorbals area of Glasgow became a centre of Jewish culture from the end of the nineteenth century, when Yiddish could be heard from tenement windows. From farther back still, pagan and other 'Celtic' religions still remain in pockets and can be seen, for example, in a Nordic influence on Shetland, which retains rituals including boat-burning and other seafaring-related rituals. 'New' religions (whatever that means) are also increasing, but these are hard to measure since, by definition, they have patterns of worship which cannot be 'counted' like church attendances, and involve more 'elective' practices, or what we might more pejoratively describe as 'pick and mix' religion.

In other words, it is not that belief in God has disappeared in Scotland, but that the Christian church has lost its hold on society. If this represents a modernisation, it is not in the sense that Scotland's world has become more materialistic, since the older Scottish Christianity was already strongly involved in material matters of reform; ironically, the decline of Christianity may even be a result of *less* materialism, or the sense that 'good works' no longer have the solid social meaning they used to. Perhaps those Scottish Christian philosophers who arrived on the scene at the time of the religion's decline, such as John Macmurray and H. J. Paton, were attempting to redress this loss by linking the spiritual and the social.

SUMMARY

- Even before the Act of Union, England was anxious to exert its religious power over Scotland.
- The Act of Union guaranteed a Protestant successor to the throne.
- Protestantism has been a central component in British imperialism.
- In 1843, the Free Church separated from the Church of Scotland; some people see this as a kind of national independence movement.
- The Church in Scotland has been, especially in the nineteenth century, a practical body, often concerned with specific social reforms.
- The Christian church went into decline in the early to mid-twentieth century, and now no longer holds the same authority it once did.
- The number of people who practise religions other than Christianity is small but growing. 'New' religions, or a 'pick and mix' of religious beliefs, are becoming common.

QUESTIONS FOR FURTHER RESEARCH AND THOUGHT

- Was the 1843 Disruption a cultural plea for national separateness?
- How powerful was the Free Church in the late nineteenth century?
- Why was the Church of Scotland so anti-Catholic in the mid-twentieth century?

- Can any contemporary or twentieth-century Scottish novelists be described as writing within a Calvinist tradition?
- What are some of the problems that might be faced by a Muslim living in a rural Scottish community?

FURTHER READING

Drummond, A. L. and J. Bulloch (eds), *The Church in Victorian Scotland, 1843–1874,* Edinburgh: St Andrew Press, 1975; A. L. Drummond and J. Bulloch (eds), *The Church in Late Victorian Scotland, 1874–1900,* Edinburgh: St. Andrew Press, 1978.
A slightly difficult to find but useful pair of books chronicling the history of the Victorian church from the time of the Disruption.

Brown, Stewart J. and Michael Fry (eds), *Scotland in the Age of the Disruption,* Edinburgh: Edinburgh University Press, 1993.
A collection of essays by influential scholars, some arguing that the 1843 Disruption helps explain the subsequent 'autonomy' of Scottish institutions, and that the Disruption was one of the most important cultural events in Scottish history.

Cheyne, A.C., *The Transforming of the Kirk,* Edinburgh: St Andrew Press, 1983.
An account of the nineteenth-century church and its relation to industrialisation.

Knox, John, ed. David Laing, *The Works of John Knox, Volumes 1 and 2: History of the Reformation in Scotland,* Eugene, OR: Wipf and Stock, 2004, first published 1543, 2 vols.
John Knox's account of the Reformation in Scotland; also available in various other editions.

Church of Scotland: http://www.churchofscotland.org.uk

Scottish Catholic Media Office: http://www.scmo.org.uk/

Free Church of Scotland: http://www.freechurch.org/

Free Presbyterian Church of Scotland: http://www.fpchurch.org/

Islamic Unity Society: http://www.ius.org.uk

CHAPTER 7

Scots Law

The independence (or, more correctly, the separateness, since independence implies a movement *from* a more significant body) of Scots law was guaranteed in principle by the Act of Union which came into force in 1707. Today, Scots law remains an institution separate from English law, and is the subject studied in Scottish universities (though in a munificent gesture of multiculturalism Dundee University offers both Scots and English law degrees). An Edinburgh law school was founded in 1707 – the very year the union was enacted – and a Glasgow one in 1714. As far as Scots law is concerned, English law is foreign, even though in terms of citizenship England is in the same state and there are many areas, for example the transfer of property, where the systems must regularly negotiate. In cultural terms, Scots law, like Scottish education, is something that Scots tend to assume is respected worldwide, although most would be hard-pressed to explain why. Here we are primarily interested in the structure of Scots law and its autonomy (rather than, for example, the details of conveyancing).

Scots law's structure has changed significantly quite recently, with the Scotland Act 1998 (enabling devolution) and the Human Rights Act 1998 (intended as an international protection). Scots law's separateness comes under Article 25 of the Act of Union (here I use the singular 'Act' though, as any Nationalist will tell you, the 'Act' has been breached so often that it is more accurate to use the plural 'Acts'), and Article 19 guarantees the independence of the Court of Session – the highest civil court in Scotland, excepting the House of Lords – and the High Court of Justiciary – the highest criminal court. The High Court of Justiciary is presided over by the Lord Justice-Clerk. As well as hearing appeals, it is a court of first instance and goes on circuit – West (in practice, it sits almost permanently in Glasgow), North, South and 'home' (Parliament House in Edinburgh). Recently, it has even travelled to the Netherlands, for the trial of Libyan citizens accused of the Lockerbie bombing (when a sabotaged passenger aircraft crashed into the Borders town of Lockerbie). Generally, criminal prosecutions are conducted by the state – the Procurator Fiscal first decides whether or not to prosecute, and whether a case merits jury trial – and are ultimately in the hands of the law officers of the Crown in Scotland. Before devolution, there were two law officers: the Lord Advocate and the Solicitor General for Scotland; there is now a third, the Advocate General.

Civil court actions are brought by the person wronged. Private prosecution, usually by the victim of crime, remains possible in Scotland where the public prosecutor has decided not to prosecute. The Court of Session, the highest civil court located in Scotland, sits in Parliament House on Edinburgh High Street, behind St Giles Kirk, in a building incorporating the site of the pre-1707 Parliament. The Court is divided into the Outer House and the Inner House. The Inner House is mostlly a court of appeal; it has a First Division, presided over by the Lord President and three Lords of Session, and a Second Division, presided over by the Lord Justice-Clerk and three Lords of Session. The Outer House is a court of first instance for civil claims, and often uses a jury of twelve people.

Scots law is nuanced differently from English Law. The rules of evidence, for example, are more stringent for criminal than for civic cases, and in Scotland evidence must be *corroborated*, or verified by two other sources. Scotland also, famously, has a 'not proven' verdict for criminal trials involving all charges right up to murder, in addition to the usual 'guilty' and 'not guilty', to be used when proof seems insufficient. *State* legislation, of course, is British, or should have become British since 1707, though again we face the problem of whether the English structure has actually changed. Scottish Acts since 1707 have typically followed English and Welsh ones, latterly merely being suffixed 'Scotland' (Acts applying to England and Wales, symptomatically, have no suffix). United Kingdom statutes are written for English law, and require 'translation' for Scottish contexts.

More broadly, although Article 25 of the Act of Union was supposed to destroy the old English and Scottish constitutions to create
a British constitution, what happened in practice was that the old
English constitution stayed in place. The instability of an English
constitution stretched to cover a lopsided union would come back to
haunt the British government in demands for constitutional change
which peaked in the late twentieth century. Moreover, recently a re-
reading of seventeenth and eighteenth-century Scottish sources has
suggested that Parliamentary rule in Scottish constitutional tradition
is dependent on popular assent, rather than the Anglo-British 'king-
in-Parliament' model – something which would have changed in 1707
were this really a union. The obvious solution, for some campaigners,
both English and Scottish, is to create a new, coherent constitution,
whether for Scotland or the UK. One such articulation was the Claim
of Right for Scotland (1988) which, despite its provocative title, was
addressed to the constitutional absence at the heart of the UK, rather
than representing a narrow Scottish Nationalism.

So from where does Scots law derive its authority? The law's major
formal sources are legislation, and the precedent created by the deci-
sion of the courts as to interpretation of that legislation; its minor
formal sources include authoritative textbooks and custom. There is
also an extant body of thought on law in the form of sources from the
time before legislation was set out as formally as it is today, that is,
before the start of the nineteenth century. And some pre-1707
old Scottish Parliament laws, unless subsequently repealed by
Westminster, still form part of Scots law 'in desuetude', in other
words they are ancient but theoretically valid, and are still sometimes
brought up. Law that cannot be referred to any legislation at all is
known as common law, and is more influenced by English law – a
context that, as in the English constitution, is more dependent on tradition, as in the major cultural division at the heart of misunderstand-
ings about what devolution really is.

The civil law/common law distinction is a pointer to a cultural
difference between continental Europe and Scotland on the one hand,
and the central principles of Britain and its empire on the other.
England is unusual in its stress of common law over Roman law;
English law, however, was also the legal *lingua franca* of the British
empire. Again this feeds into a cultural difference between
Anglophone, ex-colonial Greater Britain (as the empire was called in

late-colonial times) on one hand, and the rest of Europe on the other – with today's Scotland rediscovering its affinities with the latter. The question, of course, is how this fits with the stability of the union. Ironically, important constitutional law cases have usually taken place in England, meaning that Scots lawyers are less likely to come across them, even though these cases are, in a sense, more of a Scottish issue. This changes somewhat with the creation of a Scottish Parliament, in that some questions of jurisdiction have to be rethought, meaning that Scotland again has a serious say in shaping public law.

During that most unionist period, the mid-nineteenth century, there was a strong body of thought which tried to bring Scots law into line with English law, in large part precisely because English Law had become the basis of the law of empire. Generally, Scots law's authority went into decline during the nineteenth century, and the House of Lords, the highest civil court competent to hear Scottish cases but far removed in London, frequently simply misunderstood Scots law, or assumed it to be a less developed version of English law. And if my previous comments about Unionist Nationalism made sense, it will come as no surprise that Scots lawyers colluded in this convergence: there was even a Glasgow Law Amendment Society which sought to adapt Scots law to an Anglo-imperial standard. The absorption of the Scottish constitution at the time of union came to be seen, for example by the Victorian constitutional expert A. V. Dicey, as part of the 'evolution' of the English constitution; even today the UK is at times described in legal terms as an 'evolved state'. This situation of course renders absurd the idea of a 'union' of two previously separate states, but is in line with the idea of an 'organic' Anglo-British tradition based on precedent.

In the British (that is, English) constitutional tradition, based on a strong leader leading a strong executive (ruling party/parties) in a strong Parliament with nominal blessing from the Crown, legislation, we might argue, has become viewed as something to be *used by* the executive, rather than debated. This leads to the criticism that House of Commons debates are not really debates at all, since they are not intended to decide anything, but rather to announce legislation already decided by the executive. This situation has been shaken up, however, by both devolution and the European Union, both of which typically involve coalitions, multi-party fora and proportional representation, troubling the unitary power of the British executive, the representative of a monarch who only nominally remains head of state but whose consent is required for every law. (Where was the monarch when air strikes on Iraq were decided on the basis of stories of weapons of mass destruction? Whereas in republics such as the US, the president, as head of state, can make up non-existent intelligence reports, in the UK intelligence officers are *Crown* servants, not *civil* servants – they report to the monarch, who has a duty to veto policy based on spurious information. Scotland has an added problem here, since, should it become independent tomorrow, its Parliament is still unicameral and could even worsen the over-centralisation of the executive seen in the UK Parliament.) In traditional Scottish jurisprudence, legal authority does indeed issue from a pluralist republican thinking, one that, judging by recent readings of older sources, sees the people – rather than the Crown, or even Parliament as such – as sovereign.

Given the anti-European rhetoric of much of the British press, you may be surprised to hear that the UK was the first country to ratify the European Convention on Human Rights in 1950. European Union legislation in various forms has been in place since 1972. European law already outranks national law in both Scotland and England: where British legislation is not compatible with the European Convention on Human Rights, Parliament must change the national law or refer to the European Court of Justice. In practice, problems of clashing competence 'upwards' to Europe and 'downwards' to Scotland are usually avoided by consultation beforehand. Since 1999 the Judicial Committee of the Privy Council (formerly a colonial court of appeal, and located at 1, Downing Street) has been a final authority on the legislative competence of the Scottish Parliament relative to Britain and Europe. (The 2004 Constitutional Reform Bill, however, proposed a new Supreme Court which would combine the devolution jurisdiction of the Judicial Committee of the Privy Council and that of the Appellate Committee of the House of Lords.) The European Court sits in Luxembourg and is made up of one judge from each of the EU Member States. Of the four judges from the UK to have so far served on the European Court, two have been from a background of Scots law.

Scotland's highest civil law court is the House of Lords, the upper chamber of the UK Parliament, situated, of course, in England. The House of Lords hears Scots law-originated cases, and is deemed a

Scottish court. Usually two of its seven law lords have origins in Scots law, and the court is usually bound by its own precedents in other similar cases, however Anglocentric they may have been – so that the two Scots can find themselves in the minority even when hearing Scottish-originated cases. However, whereas in England, Wales and Northern Ireland, the House of Lords is also an appeal court for criminal cases, it does not hear appeals from the High Court of Justiciary in Scotland, which remains the highest criminal court for Scots law. As I noted above, unlike the British Parliament, the Scottish Parliament is unicameral, meaning that legislation, for better or worse, does not have to pass through an upper chamber, and can come into being more easily (and again, here we see a relative lack of importance of reliance on some kind of *precedent* in Scottish culture as compared with English culture).

At a more everyday level, sheriff courts exist all over Scotland, and are competent to try all crimes except murder, rape, treason and piracy, which go straight to the High Court of Justiciary. Today there are six sheriffdoms in Scotland corresponding to regions, each with its own Sheriff Principal. These sheriffdoms are in turn divided into sheriff court districts, each having its own sheriff court building. Like the Lord Ordinary in the Outer House of the Court of Session, the sheriff is a judge of first instance in civil matters, sitting alone. Sheriffs are appointed from amongst lawyers who have been qualified for at least ten years. Smaller crimes are prosecuted in local district courts, where procedure is always summary (as opposed to solemn) and, except in Glasgow, a Justice of the Peace serves as judge. There is also, at the time of writing, the possibility that the whole district court system may be replaced by a new 'summary sheriff'. Beneath this level again, the initial legal consultation for many people is with a voluntary advice-giving organisation like the Citizens' Advice Bureau, which gives information on debt, employment and what's left of the welfare state.

Practising Scots lawyers can be broadly divided into two categories: solicitors and advocates. Until recently, there were three areas in which only solicitors had licence to practise: conveyancing (the paperwork surrounding the buying and selling of property), executry services (wills), and the instruction of advocates. In 1990 the first two of these were opened up to those not qualified as solicitors, in order to increase competition – in line with the general trend of privatisation of the time. Most solicitors work in private practice, and much of their

Figure 7.1   Faculty of Advocates, Edinburgh. (Photograph: Michael Gardiner.)

work is still taken up by the three traditional areas, especially convey-ancing, dealing with property in the widest sense. Some of the larger law firms emphasise commercial rather than private-client work, which is less lucrative.

Advocates fulfill something like the role of barristers in England, having the right of audience in Scottish criminal courts. Their work is more varied than that of barristers, in part because of the custom that, unlike in England, an advocate accepts whatever cases come up. This is in part because of low case volume, but also in part reflects the tra-dition of intellectual generalism we saw in Chapter 5, in which wide-ranging debate is normal. Advocates are based in the Advocates Library in Parliament House in Edinburgh, one of the world's best equipped law libraries. After some experience, advocates can become QCs, or Queen's Counsel (or King's Counsel, depending on the monarch), and eventually judges. Under the Scotland Act 1998, judges' appointments are made by the sovereign on the recommenda-tion of the First Minister of the Scottish Parliament, who will have consulted the Lord President. In theory, any advocate can be appointed as a judge; in practice, only QCs are ever appointed as judges.

Finally, we might note the tendency of activists to use the contra-dictions of the Acts of Union *against* British unionism, some of which have been noted above. This tradition runs through Neil McCormick's legitimate claim that unless Elizabeth the Second is really Elizabeth the First, that British authority is only really English (a question that goes right to the heart of whether the union really is a union) to the likes of Robbie the Pict, who in *Robbie the Pict v Hingston* (1998) opposed the tolls for the Skye Bridge by appealing to the EU that the toll rendered taxation unfairly high for one 'partner' in union. This kind of literal reading of the union against itself has much in common with deconstruction, a way of reading that undoes internal contradictions in a text's logic by showing how certain sets of opposition fall apart under close reading. In other words, the Anglo-British historical tendency to *absorb* rather than *merge* is also its weakness, one that is revealed by close – we might say, *literary* – readings.

SUMMARY

- English law and Scots law are separate.
- The highest Scottish criminal court is the High Court of Judiciary in Edinburgh; the highest civil court is the House of Lords in London.
- Law which cannot be fixed to any final source is known as common law; this has more in common with English practice.
- In Scotland, in the main, there are two kinds of lawyers: advocates and solicitors.
- Many people only experience the law through advice-giving organisations like the Citizens Advice Bureau, or district courts.

QUESTIONS FOR FURTHER RESEARCH AND THOUGHT

- How true is it that, in Scots law tradition, the people have ultimate sovereignty, rather than the monarch?
- If you were accused of murder, would you rather be tried under Scots or English law?
- Find one case where devolution brought into question the relative power of Edinburgh against London, and describe how it was resolved.
- How far can the UK legally be described as a 'union'?

FURTHER READING

Ashton, Christina et al., *Fundamentals of Scots Law*, Edinburgh: W. Green, 2003.
A comprehensive short guide for law students, taking into account post-devolution changes.

Black, Robert et al. (eds), *The Laws of Scotland: Stair Memorial Encyclopaedia*, Edinburgh: Butterworth's/Law Society of Scotland, 1988–96.
A vast reference work, the title of which pays homage to Viscount Stair, who in 1681 published one of the first authoritative accounts of Scots law. Enormously expensive but authoritative and comprehensive, it contains entries by about 300 practising lawyers and academics. Necessarily out of date as soon as it appears, it was completed before recent changes in human rights law and devolution.

Crossan, Sean and Alistair B. Wylie, *Introductory Scots Law: Theory and Practice*, London: Hodder Arnold, 2004.
This is intended for general readers and those studying law as a 'minor'; it is a readable (and cheap!) guide to the basics of Scots law.

Erskine, John, *Institute of the Law of Scotland*, 8th edn, Edinburgh: Bell and Bradfute, 1871, first published 1773.
A description of classical Scots law as built from Roman Law and feudal custom; negotiates the difficult Enlightenment area of Scotland-in-Britain.

Farmer, Lindsay et al. (eds), *The State of Scots Law*, Edinburgh: Butterworth's, 2001.
A collection of critical essays taking into account the changes in Scots law over recent years.

Gloag, W. M. and Candlish Henderson, *The Law of Scotland*, 11th edn, Edinburgh: W. Green, 2001.
A vast and comprehensive guide used as a textbook by law students.

Himsworth, C. M. G. and C. M. O'Neill, *Scotland's Constitution*, Edinburgh: Lexus, 2003.
This identifies and examines the distinctively Scottish areas of law that emerge from the nation's partial, and increasing, role in state and European law.

McCormick, Neil, *Questioning Sovereignty*, Oxford: Oxford University Press, 1999.
A penetrating investigation into the relative legal powers of Scotland, the UK and Europe. McCormick has long been a champion of the movement to rethink the constitutional status of the UK and its member nations.

MacQueen, Hector, *Studying Scots Law*, Edinburgh: Butterworth's, 2004.
This is largely for students, and would-be students, of law, but also of general interest; a highly readable guide.

Stair, Viscount, ed. David M. Walker, *Institutions of the Laws of Scotland*, 6th edn, Edinburgh: University Presses of Edinburgh and Glasgow, 1981, first published 1681.
Of historical interest, this was one of the first textbooks on Scots law.

Walker, David M., *A Legal History of Scotland*, 7 vols, London: Butterworth's, 1987–2004.
The first modern comprehensive history of Scots law, running from medieval times through the Reformation, changes in the Acts of Union, the codifications of the Enlightenment, Victorian convergence, and finally the Europeanisation, human rights issues, and parliamentary considerations of the twentieth century.

The Scottish Courts: http://www.scotcourts.gov.uk

European Court of Human Rights: http://www.echr.coe.int/

Scottish Law Society: http://www.lawscot.org.uk/.

Faculty of Advocates: http://www.advocates.org.uk/

The Scottish Law Commission: http://www.scotlawcom.gov. uk/

CHAPTER 8

Sport in Scotland

Scots who have lived abroad will be familiar with the situation of being asked whether they are a Rangers supporter or a Celtic supporter (the correct answer, of course, is no). These two football clubs certainly draw huge home crowds – the 50,000 people packed into a home game at Celtic Park represent 1 per cent of the population of the entire nation. At the other end of the scale, a third-division home crowd at East Stirlingshire is likely to be less than 500 people. In all, there are forty-two clubs in the four Scottish senior leagues, plus a thriving and well supported, if frequently brutal, juniors scene (juniors meaning not young players, but teams below the senior leagues), and countless more unofficial and children's teams. Almost everyone knows at least something about football; many ordinary people are passionate about the sport and faithfully go to home games. Football is also far from being exclusively male; it's now one of the topics of everyday talk, and team support is an important pointer of cultural orientation. This is why we talk about football being central to Scottish culture, rather than, for example, golf, running or sailing, which are all also popular.

Scottish football and the national team are administered by the Scottish Football Association (SFA) in Glasgow. Of the forty-two teams in the four senior leagues, twelve are in the top league, the Scottish Premier League (SPL). Rangers and Celtic are these days expected to score a 'hatful' of goals a week against inferior opposition, confirming a common English view of Scottish football as being a two-horse race. Despite this image, in the mid-1980s Dundee United reached the semi-final of the European Cup and the final of the UEFA Cup, and Aberdeen won the European Cup Winner's Cup under Alex Ferguson in 1983. Both Old Firm clubs (Rangers and Celtic) have shown a desire to break away from the SPL into the English Premiership. The two are divided broadly along sectarian lines, a division that is often highly artificial, since many supporters have only a faint idea of how their team identity reflects religious orientation. However, Rangers' home stadium, Ibrox, 'a cauldron of hatred', is a living model of cultural cringe – British-imperial loyalism, infantile racism and testosterone-fuelled aggression. It is probably the only place in Britain, except for Orange marches (see Chapter 6) where a mass show of sectarian anger is tolerated by the police (some of whom are probably that way inclined themselves, though this is a different story). On the other hand, Murray Pittock has interestingly shown how there is still a degree of latent sectarianism at smaller clubs; his is the only recent academic account I know of to touch on this tough subject.

On the other hand, Celtic Park is not exactly an ideal of modern community. Founded in 1888 with the laudable aim of becoming a kind of social club to support Irish immigrants, Celtic nevertheless recently became the first Scottish club to show a serious desire to join

Figure 8.1   Ordinary SPL (non-Rangers/Celtic) home crowd. (Courtesy of Dundee F.C.)

the English Premiership, for more or less corporate reasons. The English Premiership has been transformed since the 1980s by vastly increased revenues, undergoing something like an economic rationalisation befitting the 1980s privatisation of everything in sight, and distancing the boardroom from the supporters. Maybe the SPL *would* be more interesting if the Old Firm left to join the English Premiership as they seem to want to do: the football match might regain more of the local significance it used to have. Whereas every member of the Celtic team who participated in the 1967 European Cup victory came from within 30 miles of Celtic Park, the current team is put together from expensive players available on the international market. Football commentary in newspapers and on TV increasingly centres around business and club management, begging the question of whether there is a difference between supporting Motherwell over Kilmarnock and supporting Beecham over Unilever.

Of course, as Celtic manager Jock Stein realised in 1967, there is a difference: football is deeply embedded in Scottish culture as the expression of a local place. It can even have a serious political edge: when Margaret Thatcher attended the 1988 Scottish Cup Final (it is not recorded whether she supported Celtic or Dundee United), at a time Scots were feeling least politically represented, fans of both teams showed the prime minister 'red cards' which had been distributed before the kick-off. Also in the 1980s, the British national anthem, which was always drowned out by booing when it was played before Scottish international football matches, was replaced by 'Flower of Scotland', an unofficial Scottish national anthem (written by the folk group The Corries). The English team still has no national anthem, though many English supporters (stop me if you've heard this one before) seem not to have noticed this.

The corporate restructuring of football has had harsh effects on smaller senior clubs. It is not only that Celtic and Rangers are seemingly always televised in preference to other clubs and that their minor gossip perpetually occupies the back pages of the tabloid newspapers in preference to games by other teams, but also, for example, there are now strict regulations which include having an all-seater stadium (based on an interpretation of the Hillsborough disaster of 1989 when ninety-six people died in part because of unsafe stadium design, to the effect that all-seater stadia are necessary for safety). A number of clubs have recently gone out of business, where over the previous few decades, the club situation had been reasonably stable. Some minor contenders have built soulless all-seater stadia (perhaps the ugliest stadium in the UK belongs to Clyde FC – it can be seen from the right-hand-side window of a train going from Glasgow to Edinburgh), replacing the terraces, one of the stages of working-class Scottish narratives to disappear along with the factory floor and the working men's club – see Chapter 11.

The point of the survival of smaller clubs is not merely a *Guardian*-reading liberal argument about biodiversity; it is also, more importantly, that home games can unite small and medium-sized towns and create the kind of local and free-forming *crowd* which would not otherwise exist (in an era when crowds are increasingly subject to governmental control). The historian T. C. Smout has remarked that in the early twentieth century football took on a 'quasi-religious' character, but Smout's 'quasi-' itself reveals a lot about what he expects religion to be like, while for post-war Christian philosophers like H. J. Paton and John Macmurray, religion is represented by any communion in which personal connection becomes the structuring stuff of the individual. The football match as a kind of religious ceremony: this idea is not as intellectually lazy as it seems at first.

There is in Scotland, as in England and most European countries, a subculture of 'soccer casuals' – originally so called because of their taste for the casual lines of designer labels, a style that invites comparisons with 1980s New Romantic style, but which could also be seen in terms of the early 1960s smart-but-casual Mods. This subculture is not as big as is sometimes assumed by people who don't go to football matches; certainly a 1990s version of it features in the fiction of Irvine Welsh and Duncan Maclean, but these two writers happen to be describing two football teams notorious for their casuals scenes (Hibernian and Aberdeen). Unlike in England, organised soccer violence tied to right-wing racist groups has never really taken off in Scotland. And if football's history is primarily about men, today the terraces' maleness should not be exaggerated – organisations like the Scottish Football Association (SFA) are vigorously promoting women's football, the proportion of female supporters at matches has rapidly increased since the 1980s, and football grounds are no longer unsafe places for women (except possibly for Ibrox, which is unsafe for anyone with the wrong kind of face).

Football then, despite the Scottish national team's terrible performance on the world stage, is *the* Scottish sport. But in all there are eighty national governing bodies of sport in Scotland, and around 13,000 sports clubs, mostly small and geared to a single sport. Among these are sports that have a unique relationship to Scotland. Golf's world headquarters, the organisation that first codified the sport and even now makes the rules, is the Royal and Ancient club in St Andrews. High quality and relatively cheap municipal courses abound, as well as the more famous private ones sometimes used as venues for international competitions (Turnberry, Royal Troon, St Andrews Old Course, Muirfield, Carnoustie). Golf has its own protocol, one that is relatively inter-class – and this is hard to explain to visitors, who often associate golf with the middle-class 'country club'. Scotland has produced a number of champions over the years (Sandy Lyle, Bernard Gallacher, Colin Montgomery), though the sport goes through phases like football – at times there are a large number of talented pros who do not quite achieve an international profile.

Also popular in parts of Scotland is rugby, a sport played, according to the popular car sticker, by men with odd-shaped balls. It has strongholds in the Borders, and perhaps has more of a class-fix than golf, since most working-class boys prefer football to rugby. Rugby is properly leagued and, again, the Scottish national team has had its glorious eras. Bowls (lawn bowls) is popular especially, though not exclusively, among older people, and is also important for the social clubs usually attached. Bowling (tenpin) is a relatively new phenomenon: it tends to be seen as a leisure activity rather than a sport, and does not have the depth of culture it has in the US. Curling is like lawn bowls transferred onto ice, originally frozen lakes (begging questions about global warming), and is common in Scotland, whereas there is almost no culture of curling in England. In the Winter Olympics, it is almost always the case that every member of the British curling team is Scottish, giving rise to uncomfortable moments when a BBC commentator has to talk about the 'British team' (which is usually solved by 'devolving' the commentary to a Scot). Snooker, played with twenty-three balls on a twelve-foot-by-six-foot table (four times the size of a pool table) also has its own culture, traditionally male and belonging to dingy clubs – see the early stories of James Kelman. Scotland has produced some of the sport's greatest players, in particular Stephen Hendry, who dominated the sport in the 1990s. Snooker should not be confused with billiards, played on the same table with only three balls – the sport played after dinner in nineteenth-century novels – which has died down but still has a cult following. Nor should it be confused with pool, which is played in various ways (though Scotland has nothing like the American rank-and-file culture of nine-ball) on a smaller table. Darts – drunk people throwing arrows at a numbered board – has also had a number of Scottish international players rising up through pub leagues. Like snooker, there is a gulf between the professional game and the game most of us play – the treble twenty is a lot smaller in real life than it is on TV.

Cricket does exist in Scotland, though unlike in England, it is not usually played in schools and is seen as something foreign (ironically, unlike in Trinidad or Pakistan, places where the British empire concentrated its power). Most Scots either do not understand the rules of cricket, or at least pretend not to. Very few could sit through an entire five-day Test match. This flags up a serious cultural difference: the imperial role of cricket as a model of gentlemanly fair play and gradualism – of cultural and constitutional stability arising from knowing one's place – has little to do with Scottish culture, and the gentlemanly ideal was propagated through a public school system that never took hold north of the border. (And if you are reading this in one of the many countries with a language that does not distinguish between England and the UK, you should remember that the gentlemanly ideal *in general* is English, and was tuned to English education.) Tennis is also viewed as a mainly-English sport, though this may change with a young generation of highly talented Scottish players now emerging.

For horse racing (see, again, the early stories of James Kelman for a cultural focus) there are courses at Hamilton Park, Musselburgh and Ayr. Studying the form for races at Scottish and English courses is a regular feature of Saturday morning for some. The activity of going to the racecourse itself has doubtless declined, but events like the Scottish Grand National still attract big crowds. Ice hockey has grown as a 'super-leagued' spectator sport, in part drawing on the Scottish-Canadian diaspora and the once-frozen lakes (see above). There is also a significant culture of sailing, which has a couple of dozen clubs and thousands of participants, overseen by the Scottish Sailing Institute. Angling (fishing) is popular – it is the most popular sport in Britain, according to urban myth – though the image of easily accessible fishing in picturesque rivers is largely a hangover from Scotland's early Victorian rebranding.

There are judo clubs throughout Scotland. So too are there karate clubs, a sport that arrives in Scotland having picked up a flavour of zenned-up respectfulness not present in its own country. In Scotland *muay thai* (kick boxing) also loses its original class-fix (Thai boys coming to cities to fight for money); ironically, on the other hand, Scotland's strong working-class tradition of boxing may have lost out by being seen as brutal. This is unfair on boxing, given that karate is potentially a lot more brutal – one interpretation of *ippon* is as a single strike able to kill an opponent – and boxing clubs have been one way to draw boys away from crime, alcoholism, and latterly, drugs, offering a kind of discipline that schools often can't reach. Whether there is a significant culture of illegal bare-knuckle boxing is, to me anyway, uncertain; its context is one of many appropriated by the film director Guy Ritchie, relocating from central Ayrshire coal mines to East London warehouses (compare the films *The Big Man* (1990) and *Snatch* (2000)).

Shinty, a game like the Irish hurling (the closest North American sport might be lacrosse), is properly leagued and is played mostly in the north-west of Scotland. Highland games are a different kind of sporting spectacle again – celebrations with vaguely Jacobite overtones (gatherings of the clans) which include traditional dancing, games and sports, most famously tossing the caber (a large pole) and heaving iron weights over a bar. Despite the generic name, they do not take place exclusively in the Highlands, but reach as far south as Dumfries and Bathgate. While Highland games – the 'traditional' face of Scottish sports – are relatively flourishing, high street sports shops have in part turned into quasi-American clothing outlets, with little connection to the sports in question (thus the baseball bat, despite the fact that no-one plays baseball: in some parts of Glasgow, taking a cricket bat to someone's head would just seem too effete).

These are some of the sports practised. The wider picture is that sport has blended with leisure and tourism. If there has been a major change in Scottish sports over the past few years, it has been in the attempt on the part of government to organise sport formally and to tie it to a *culture* of a healthy outdoor nation. This is true of the UK as a whole: the governmental position of minister for tourism, culture and sport shows how sport has been linked to cultural image. In

Scotland, outdoor sports like mountain biking and climbing have been increasingly used by tourism organisations like Visit Scotland to rebrand (or re-rebrand) Scotland's 'natural resources' to encourage people to do more sports: 'Scotland itself is a large natural resource which gives opportunities to a large number of sports, such as sailing, orienteering, equestrian events and mountain biking'. The ideal, of course, would be to use these natural resources to revitalise the local communities around them, rather than repeating the moment of the 1850s, in which Scots participated in the marketing of an area which had been 'cleared'.

In April 1999, an organisation called SportScotland, chaired by the deputy minister for tourism, culture and sport, Elaine Murray, and anticipating the strong support and funding of the Scottish Executive, set in place a national strategy for sport which would become 'Sport 21', a strategy aiming for '[a] country where sport is more widely available to all. A country where sporting talent is recognised and nurtured. A country achieving and sustaining world class performances in sport'. Its strategies include setting in place various partnerships between local authorities – the main providers of facilities – and national bodies and educators, and extending membership of sports clubs, and the opening of facilities, for example in schools and universities. In 2000, as revised in subsequent years, the national cultural strategy *Creating our Future: Minding our Past* stated that sport and other aspects of culture 'play an important role in bringing people together and promoting social inclusion'. This can be interpreted quite widely: according to SportScotland, '[i]t is the simplest sports: walking, swimming and cycling, which have grown the most quickly over recent years'.

SportScotland also aims to increase the frequency of exercise taken by Scots of all ages, and especially young people and especially girls, and to increase the amount of time spent on sports in school. It points out the importance of athletes in popular sports visibly participating at world-class level (wishful thinking given the condition of Scottish football) and claims that 90 per cent of people agree that public money should be used to support world-class Scottish athletes. Scottish sporting strategy is also bound by UK policy, as contained in the policies and strategy of the Department for Culture, Media and Sport's *A Sporting Future for All* and the think-tank report *Game Plan: a strategy for delivering Government's sport and physical activity objectives.*

These objectives are numerous and often quite specific, aimed at improving 'community', and at improving Scotland's terrible health record.

Sport 21 thus increasingly sees sport as a social tool – in a post-industrial society estimated figures of *participants* replace those of *production*, and sport is used to 'combat anti-social behaviour', and 'to teach lessons of endeavour'. Making the body public in this way shows how sport is increasingly described in terms of management and marketing, as in figures of 'delivery'. Put more negatively, the attempt to turn sports players into accountable consumers could be seen as a remaking of the individual, as in the social engineering tendencies of parts of the post-1945 welfare state (see Nikolas Rose's book *Governing the Soul* (1990)). Sport 21 can also sound oddly like late-Victorian English public school cricket ('lessons of endeavour'), seeing one of sport's aims as to 'promote the values of democracy, integrity, fairness, respect, social justice and equality'. The aim to get more people doing sport could be seen negatively as diverting political energy, or positively as getting people together in an active mode and combatting depression and drugs problems. In 2003 Sport 21 laid out quite specific aims about numbers of people it wanted to participate in sport by 2007, and also set out a vision for 2020.

Finally, there is the seemingly complicated question of international representation: in the Olympic Games, Great Britain is represented without reference to individual nations; in the Commonwealth Games – a meeting for countries with the British monarch as their head of state – Scotland and England have their own teams; in football and most other sports, Scotland and England have their own teams and there is a rivalry that makes a UK team hard to imagine; in rugby, Scotland and England have separate teams but sometimes tour together as the British Lions (and in a strange twist, in rugby, Northern Ireland and the Republic of Ireland are unified as Ireland). But the rivalry between Scotland and England in sports (especially football) should be seen for what it is: a local rivalry, rather than some kind of ethnic hatred, as some fuming right-wing journalists seem to imagine. In sports as in other forms of culture, Scotland and England have a lot in common and give a lot to each other, as should be borne out by devolution and possible independence. In modern times, Scotland and England are culturally close, and all Scots realise this on some level – even those of us who are willing David Beckham to miss a penalty.

SUMMARY

• In cultural terms, Scotland's most important sport is football (soccer). There are four main leagues and a national team which, at the time of writing, is faring badly.
• The supporters (and sometimes the players, board, and management) of Scotland's two biggest football teams, Rangers and Celtic, roughly correspond to Glasgow's sectarian divisions. Celtic was set up as a support society for Irish Catholic immigrants.
• Golf is played very commonly in Scotland; the sport's rules are still globally codified by the Royal and Ancient Club of St Andrews.
• Other popular Scottish sports include curling, rugby, fishing, running and martial arts.
• Highland games are 'traditional' gatherings which involve sports more or less specific to Scotland, as well as dancing and other activities.
• Both the New Labour administration and the Scottish Parliament have made serious plans to encourage more people to participate in sport; by European standards, Scotland has a reputation of being lazy as far as participation is concerned.

QUESTIONS FOR FURTHER RESEARCH AND THOUGHT

• How do people take care of their own bodies in Scotland, and how does this compare with other nearby countries? Or with Scotland thirty years ago?
• Scottish athletes compete for Britain at the Olympics, but for Scotland at the Commonwealth Games. What does this say about the idea of Commonwealth? Or about the Olympics?
• Why is the British national anthem no longer played before Scottish football matches, but still played before English matches?
• Why do Rangers and Celtic draw so many supporters from smaller towns which have their own teams?
• Is Sport 21 making Scotland a fitter nation? Is it having any other effects?

FURTHER READING

A Sporting Future for All, London: Department for Culture, Media and Sport, 2000.

Sport 21 2003–2007, the National Strategy for Sport, Edinburgh: SportScotland, 2003.

Scottish Football Association: http://www.scottishfa.co.uk/index.cfm

Royal and Ancient Golf Club: http://www.randa.org/

SportScotland: http://www.sportscotland.org.uk/

National Trust for Scotland: http://www.nts.org.uk/

Glasgow Survival: http://www.glasgowsurvival.co.uk/ (a fascinating insight into 'ned' culture).

Off the Ball: http://www.bbc.co.uk/scotland/sportscotland/offtheball/(football banter)

CHAPTER 9

Scotland's Languages

Like every other nation, Scotland is home to native speakers of a range of languages. In Scotland's case there are significant pockets of Urdu, Arabic, Italian and Chinese. Usually, however, these 'other' languages are forgotten in favour of what are viewed to be Scotland's three 'native' languages: English, Gaelic and Scots. The idea of these three being more 'native', an idea common throughout cultural and literary studies, is entirely nonsensical: languages grow and fall, but none is simply tied to any nation. Nations are not 'racial' bodies.

The other two points to clarify from the outset are the distinctions between *language* and *dialect*, and *dialect* and *accent*. Firstly, a language is usually defined as a discrete system within which various varieties – *dialects* – exist. Secondly, dialect brings in lexical and grammatical differences, though still within the same language, while *accent* is merely the sound of the voice, the phonetic difference. So a person can speak perfectly good French with an English accent, or perfectly good English with a Chinese accent. Accent does not affect grammar.

'Scots' can be understood in three senses: firstly, it is the artificial literary dialect pioneered in the 1920s from reference sources; secondly, it is a dialect of English with many sub-varieties; thirdly, as 'Broad Scots', it is the language spoken by most people living in Scotland, with dialects corresponding to area but all constituting one linguistic continuum, one that went underground in the sixteenth century and stayed underground as the royal court moved to London and the Enlightenment encouraged English speech. This last explanation is the current academic consensus. On the other hand, there are important reasons why we might want to view Scottish English as a dialect of English instead of a language: the 'dialect' explanation makes it clear that when most Scots speak they are often having to *choose* between mutually intelligible varieties, as does, for example, the Francophone Martinican native in Frantz Fanon's *Black Skin, White Masks*. In this sense most Scots would be described as *diglossic*, meaning that they speak two discrete dialects, rather than *bilingual*, meaning that they speak two languages and are fixed in a single language at any given time. Peter Trudgill, perhaps the world's most famous sociolinguist, has often brought up Lowland Scotland as an example of diglossia (and it is worth noting that Trudgill did his PhD in Edinburgh).

If we do, hypothetically, assume that what most Scots speak is a dialect of English called Scottish English (ScE), what is remarkable is this dialect's similarity throughout the country, one that corresponds very closely to national borders. Thus, Trudgill describes people *deciding* (albeit often unconsciously) to use specific words and grammars to accentuate national borders, showing their Scottishness in specific contexts by 'style drifting', and 'dialect switching'. If we see most Scots as speaking a language called Scots, then Scotland is a single language community; if we see them as speaking the dialect ScE, then they use various ways to equate their dialect with their nation, and sharing a dialect becomes an active way of showing their belonging to the nation. The Scots-as-language thesis may seem more nationalist at first view, but, by making English a discrete foreign language, it takes away the power of individual Scots to show their belonging by word-choice and grammar-choice. This is a real situation which faces Lowland Scots every day, like Fanon's Martinicans, who have studied in Paris and are constantly negotiating, in every mouthful, between two forms of French. Thus, there are good reasons, taking in postcolonialism, why Scottish English-as-dialect might be seen as a more nationalist stance.

This ebb and flow structures Scots' linguistic existence: there are places where using an English which is too Standard is positively dangerous (see 'The First Day of the Edinburgh Festival' section of the film *Trainspotting*), and others – almost any official context – where people will try to speak an English as Standard as possible. One good example of this is on Scottish trains, where announcers seem to be constantly undergoing customer care courses which teach them to associate Standard English (SE) with politeness – and which, being native speakers of ScE, they usually handle badly: 'this train shall stop at' instead of 'this train will stop at'; 'disembark' instead of 'get off'; 'require' instead of 'want'. In popular imagination, the SE form equals the more polite form equals the more complicated form – a defensiveness which writers like James Kelman have seized on and used to great effect.

In any case, the question of whether Scots/ScE is a language or a dialect is somewhat moot; linguists have agreed that Broad Scots – Scots taking in a great deal of dialect variation – is indeed a language and that this is what most Scots speak. If Scots is a language, as described by Corbett, McClure and Stuart-Smith (2003), it runs from Broad Scots to Scottish Standard English (SSE), the 'perfected' form; Broad Scots is more recognisably divergent from English, whereas SSE is a discrete and strict variety whose written form only differs from Standard English in 'certain idioms, vocabulary items, grammatical uses and possibly distribution of such linguistic features as modal auxiliary verb uses'. In this chapter, despite my complaint that separation of discrete languages ignores the question of choice, I go along with the definitions of these prominent linguistic scholars.

This book, like the overwhelming majority of English books, is written, more or less, in SE, a dialect originally arising from around London and tied to the authority of Oxford and Cambridge (and note the 'author' in that word 'authority'). If this book wasn't in SE, it would have great difficulty getting published, even if the Scots it was written in was comprehensible to all of its readers – though this publisher, to its great credit, *has* taken the step of publishing serious books in Scots. Similarly, the dialect of English that almost all non-native speakers learn is SE (or a mixture of SE and American English (AmE): the AmE that language students study is still very close to SE). 'Foreigners' can be spotted, like ScotRail announcers, in trying to speak too 'correctly'. What learners of English often do not realise is how few people speak SE natively. Most linguists estimate the number of native speakers of SE to be less than 2 per cent of the *British* population – and thus a tiny percentage of the world Anglophone population – and mostly middle-class and elderly residents of the south-east of England.

In other words, SE is pretty much only a written dialect. This raises serious ethical questions about its global reach, since SE is not really a *lingua franca* taking in elements from each area – it is a highly place-and class-specific version of English, coming from the old imperial centre (or that plus a mixture of the new imperial centre, the US). The point that can be hard to get across to English learners is that SE may be more useful in certain situations, but it is no more correct than any other dialect – this idea of abstract absolute correctness makes no linguistic sense. This is something that most Scots realise on some level, and yet, like the ScotRail announcers, we often continue to behave as if we should be using SE – as I am doing, in a typical act of bad faith, right now. Most Scots – though to a lesser extent than a couple of decades ago – tend to have a kind of a complex about their English, and feel the need to struggle to make their speech more SE in formal situations.

Spoken examples of Scots are to be heard everywhere on the streets of Scotland; written examples tend to be limited to literary subjects (if you find a DVD player manual written in Scots, let me know), and even then have only been acceptable at times of vernacular revival, and have usually been in formal modes close to SSE. This ironically lends a class-fix to the use of Scots which is the opposite of what was intended: while many working-class Scots want to learn more about English, graduates of the ancient universities (especially in the subject of 'English') want to push SSE-style Scots, or Lallans, rather than English, since they already have 'good English' under their belts. In other words, Scots is not necessarily democratising – at times it has had the opposite effect. At roughly the same time as Hugh MacDiarmid was creating his Synthetic Scots literary revolution (see Chapter 11), John Reith, another Scot, was making sure that the BBC be run along lines that were strictly SE and also strictly Received Pronunciation (RP), the now-archaic prestige accent of the southeast. Some Scottish academics tend to forget that the BBC has wielded more cultural power than Hugh MacDiarmid, and that BBC presenters in Scotland still tend to be well within SE (besides the occasional SSE phrase delivered with an ironic smile).

The Scots-as-language thesis is backed up by a strong historical argument, of which Derrick McClure, editor of the journal *Scots Language*, is probably the foremost scholar. Scots was shaped by Old English and then by a *Norman* version of Middle French, rather than the more *Parisian* version which appeared in the south of England. Scots is also influenced by the Old Norse of the Viking invaders who, until the fifteenth century, occupied the Northern Isles (Shetland and Orkney) as well as large areas of north-east England. From the second half of the fourteenth century, Scots was used in Parliament, and found its own literary epic in John Barbour's *Brus*, in 1375 (that is, exactly contemporary with Geoffrey Chaucer, champion, albeit unconscious, of 'vernacular English'). The Reformation saw a swing back to English, in part through the influence of the Geneva Bible of 1560, and Scots language went underground soon afterwards with James VI/I's determination to 'improve' – that is, Anglicise – the government. The Enlightenment saw a strong adjustment to – in one reading, the *creation of* – English Literature, which became the guardian of the SE form, especially in the canon of English poetry. In Scotland there was little hostility to the encroachment of Anglo-Saxon, which had become associated with commerce and prosperity. The fourteenth and fifteenth century *makars* (poets) who are seen as exemplars of the height of Scots also saw themselves as participants in an emerging *English* tradition, as would post-union writers from Tobias Smollett to Thomas Carlyle.

Unsurprisingly, there was a boom in elocution lessons during the Enlightenment; it was typical for Scots now to admit that they would never speak really good English (meaning SE), but that they could learn to work with their disabilities so as to pass in polite society. (Compare this with today's 'globalisation', in which the idea of English as a World Language is often taken for granted.) A Scots literary revival was staged by mid- to late-seventeenth century writers including Allan Ramsay. Ramsay nevertheless disingenuously introduced the inverted comma (') to show deviation from the SE norm, a habit copied by the twentieth-century nationalist Hugh MacDiarmid, even though this inverted comma undermines Scots language's status by making it look like adapted English.

For English Romantics such as William Wordsworth, the Scots Robert Burns and James Macpherson were a useful model of vernacular, yet in general the likes of Burns tended to be seen as a 'folk poetry' rather than a properly literary one. Most nineteenth-century writers used Scots almost exclusively in dialogue and usually to indicate local colour, rather than mixing it with their own authorial voice, which maintained an educated authorial distance. Scholars like James Murray and John Wilson revived interest in local dialects (especially of the Lowlands) at the turn of the nineteenth century, that is, in the environment immediately preceding MacDiarmid's Synthetic Scots. Acceptance or rejection of MacDiarmid's overhaul of Scots as Synthetic Scots became a fundamental question for literary writers of the mid-twentieth century; from about the 1960s more widely spoken urban varieties began to be used – in a sense another revival and rethinking of vernacular tradition.

In part due to the influence of English Literature's tendency to standardise along Anglo-British lines, urban Scots used to be virtually ignored by scholars, until at least the second half of the twentieth century. In recent years there has been a strong reaction to this, and there is now a large body of study on all aspects of Scots – rural and urban, working-class and middle-class. In 2002 the final volume of the *Dictionary of the Older Scots Tongue* was published, and the Scottish Language Dictionaries set up. The SCOTS corpus collects and organises data from all forms of Scots. All of this represents an academic corrective to the way in which the majority of Scottish people have been educated from infancy to believe that their own native speech is wrong. This well-known poem by Tom Leonard sarcastically shows how BBC newsreaders maintain their own SE and RP over their working-class audience – 'scruff' – keeping up the appearance of SE speech being more 'true'. In the poem, SE is ironically 'translated' back into ScE/Scots, even though the newscaster is saying that he must speak 'properly' – 'talk wia/BBC accent' – since otherwise people would not believe his authority:

this is thi
six a clock
news thi
man said n
the reason
a talk wia
BBC accent
iz coz yi
widny wahnt
mi ti talk
aboot thi
trooth wia
voice lik
wanna yoo

scruff. if
a toktaboot
thi trooth
lik wanna yoo
scruff yi
widny thingk
it wuz troo.

This marks a move forward from Scottish Renaissance thinking of the 1920s – the period when Scots is usually seen as becoming literary again – when there remained a real danger of reinstating a form of classism within Scots in over-relying on Synthetic Scots or what A. J. Aitken has called 'Ideal Scots' (like our SSE). Ideal Scots relates to Broad Scots somewhat in the way that SE relates to English, tending to be seen as more correct and therefore somehow more true, and assuring advantages to certain sectors of society – particularly those educated enough to write in Ideal Scots – meaning that Ideal Scots tends to *repeat* the class-fix. As I suggested above, many of those who worry most about the 'dilution' of Scots by English are also those who also benefit most by having good SE, such as scholars and teachers (thus, for example, the starchy version of Lallans or SSE which has recently been allowed in the upper years of 'English' in schools).

Leonard's poem is reprinted here as an example of Scots/ScE in a Scottish 'accent'. Since there were few precedents when Leonard wrote the poem, he had to make up the spelling and grammar (the *orthography*) himself. In preference to sticking with everyday speech/ Broad Scots, MacDiarmid, however, had used old reference books to gather together an artificial language from archaic writing, aiming at a kind of Ideal Scots. Rather than looking like how people speak, it resembled a series of substitutions, meaning that, ironically, it followed Standard English quite closely, mostly just substituting individual words. As an example, I quote the opening of MacDiarmid's classic poem, the nationalist epic 'A Drunk Man Looks at the Thistle':

I amna fou sae muckle as tired – deid dune.	fou – drunk
	sae muckle – as much as
It's gey and hard wark coupin gless for gless	gey and – very
Wi Crouvie and Gilsanquar and the like,	coupin – lifting
And I'm no juist as bauld as aince I wes.	bauld – bold

The elbuck fankles in the coorse o time,	elbuck – elbow
The sheckle's nae sae souple, and the thrapple	fankles – twists
Grows deef and dour: nae langer up and doun	sheckle – wrist
Gleg as a squirrel speils the Adam's apple.	souple – supple
	gleg – quickly

Once we substitute the SE words on the right of the page, it becomes clear that the grammar of this Scots is not as distant from SE as it seems. There is an important difference between this Synthetic (or Ideal) Scots, used during the middle of the twentieth century, and more recent writing by the likes of Tom Leonard, James Kelman, Janice Galloway and Irvine Welsh. The latter type of Scots engages to some extent with SE, often moving between SE and Scots according to context and nuance, as do most Scottish people (thus, one might say, making it more social-realist). And although British television has from the 1990s more commonly used 'regional accents' (an infuriating phrase which implies that RP is somehow *not* regional), the move away from RP in television in fact dates from experiments in the late 1950s. Native RP these days is rare and vaguely comical (and indeed is used as such by comedians like Harry Enfield).

Scotland has another entirely separate language which is official in many contexts and spoken natively by a large group of people: Gaelic. As I said at the head of the chapter, I have no intention of describing Gaelic as one of Scotland's 'indigenous' languages, which suggests that speakers of Arabic and Chinese are automatically not real indigenous Scots. However, Gaelic has been widely spoken in Scotland for a longer time and, as historians of language such as A. J. Aitken have shown, at one point covered much more of the nation than used to be thought, stretching down as far as the Lowlands. Moreover, as Trudgill has shown, the grammar of Gaelic has on occasion leaked into ScE: for example, the present continuous (present progressive) in ScE 'what is it you're wanting?' (SE: 'what do you want?') originates in Gaelic's reliance on the present continuous.

Gaelic was delivered a double blow, firstly by the union and its push towards cultural 'improvement', and secondly by the Highland Clearances, which tore apart once heavily populated Gaelic-speaking areas. The language is partially mutually comprehensible with Irish Gaelic, which maintains a larger number of native speakers, but is not at all comprehensible with English, or with Welsh. Today, Scottish

Gaelic has around 70,000 native speakers, mostly in the north-west, but increasingly it is being given academic protection, and if anything is liable to grow. Non-British people now sometimes show an interest in learning Gaelic (almost unthinkable 100 years ago), the Scottish Parliament produces many documents in Gaelic and has a cross-party Gaelic pressure group, and there have been great efforts to make Gaelic available in schools. After almost being wiped out in the nineteenth century, in the twentieth Gaelic was well represented in literature, especially poetry. Today the vast majority of Gaelic speakers are bilingual, also speaking English natively. Yet as some of these people study Standard English at school as a 'second language'; they sometimes speak an English *more* Standard than that of most Scots.

As an example of Gaelic, I quote four lines of 'The Cuillin', by the renowned poet Sorley MacLean:

an Eilean uachdrach
a' Cuilithionn ghruamaich,
nan loch suaineach
mo luaidh's mo ghaol;

which is translated as:

in the high island
of the grim Cuillin,
of the winding lochs,
my glory and my love.

MacLean's total output is brave and renowned; on the other hand, languages other than English Scots, and Gaelic are not yet often discussed seriously as Scottish languages. And however much we support Gaelic, it has to be said that the exclusion of other languages is simply racist. As hinted above, this exclusion also, ironically, echoes the Anglophone and Eng. Lit. belief that the status of English as a 'world language' is natural, an imperial attitude *that Scots helped create*. In other words, the vague feel of multiculturalism afforded by using Gaelic and Scots seems to allow Scottish culture to get away with more chauvinism than it should. For example – to my knowledge anyway – no major anthology of Scottish literature yet contains any work at all in any language other than 'Scotland's three'. Of course, there is an argument that says that if people 'come here' (whatever this means), they should also learn the language. This does have a logic to it in terms of language-protection (though English is scarcely in danger of extinction). However, if we were really fascistic enough to equate nation and language, we would in any case be forced to choose between Gaelic and English, and English would win, meaning that Gaels would also be seen as belonging to 'elsewhere' – a retreat to a nineteenth-century vision of the Celt as savage. In short, the equation of nation and language gets us nowhere; it gets no nation anywhere. And in a nation with no state boundaries, and therefore no citizenship of its own, the idea that Gaelic speakers are more Scottish than, for example, Urdu speakers, is positively a liability.

SUMMARY

- Scottish people usually speak a number of languages; by far the biggest is English, usually in a Scottish dialect (ScE), or, if you prefer to see it as a separate language, Scots.
- Scots can be split into Broad Scots, spoken by most people, and the grammatically perfect 'Ideal Scots' or SSE.
- Scots is more often described as a language when it is in its Broad form.
- If we call ScE a dialect, then the condition of being able to speak two discrete dialects, known as *diglossia*, is common amongst Scottish people. This gives most Scots a linguistic flexibility which most do not even realise they have.
- *Languages* are mutually comprehensible; *dialects* are varieties of a single language. *Accents* are the sounds of speech. Received Pronunciation (RP) used to be Britain's prestige accent.
- Scots poetry, dubiously called 'vernacular' poetry, has had an important place since Allan Ramsay in the eighteenth century, and it later influenced English Romanticism; an artificial vernacular, 'Synthetic Scots', was remade by Hugh MacDiarmid in the 1920s.
- There is now great enthusiasm to revive Gaelic, once spoken by much of Scotland, and today spoken natively by about 70,000 people, mostly in the north-west.
- Many people born and brought up in Scotland speak other languages. These people are as Scottish as their next-door neighbours.

QUESTIONS FOR FURTHER RESEARCH AND THOUGHT

• Is the connection between social class and dialect simple and direct
  in Scotland?
• Can you think of any other diglossic communities? How do they
  compare to Scotland?
• Would elocution lessons be generally regarded as an advantage for
  a Scot today?
• Find out some of the ways in which 'other' (that is, not English,
  Scots or Gaelic) languages are being promoted in Scotland.

FURTHER READING

Corbett, John, J. Derrick McClure, Jane Stuart-Smith, *The Edinburgh
Companion to Scots*, Edinburgh: Edinburgh University Press, 2003.
A valuable collection of essays describing the history, sociolinguistics
and phonetics of Scots, here regarded as a discrete language.

Haugen, E., J. D. McClure and D. S. Thomson (eds), *Minority
Languages Today*, Edinburgh: Edinburgh University Press, 1990.
Takes a strong Scots-as-language line and attempts pioneering com-
parisons with other languages.

Jones, Charles (ed.), *The Edinburgh History of The Scots Language*,
Edinburgh: Edinburgh University Press, 1997.
A ground-breaking overall history of the language, heavily drawn on
by later studies.

McClure, J. Derrick, *Why Scots Matters*, Edinburgh: Saltire, 1997, first
published 1988.
Originally a pamphlet, glossing a complex subject, this redefines the
parameters of the language/dialect debate and makes a case for the
expressive powers of Scots language.

Smith, Adam, *Lectures on Rhetoric and Belles Lettres*, Oxford:
Clarendon, 1983, originally published 1958 (arguably).
See ch. 2.

Trudgill, Peter, *Accent, Dialect, and the School*, London: Edward Arnold, 1973.
An early and important account of how the policing of non-standard dialects negatively affects the development of children.

Trudgill, Peter, *Sociolinguistics: An Introduction*, 4th edn, London: Penguin, 2000.
This is an indispensable introductory guide to this field of linguistics, clarifying many of the basic terms of linguistic analysis.

Withers, Charles W. J., *Gaelic Scotland: The Transformation of a Culture Region*, London: Routledge, 1988.
A weighty account of the movement of Gaelic by a renowned Gaelic history scholar.

CHAPTER 10

The Scottish Parliament

On 11 September 1997, a large proportion of those registered to vote in Scotland (and a smaller proportion in Wales) voted on a referendum on devolution which had been promised by New Labour before it was elected to government in May of that year. The vote in Wales was close; in Scotland it was much more decisive. Two questions were asked, and both were answered in the affirmative: 73.4 per cent of those who voted in Scotland were in favour of a Parliament, and 63.5 per cent in favour of the Parliament's right to alter taxes. The Parliament was duly set up and convened on 12 May 1999, and Scotland had its first Parliament for almost 300 years.

On 1 July 1999 the turnout for the first Scottish national election was a bit smaller. Occasionally it has been argued that this was due to a complicated voting system – it was the first ever national election in Britain to use any kind of proportional representation (PR). This explanation is hard to believe, since post-election research has shown that most people were content that they understood the voting system well enough to make proper choices, and that the use of PR, common to most of Europe, was overwhelmingly popular. A more likely reason for the low turnout was a dip from the excitement of 1997, a year that represents the conclusion of a long period of mixed, and often vague, cultural demands for increased democracy. As people realised after 1999, the Scottish Parliament's powers inevitably reconfirmed the old division between nation and nation-state, as described in Chapter 1. In short, although the Parliament provides a vital area of debate and representation, and includes more voices from women and smaller political parties than is possible in London, its actual powers are not very different from those of pre-1999 Scotland-as-region.

The official models given by the Parliament itself for Scotland's position were Catalunya (a region of north-east Spain and south-west France with strong separatist feeling), the German *Länder* (semi-autonomous 'states' of the federal government), and the Cantons of Switzerland. These models are misleading, since Scotland represents a unique example: for one thing, until 1707 Scotland really was a nation-state, and the new Parliament was opened with the statement that it was being '*re*-convened'. Secondly, Scotland has retained all the civic structures usual to nations, especially separate systems of education, law and religion. Thirdly, although there are passionate nationalists in Catalunya, Scotland's status as a nation is established as common knowledge, and is not really up for debate. The question is whether the next step will be independence within Europe, and whether it will occur naturally without any need for great upheaval, as a result of questions about democracy raised by the Parliament. For some, the Parliament signals a renegotiation of the unsatisfactory agreement of 1706.

Every four years beginning in 1999, 129 MSPs (Members of the Scottish Parliament) have been elected by people aged eighteen and over and registered as resident in Scotland. Unlike British Parliamentary elections, people do not simply vote for one individual in one constituency, but make two votes, the second of which counts towards a list of potential MSPs submitted by each party. This means that votes for the second-placed candidate are not wasted, unlike in UK elections, where only the first-placed candidate's votes in each constituency are counted, and a relatively large section of the vote for a party can produce very few or no MPs for that party. This creates a closed two-party system, since even if, for example, the Liberal Democrats win 20 per cent of the overall vote, they might still only end up with 5 per cent of the Parliamentary seats. The Scottish system, like most European voting, is fairer, in that other parties' votes count. Smaller parties, such as the Greens and the Scottish Socialists, can have a voice in the Parliament if a certain proportion of people vote for them. Additionally, in the Scottish Parliament lists can be 'zipped' by each party, ensuring an equal number of men and women. This voting system means that after 1999 there was almost twice as high a proportion of women MSPs than women MPs. It also encourages a higher turnout since, in UK politics, Labour voters often do not bother voting in a safe Conservative seat, and vice-versa. Seen in this post-devolutionary light, British democracy looks a bit knackered.

In the Scottish Parliament, the party with the majority of votes makes up the Scottish Executive, or the 'government' of the Scottish Parliament. In practice, this is liable to remain either the Scottish Labour Party or the Scottish National Party (in which case things become interesting) or some kind of coalition using smaller parties, especially the Liberal Democrats. The Parliament meets in 'full meetings' attended by up to all of the 129 MSPs, and 'committee meetings' made up of smaller groups, which usually present reports on specific topics to the Parliament as a whole. The head of the Scottish Parliament, the Scottish equivalent of the British prime minister, is known as the 'First Minister'. The first First Minister, Donald Dewar, passed away soon after he helped to midwife the devolutionary process.

The Parliament building itself was estimated in the government's White Paper on Devolution as costing £10 million to £40 million. Eventually however, as a result of managerial mix-ups, the deaths of

Figure 10.1   Interior of the Scottish Parliament – note how the seating is in an arc rather than adversorially opposed. (Source: Scottish Parliamentary Corporate Body.)

the Spanish architect Enric Miralles and Donald Dewar, arguments between Miralles's widow and their Edinburgh partners, the complexity of the structure (based on upturned boats), the hasty desire to establish the Parliament as a symbol, the preference for style over cost, the speed of the architectural competition, the contractual practice of 'construction management' (which means that the final cost is never known until a building is completed), and most seriously, the possible withholding of information from MSPs by civil servants when the Parliament voted on the building in its first weeks, made the final cost of the building £430 million – a staggering amount for a nation with a population of around five million. To an extent the final bill is down to the enthusiasm of Donald Dewar and others prominent in the devolution process to put in place a spectacular and epoch-making structure *quickly* – though in the end it was a terribly slow process only completed in September 2004, and occasioning a report by Lord Fraser of Carmylie, which apportioned blame, predictably, across the board. Most serious, however, is the idea that civil servants were at a very early point deceiving MSPs, when the Parliamentary move from Westminster to Edinburgh was intended as a step towards democracy.

In Scotland, issues of government are now divided into two categories: *reserved* matters remain with the British government, and *devolved* matters, as the name suggests, are those that have moved to the Scottish Parliament in Edinburgh. Reserved matters include defence, foreign policy, social security (for example, money paid to the unemployed or the disabled), immigration and employment. Devolved matters include social work, health services, local councils, housing, transport, sport, law, police, farming and fisheries, and the arts. We should always bear in mind this distinction between reserved and devolved matters when considering the powers of the Scottish Parliament, and the changes occurring in Scottish society. What many people fail to notice is that devolved powers have not (yet) increased greatly, despite the proliferation of committees and think-tanks in Edinburgh.

The continued British tendency to see Scotland's powers as 'regional' would confirm the 'pessimistic' interpretation of commentators like Tom Nairn, which suggests that devolution is a British policy designed to give the appearance of changes in power, while actually retaining serious state power in London. The thing to bear in mind is that the New Labour British government that engineered devolution tended to see it as a means of strengthening local government, rather than creating anything specifically national, while most Scottish people felt that a national political change was taking place. As I have suggested elsewhere, perhaps it is not devolution *itself* that shows a great shift, rather the misunderstanding between the British state and the Scottish people over what devolution represents.

Citizenship has not changed, and is still administered by the UK, meaning that, as suggested in Chapter 1, a person can never officially 'become' Scottish or English – the citizenship of immigrants is British, and they have to see their Scottishness or Englishness as a *cultural* phenomenon (which is one reason why this book has been written). We often read that the moment of devolution in 1999 was unrealistically 'euphoric'. In part this arises from the fact that devolution as it was understood 'from beneath' was an expression of something much more important than simply granting some political power to a group of people; it was also about much more fundamental ideas of democracy and the end of the wider empire which had required union. In this sense the fact that large claims were made, and are still being made, for devolution is not downgraded by any amount of disillusion with the workings of the parliament itself. If the Scottish people made one oversight in creating their Parliament, it was in forgetting that any Parliament is run by politicians, and that politicians tend to behave like politicians. This is an easy mistake to make, and does not take anything away from the remarkable achievement of denting an Anglo–British constitutional tradition which seemed never to be going anywhere.

The experiment with a partial system of PR was warmly welcomed by most of the Scottish electorate. Given the range of voices and the relative freedom from 'precedent', politics in the Scottish Parliament should be less a matter of management than one of ethics. In the British system both New Labour and the Conservative Party had increasingly come to occupy a 'middle ground', appealing to the public as moderate and sensible managers – 'consensus politics'. The non-PR system means that there are no Green Party MPs at all, even though many people broadly support the party's aims. And although New Labour were taking their own UK-based steps to equalise male/female representation, the Scottish Parliament speeded this up by remaking the rules immediately; a much larger proportion of women MSPs were at once elected to the Scottish Parliament in 1999 than sat in the British one – 37 per cent in Edinburgh as opposed to the 18 per cent the British Parliament had slowly struggled towards (and the Scottish figure would have been almost half had the Conservative Party not refused to 'zip' its list candidates). Nevertheless, at the time of writing the Scottish Parliament has so far failed to elect *any* MSPs from ethnic minorities. There is an element of 'racial' mistrust in this, but it may also be in part due to the fact that stateless nations cannot offer citizenship, and therefore cannot confer the rights that come with citizenship. Some Scottish nationalists would argue that, if Scotland became independent and could therefore offer full citizenship, the problem of 'what it means to be Scottish' would be formalised and people would feel more enfranchised.

The era of the Parliament, then, raises potential questions not only about who can be Scottish, but contrasts them with more immediate questions about who 'feels' Scottish. The question of who would be allowed to become a Scottish citizen after independence, for example, is not that simple. According to research conducted in the devolutionary year of 1999, 'being born in Scotland' is slightly more convincing than 'living in Scotland' as a qualification for hypothetical future Scottish state nationality. Still, more than half of people living in Scotland, when asked by researchers, thought that even people born outside Scotland should be allowed Scottish citizenship if currently living there. It is possible that, if Scotland becomes independent, citizenship will be offered to both of these groups – those born in Scotland but living outside, *and* those born outside Scotland, but living inside. This would be a relief to those immigrants who 'feel Scottish' and who are part of Scotland's cultural life, yet find themselves victims of a kind of colloquial racism; it would also be a relief to those who were born in Scotland and 'feel Scottish' but don't live there (like me).

Then there is the question of social class. Previous chapters have shown that, in very simple terms, Scotland is slightly more working-class than England, and that it is more enthusiastic about preserving social welfare, and free health and education (thus the referendum vote in favour of the Parliament's ability to raise taxes – where 'raise' has the double meaning of 'collect' and 'increase'). In general, more people support higher benefits for the unemployed in Scotland than in England, and Scots were central to the creation of the welfare state as it existed from the late 1940s to the 1990s, the partial dismantling of which coincided with a strong desire for devolution. The interesting thing is that 'feeling Scottish' and social class are closely linked; individual Scots have tended to see the Scottish part of their own double identity as a more working-class element, and the British part as a more middle-class element. Although Labour has traditionally been the party of the working class, the British New Labour Party in England attracted an increasingly middle-class vote in the 1990s in order to get themselves elected. In Scotland, on the other hand, New Labour and the SNP fight one another for the same working-class ground, showing that, as in the 1920s, the Scottish sense of national community is strongly class-fixed. However, 1999 research by Lindsay Paterson et al. showed that 'Scottishness' had become a *more important* marker of personal identity for many people than class identity, a serious deviation from the history of the Scottish labour movement. Meanwhile, the growth of the Scottish Socialist Party has been another phenomenon of devolution, explicitly linking class and nation, while in the UK Parliament any remaining socialists were mostly purged by New Labour in the 1990s.

Finally, another interesting dimension of 'feeling Scottish' is age: generally, younger people have felt more disillusioned with the changeless form of Britishness, even when Britishness was presented in the late 1990s as 'Cool Britannia'. 'Cool Britannia' was pushed by a New Labour think-tank around 1997 and was intended to 'rebrand' Britain (notice that I have used this same verb to describe the Victorian 1850s) as diverse, fashionable, young, hip and so on. It encompassed a wide range of individualistic films like *Shallow Grave* (1995) and *Billy Elliott* (2000), pop bands like Oasis (who attended parties at prime minister Tony Blair's house soon after his election) and Blur, and the now often-lampooned Young British Artists, like Damien Hirst. Despite the push of British cultural organisations such as the British Council and the Lottery Fund to represent this 'cool' British diversity, many British young people, especially Scottish young people, have preferred local and national cultures, and were nonplussed by Cool Britannia, which rapidly disappeared. Most Scots in their teens and twenties regarded 'Cool Britannia' as uncool at best, and at worst as patronising. As Billy Bragg sings in 'Take Down the Union Jack', 'Gilbert and George are taking the piss aren't they?' They certainly are, but it's easier to see these things when you live more than five miles from the Tate Modern Gallery.

The union jack (the British flag) was one particularly hated manifestation of Cool Britannia style which was revived around 1997 as the government tried to put a cultural cap on devolution. Union jack designs were worn, famously, by bands like the Spice Girls, and were primarily intended for export (living in Tokyo, I found the proliferation of union jack designs around 2000 staggering). Cool Britannia, mercifully, was parodied in front of a global audience in the 'Austin Powers' films; the retro-1960s bungling spy himself (Mike Myers) is Scottish Canadian. To bring us back from Hollywood to Holyrood: youthful cynicism over Cool Britannia was matched by positive expectations for the Scottish Parliament: in 1999: amongst all age groups, those between the ages of eighteen and twenty-four were the most enthusiastic about devolution; an extraordinary two-thirds of these people expected that devolution would lead to full independence within twenty years. It is clear that, since this generation is growing up to occupy positions of power within a devolved Scotland, attitudes towards Scottish sovereignty in the 2020s will look very different from those of the 1990s.

SUMMARY

- In the 1990s, the New Labour Party promised a referendum on devolution, which they delivered on coming to power in 1997.
- In September 1997 the Scottish people voted in favour of devolution.
- In May 1999 Scotland convened its first Parliament for almost 300 years.
- 129 MSPs are voted into the Scottish Parliament every four years; the voting system, like most of Europe, uses elements of proportional representation, meaning that percentages of the vote are linked to percentages of representation for each party, offering a voice for smaller parties.
- In the first Scottish Parliament, there were about twice the proportion of women MSPs than there were women MPs in Westminster.
- The two biggest parties in the Scottish Parliament are Scottish Labour and the Scottish National Party.
- The ruling party, or parties, make(s) up the Scottish Executive; its head is the First Minister.
- Devolved matters are controlled by the Scottish Parliament, reserved matters by the British Parliament; except for taxation,

these powers have not changed much since before 1999, but the system has become more accountable.

- The scope of the Scottish Parliament is still extremely uncertain. It is viewed differently inside and outside Scotland – Scots tend to see it as a *national* body, the English as a *regional* body.
- Most Scots believe that the Parliament will improve most aspects of their life, for example in maintaining education and the welfare state.
- 'Feeling Scottish' has a strong correlation with youth, class and social responsibility; the young are the most enthusiastic about the new Scottish identity brought by the Parliament, and are increasingly turning their backs on British culture.
- The Scottish Parliament building in Holyrood cost over ten times more than originally budgeted; Lord Fraser of Carmylie found fault for this throughout the construction process.

QUESTIONS FOR FURTHER RESEARCH AND THOUGHT

- Why did the 1979 devolution referendum fail (excepting the obvious reason that the British government 'cheated')?
- Why did Scottish culture show an extraordinary revival in the 1980s, after the referendum failure?
- What *new* powers does the 1999 Scottish Parliament have?
- Aside from regular Parliamentary business, what is the symbolic importance of the Parliament?
- Is the Scottish Parliament a protector of the welfare state?
- Who was most to blame for the Holyrood Parliament building being massively over-budget, and why did Lord Fraser of Carmylie apportion blame so evenly?
- Was all Scottish culture in unison on the opening day of the Holyrood Parliament?

FURTHER READING:

Aughey, Arthur, *Nationalism, Devolution, and the Challenge to the United Kingdom*, London: Pluto, 2001.
A thorough and highly readable reflection, moving across traditions left and right, political and cultural, taking in Eric Hobsbawm, Simon Heffer, Billy Bragg, and others.

Bromley, Catherine, John Curtice, Kerstin Hines and Alison Park (eds), *Devolution – Scottish Answers to Scottish Questions?*, Edinburgh: Edinburgh University Press, 2003.
A thorough guide to the attitudes and thinking of Scottish people post-devolution, and how they relate to policy.

Edwards, Owen Dudley (ed.), *A Claim of Right for Scotland*, Edinburgh: Polygon, 1989.
An edition of the historical milestone in which a wide range of Scots demanded constitutional change.

Harvie, Christopher, and Peter Jones, *The Road to Home Rule*, Edinburgh: Polygon, 2000.
A pictorial account of campaigns for a Parliament.

MacCormick, Neil, *Questioning Sovereignty: Law, State, and Nation in the European Commonwealth*, Oxford: Oxford University Press, 1999.
See ch. 8.

Mitchell, James, *Strategies for Self-Government: The Campaigns for a Scottish Parliament*, Edinburgh: Polygon, 1996.
A classic consideration of the forms and contexts of British devolution and Scottish independence.

Murkens, Eric Jo et al., *Scottish Independence: A Practical Guide*, Edinburgh: Edinburgh University Press, 2003.
Despite the seemingly polemical title, this is an informative and fascinating guide to the constitutional possibilities and difficulties raised by devolution; an extremely thorough answer to the question 'does devolution bring independence closer?'

Nairn, Tom, *After Britain*, London: Granta, 2000.
See Introduction.

Paterson, Lindsay et al., *New Scotland, New Politics?*, Edinburgh: Polygon, 2001.
See Introduction.

Paterson, Lindsay (ed.), *A Diverse Assembly: The Debate on a Scottish Parliament*, Edinburgh: Edinburgh University Press, 1998.
A collection of documents from various types of campaign for a parliament.

Pilkington, Colin, *Devolution in Britain Today*, Manchester: Manchester University Press, 2002.
An interesting introductory textbook; a not-so-basic guide to the political history of devolution in Scotland and Wales and quasi-devolution in the English regions. Perhaps unsurprisingly for an English guide, it does not touch on the difference in perceptions of *national* devolution on the one hand, and *regional* devolution on the other.

Scottish Constitutional Convention, *Scotland's Parliament, Scotland's Right*, Edinburgh: SCC, 1995.
Read this alongside the 1988 *Claim of Right*.

Taylor, Brian, *The Scottish Parliament*, Edinburgh: Polygon, 1999.
Highly anecdotal account of the parliament by a leading political journalist in Scotland; it is insightful in terms of particular insider stories, though doesn't seriously touch the larger issues.

Wright, Kenyon, ed. Harry Conroy, *The People Say Yes: The Making of Scotland's Parliament*, Glendaruel: Argyll, 1997.
Here the clergy weighs in; Wright, who was central in devolution campaigns, puts an ethical case for devolution.

Scottish Parliament: http://www.scottish.parliament.uk

Holyrood News: http://www.holyroodnews.com/

Scottish Executive: http://www.scotland.gov.uk/

Scotland Office: http://www.scotlandoffice.gov.uk

Westminster Parliament: http://www.parliament.uk/)

European Commission: http://europa.eu.int/comm/index_en.htm).

European Parliament: http://www.europarl.eu.int/home/ default _en.htm

CHAPTER 11

The Contexts of Modern Scottish Literature

Scottish literature is thriving, and yet it is as much in need of a total overhaul as it was in the 1920s. The problem is not that there is a lack of writers: recently, Scotland has produced an abundance of provocative authors, and many have found international fame. The problem, I suggest, is the persistence of *genres* which arise largely from the separating-out of types of thought that took part in the Scottish Enlightenment. 'The novel', 'the poem', 'criticism': they tend to still be as discrete and as individually demanding as they were in the time of MacDiarmid. This separation may seem natural, but it goes against Scottish generalist educational tradition (see Chapter 5), whereas in France, for example, a country that has been forced to come face to face with the consequences of its own Enlightenment as recently as the Algerian War of Independence (1954–62), genres have tended to disappear under the importance of *writing itself*. Only when writing is simply writing, and the encampments of genre open up to mutual influence, can literature confidently participate in cultural life, rather than being seen in terms like 'generations of novelists', as if novelists were as ephemeral as good national football teams. Yet even in university departments which have absorbed 'French theory' and should know better, book lists are still often separated into 'primary' and 'secondary' categories. What *is* this difference between primary and secondary? Why this addiction to *types*?

Or rather, why is this addiction a problem? Separating out genres, which are then required to stay in their own places, involves a kind of *violence*, since it is bound to a world in which each type of writing is known and bound by Eng. Lit.-style rules. The modes of writing that are seen as most 'literary' tend still to be the favourites of that most British discipline of English Literature, which developed along with empire. And from the viewpoint of the small nation, if some genres are seen to represent 'real', 'immediate' experience more than others (as some contemporary Scottish novelists have claimed), we are still not in a healthy literary environment. Ironically, the Scottish Enlightenment, which helped set up the now-suspect discipline of English Literature, is a prime example of such an inter-disciplinary environment: describing David Hume as a literary figure would have raised no eyebrows in 1760.

Today's secondary reading, then, could be tomorrow's primary reading, and vice-versa. The point is, if there was a normal mutual influence and ideas circulated beyond the 'primary', as in eighteenth-century Scotland or twentieth-century France, it might not be neces-sary to stack all bets on a generation of saleable novelists, as Scotland tends to do. This chapter is neither an explanation for, nor a criticism of, the internationally known names or those of previous generations, and does not include examples of writing. For this, you should turn to the excellent *Scottish Literature*, edited by Gifford, Dunnigan and MacGillivaray, which has about 1,000 pages more to spare than I do here. Here I suggest something different, by speculating on the con-ditions necessary for a healthy literary culture, and holding up Scottish writing against this speculation.

As many commentators have recently shown, there is a seam of anti-intellectualism in the English aspect of Eng. Lit.'s conception of genre, centred on poetry, which has been a guarantor of 'good' English, and has served England well in its centrality to empire. One of the heroes of Virginia Woolf's *The Waves*, aptly named Percival – an English hero rather than a British hero, is a figure of envy because he has the kind of education that eschews 'cleverness', but gives him a stance of well-meaning practicality which helps him through situa-tions like wheels coming off carts in colonial India. In Scotland, this figure of the *good bloke* does not work so well; for all its faults, Scotland has never really been anti-intellectual, nor has it ever elevated gentle-manliness over ideas. Eng. Lit.-style, generic, anti-intellectual think-ing also implies that the audience of, for example, a poetry book are more vital in being 'beyond the university'. This means that thou-sands of students who have struggled to reach an environment where they are relatively free to take on the ideas that will arm them against a lifetime of corporate brainwashing, are compared unfavourably to the handful of readers of contemporary poetry, all still in the name of literature. Here I suggest that Scotland in particular needs some kind of post-generic connectedness to recreate itself as a national literary community, not merely because it is a small nation and will have fallow periods like the football team, but because the Scottish Enlightenment itself eventually coded the types of thought that became genre, and the ethics of this have not yet been thought through.

A slightly different problem we face here is that 'modern' has more than one meaning. Under the umbrella of philosophy or social history, the term can refer as far back as the seventeenth century, or even earlier. Under the umbrella of English Literature, there exists this same tendency to refer the 'modern' back to a shift in thought in the seventeenth century, but this is complicated by another tendency to equate 'modern' with 'modernist', putting the starting-point sometime in the 1910s. So, only in a problematic sense can we describe as *modern* important eighteenth-century poets such as Robert Fergusson and Robert Burns – the former influencing the latter, and the latter having a great influence on English Romanticism in his cadences of speech from the Ayrshire countryside, and in his egalitarian reaction to the French Revolution. Nor, in the modern-as-kind-of-modernist sense can *modern* describe James Hogg's important crypto-Calvinist tale *The Private Memoirs and Confessions of a Justified Sinner* (1824), although it is obvious that this book is central to descriptions of the alienation of the modern self as it would later reappear in Robert Louis Stevenson and then Hugh MacDiarmid.

Yet the seeds of the modern-as-kind-of-modernist are at the roots of the Enlightenment itself. Allan Ramsay's Vernacular Revival of the 1720s joined literary high culture to folk speech; he also ran Scotland's first lending library which, in an episode telling about the tensions which led up to the Enlightenment, was raided by magistrates in 1725 on suspicions of harbouring heretical material. The kirk also set itself against the theatre, as it did, in a different sense, against some of the ideas of David Hume, sensing an oncoming secular nation. James Macpherson's *Ossian* (1759–63) was a rewriting of ancient Celtic myths, often described as 'controversial' since it went under the authorial name of Ossian himself, the narrator of the legends of Fionn mac Cumhail. Though 'exposed' as a 'forgery' (genre again),

Macpherson's work was influential not only on Scottish but also English literature, and provided a mythscape for the Enlightenment period, as it would again in the early twentieth century. Others had already laid their bets on a pan-national British history, with Edinburgh functioning as a miniature London, an attitude reflected, albeit in humorous form, by Tobias Smollett's *Humphry Clinker* (1771): '[a]ll the diversions of London we enjoy at Edinburgh, in a small compass'.

If the 'literature' of the Enlightenment was wide-based, its separation of experience into objects – later on the problem of types, *genres*, of English Literature – would come home to roost. It is only in about the 1810s that the Eng. Lit. canon starts to 'narrate' Britishness via the distinct genres of poetry, the novel, drama and criticism. In a famous reading of Jane Austen's 1814 *Mansfield Park*, Edward Said shows how 'the novel' as an emerging *genre* centres characters' sense of home, which is in turn reliant on Anglo-Britain's centrality to empire. Walter Scott's *Waverley* novels also begin from 1814, but repeatedly cover the ground of the Jacobite rebellions which *troubled* the idea of a Scottish national home in a new British state. Scott is notoriously ambivalent, since although the Waverley novels bring the Jacobite rebellions back into public memory, they do so in a nostalgic way which presents the rebels as ancient heroes of a long-gone culture.

Figure 11.1   Bank of Scotland note, featuring Walter Scott, one of Scotland's most celebrated writers. Scottish notes are in pounds sterling, like English notes; Scott fought for Scottish banks' right to keep producing distinctive notes. (Courtesy of the Governor and Company of the Bank of Scotland.)

Between Scott and Hogg in the 1820s and later writers such as Robert Louis Stevenson in the 1870s, there is a deafening silence, the likes of which does not exist in English literature, or in most other national literatures. It is not that there were no writers, but that Scottish literature, as such, suffers the 'strange death' we have seen in Scottish history: its narration either simply 'becomes English' – as in the Anglocentric work of Thomas Carlyle, who would anyway fail the 'genre test' today since he was a 'critic' – or it shrinks back into anonymous kailyardism. The kailyard story is said to peak about 1885–1900 (estimates vary); this high-selling format is associated with J. M. Barrie (perhaps unfairly) and Ian McLaren (perfectly fairly). In kailyard, familiar characters (the minister, the dominie (school-teacher), the lad o' pairts) play familiar roles, centred round a country house or small farm with little relation to the outside world. It is an odd post-devolutionary irony, or perhaps a show of confidence, that although the kailyard novel has been seen so negatively as to make calling someone's work 'kailyard' akin to a handbags-at-twenty-paces insult, kailyard fiction itself is now receiving some attention, not all of it simply condemnatory, and some of it teasing out different thematic seams. Moreover, as William Donaldson has shown (as amplified by Christopher Harvie in *Scotland and Nationalism*), there *was* a thriving non-kailyard literary journal culture in the final decades of the nineteenth century, one that was surprisingly social-realist, but survived less well in future anthologies. In any case, the kailyard idiom is generally seen as being broken by George Mackay Brown's painfully naturalistic *The House With the Green Shutters* (1901), and later shattered entirely by Lewis Grassic Gibbon's Renaissance classic *A Scots Quair* (1932–4), which uncompromisingly shows the interaction of the local (here, Aberdeenshire) and the global.

If modern does indeed imply kind-of-modernist, we might extend our modern selves back to Robert Louis Stevenson, a figure who was by his own account influenced by his predecessor Walter Scott's attempts to write historical fiction (which says something about the silence between the 1820s and the 1870s), circling back over Jacobite themes, for example in *Kidnapped* (1876), as did Scott. Although known to the world as a writer of adventure stories (a title better fitted to the later J. M. Barrie (of 'Peter Pan') and John Buchan (of *The Thirty-Nine Steps*)), Stevenson can today be read in a political, and even a postcolonial, sense. His stories set in the South Pacific cleverly

THE CONTEXTS OF MODERN SCOTTISH LITERATURE 149

critique colonial exploitation, and exert a visible influence on Joseph Conrad's more famous *Heart of Darkness* (1899). Both Stevenson's 'The Beach at Falesà' and Conrad's *Heart of Darkness* are set in confusion and half-light; both involve journeys following mad predecessors; and both are written with an eye on the exploitative nature of the relationship between colonists and natives. Scotland in general had a great influence on Conrad, his key informant about the state of contemporary Britain being R. B. Cunninghame Graham, a co-founder of *both* the Scottish Labour Party and later of the Scottish National Party, and an important fiction writer in his own right.

Stevenson's most famous moment is doubtless his popular horror story 'The Strange Case of Dr Jekyll and Mr Hyde' (1886), which, although he does not say so in the story, can easily be read as thematising the identity split between Scottishness and Britishness. The story is supposed to be set in London, but closely resembles the shadier parts of Edinburgh frequented by Stevenson in his youth. (Does a drug-culture-based, ambivalent, world-famous, unloved-by-academics story of the dark side of Edinburgh sound familiar?) Stevenson's doctor/monster battles within himself over which is his primary identity, anticipating the philosophical splits noted above. The doctor feels a kind of longing for the savage: 'I was still cursed with my duality of purpose; and as the first edge of my patience wore off, the lower side of me, so long indulged, so recently chained down, began to growl for licence' (p. 92). Despite the appropriateness of this 'duality of purpose', in which the less respectable, Scottish side of the self is 'chained down' by British tradition, twentieth-century critics became wary of the story's ambivalence, since it seemed to indicate a national sense of indecision. However, Stevenson, for example in his South Pacific stories, shows stylistic splits and 'cuts' in narrative which seem to anticipate modernism, as Alan Sandison has recently pointed out.

A decisive break came in the early 1920s. The term 'Scottish Renaissance', originating with Patrick Geddes at the end of the previous century, was popularised by Alexander McGill to describe a rebirth of confidence in Scottish culture. Its key figure was Hugh MacDiarmid, whose artificial literary language, Synthetic Scots, and epic poem 'A Drunk Man Looks at the Thistle' (1926) are remembered as *the* literary story of the period. Turning on the doubleness of Scottish identity, the drunk man moves between self and society, between image and experience, saying of himself:

To prove my saul is Scots I maun begin
Wi what's deemed still deemed Scots and the folk expect,
And spire up syne by visible degrees
To heichts whereo the fules hae never recked.

But aince I get there I'll whummle them
And souse the craturs in the ether deeps

In other words the drunk man moves 'up' to high culture and back 'down' to his own experience, to baffle ('whummle') readers used to the familiarity of Good English, and authorial distance from the kail-yard. Re-cast in Marxist terms, this double movement is *dialectical* – a clash of the thesis, and a challenge and modification of the thesis, the antithesis. The familiar identity split which we have seen passed down through Stevenson is redefined more aggressively as 'antisyzygy', and made the basis of a modernist aesthetics aiming to be both national and international. Renaissance writers were largely atheist and marxist. Some, for example Edwin Muir and Neil Gunn, even described the Protestant Reformation as a movement damaging to community; while this is a hopeful sign pointing towards ideas of community to be found in John Macmurray, it also runs the risk of relying on an 'organic' community also common to the English New Criticism of F. R. Leavis, a kind of rearguard movement for Eng. Lit. in its imperial form. (As I have argued elsewhere, the Scottish Renaissance is closer to New Criticism than it would like to think, MacDiarmid closer to T. S. Eliot than he would like to think.)

MacDiarmid continued in this vein until various frustrations caused a change in his style in the mid-1930s. By this time, however, the Renaissance had caused a complete renewal of Scottish literature. Gibbon's Chris Guthrie's movement between her Scottish self and an 'English' self forced on her by education is matched by the authorial movement between 'dialect' (see Chapter 9) and 'English', which for Chris means both Standard English dialect and Britishness. At about the same time Neil Gunn was also writing powerful stories of the north with something of a Renaissance approach, often subtly thematising the Highland Clearances, as would the poets Iain Crichton Smith and Sorley MacLean – the latter considered by many the greatest Gaelic language poet ever. In addition, a range of MacDiarmid-influenced poets including Helen Cruickshank and Robert Garioch all wrote in something like Synthetic Scots before the war. The Scots movement was supported by various linguistic societies, and it was boosted by a much bigger readership when MacDiarmid's work was rediscovered in the mid-1950s after twenty years of relative obscurity, triggering a 'Second Scottish Renaissance'. Meanwhile, Muriel Spark, while about to enjoy international success, tended to be ignored as a *Scottish* writer, especially during the period when she set her stories in London. This is unfortunate, since her finely-tuned irony (in, say, *The Ballad of Peckham Rye* (1960)) is often a key to understanding how Scots placed themselves relative to Britain. Her famous *The Prime of Miss Jean Brodie* (1961), a semi-autobiographical story of an Edinburgh private school, brilliantly shows the over-individualistic (and at the time, fascistic) tendencies of the respectable Edinburgh middle classes.

MacDiarmid's Synthetic Scots was not to remain authoritative forever. By the early 1960s Edwin Morgan and Ian Hamilton Finlay, and later Tom Leonard and Liz Lochhead, turned to linguistic forms

Figure 11.2   Edwin Morgan, one of Scotland's premier twentieth/twenty-first century writers, who was officially recognised as 'Scotland's Poet' (a parallel position to the British Poet Laureate), and who composed the poem 'Open the Gates' for the Scottish Parliament's move to Holyrood in October 2004. (Photograph: Michael Gardiner.)

much closer to Broad Scots as spoken form (see Chapter 7) – particularly Glasgow speech – rather than the dictionary-based Synthetic Scots. Morgan is an especially important figure, sympathetic to MacDiarmid's project yet moving it onwards to something less stiff than Synthetic Scots and more like the voices in Glasgow streets, and so, arguably, clearing the way for the 'dialect novel' which took off in the 1980s. Morgan was trained as a linguist, and built on this linguistic sensitivity as a translator; indeed, some of his readings of European and South American modernism border on translation. His *Emergent Poems* (1967) make a poem rise up from an original phrase *in another language*, as in his 'Manifesto', which makes 'translated' phrases rise up from the original – 'proletarii vsekh stran

Manifesto

```
        r      i   se
                   st an    d
     pro        v e
                   st a        y
          t r                  y
        r et r                 y
        le ar            n
            r    e       a    d
            t r          a    in
                s     tra     in
                v             i    e
        le a                  d
          t      e   st
        r et      e   st
       pro  t     e   st
       ro   a        r
       p     r   e   s              s
       p     ri      s              e
       pr    i           n          t
        e                   di   t
                s       a        y
       proletari        an s   in
          e    v e      r        y
          l             an   d
             a          r           e
          o             n           e
       proletarii vsekh stran soedinyaites
```

Figure 11.3   Edwin Morgan's poem *Manifesto*. (Courtesy of Edwin Morgan.)

soedinyaites' – seemingly without the author-ity we usually associate with the great individual.

Morgan's method here is arguably still a form of MacDiarmid's 'dialectic', 'translating' from original to ghost-phrase (and thus also rejecting the 'authority' of genre). Morgan is also a genuinely popular poet; the Scottish Executive created a laureate-like position for him, and his work is frequently taught in schools. And the method of using shifting dialects has been highly influential on what I have called the 'Third Scottish Renaissance', that highly promoted group of writers which probably starts with the mid-period Morgan and leads to Alasdair Gray and James Kelman, and, later, Irvine Welsh, Alan Warner, Duncan Maclean and Janice Galloway, who emerged in the 1980s and 1990s. This movement coincided with an international recognition of Scottish painters such as Ken Currie, whose murals decorating the People's Palace in Glasgow are another symbol of the confidence of the time. Alisdair Gray's epic novel *Lanark* (1981) is an early classic of the era, re-mapping Glasgow in a new and disturbing way, and published only two years after the British election of the Thatcher administration.

Figure 11.4 James Kelman, Booker Prize winner and hugely admired fiction writer. (Photograph: Michael Gardiner)

Figure 11.5   Frontispiece to Alasdair Gray's celebrated novel *Lanark*, illustrated by the author himself. (Courtesy of Alasdair Gray.)

A key figure in this revival is James Kelman, who since the early 1980s has successfully negotiated with Glasgow speech. Kelman developed a new system of orthography, ignoring the inverted commas and apostrophes of previous fiction which visibly separated one person's speech from another and from the author's, and which had given the writer the author-itative distance of 'really' writing in Standard English. In this scarcely publisher-friendly idiom, Kelman eventually won the prestigious Booker Prize in 1994 with his novel *How late it was, how late*, which begins with a working-class, middle-aged man waking up after a beating he doesn't remember:

Ye wake in a corner and stay there hoping yer body will disappear, the thoughts smothing ye; these thoughts; but ye want to remember and face up to things, just something keeps ye from doing it, why can ye no do it; the words filling yer head: then the other words; there's something wrong; there's something far wrong; ye're no a good man, ye're just no a good man.

Almost 400 pages of narration follow, moving between 'I', 'you', and 'he' forms, all used to describe the self – mixed with dialogue with unseen interlocutors. Here speech and writing have a new relationship, without the boundaries that from the Enlightenment defined 'Good English', and to which even MacDiarmid was to some extent obedient, by making a point of opposing it. Moreover, along with the popularity of the Edinburgh writer Irvine Welsh, Kelman's rise came at a time when Scots were literally finding a political 'voice' in the form of the new Parliament. Indeed, rather than thinking that devolution has created a situation where it is fashionable to write in Scottish dialects, we could reverse the proposition – the long struggle to find a modern means of expression has pushed a national sense which, dissatisfied with being politically silenced in the 1980s and 1990s, had to find a creative solution.

SUMMARY

- Scotland's tendency to rely on literary genres, though it allows for the marketing of groups of authors, may be its weakness, arising from its own residual pro-British Enlightenment thinking.

- From medieval times through to the time of Robert Burns, there was a strong tradition of Scottish poetry in the vernacular; this fed into, and to some extent disappeared underneath, English Romanticism in the early nineteenth century.
- The nineteenth century saw some important historical fiction but a lot of late nineteenth-century fiction took on a nostalgic, narrow tone; this is known as 'kailyard fiction'.
- Kailyard fiction was the immediate target of the 1920s Scottish Renaissance, a rebirth across many forms of the arts, whose most remembered figure is Hugh MacDiarmid.
- MacDiarmid and his generation were rediscovered in the 1950s, and Scottish writing revitalised; this revitalisation fed into the work of important poets like Edwin Morgan and Ian Hamilton Finlay, who nevertheless were critical of MacDiarmid's use of Synthetic Scots.
- The 1980s saw another rebirth of Scottish fiction, in a movement whose most successful exponent has been James Kelman. Kelman has arguably led the way for other 'dialect' writers, such as Irvine Welsh, Alan Warner, Duncan Maclean and Janice Galloway, who have rethought the literary presentation of a particularly Scottish – not British – experience.

QUESTIONS FOR FURTHER RESEARCH AND THOUGHT

- How is the Scottish Enlightenment responsible for the idea of literary genre?
- Is there a significant body of late eighteenth-century Scottish literature which is anti-British?
- Who were the major women writers of the nineteenth century, and why don't we know more about them?
- Was the 'kailyard literature' of the late nineteenth century really damaging to the image of Scotland?
- Who were the first Scottish modernists?
- How successful was Hugh MacDiarmid's project of the 1920s?
- Can the thematising of the Highland Clearances, for example in Neil Gunn or Sorley MacLean, be read as a postcolonial phenomenon?
- How did the setting of the Scottish novel change from mid- to late-twentieth century?

• How does the cultural politics of the best-known Scottish writers of the 1980s and 1990s compare with those of the 1920s and 1930s?

FURTHER READING

Brown, George Mackay, *The House With the Green Shutters*, Edinburgh: Canongate, 1996, first published 1901.
The genre-breaker; see above.

Burns, Robert, *Selected Poems*, London: Penguin, 1993.
Read them again and think about Revolutionary and Romantic contexts.

Craig, Cairns (ed.), *The History of Scottish Literature*, 4 vols, Aberdeen: Aberdeen University Press, 1987–8.
Very exhaustive, and surprisingly undated; worth seeking out.

Craig, Cairns, *The Modern Scottish Novel*, Edinburgh: Edinburgh University Press, 1999.

Craig, David, *Scottish Literature and the Scottish People*, London: Chatto and Windus, 1961.
A highly readable literary history, going from theme to theme, taking in communality, the town and the country, religion, audience, language and emigration, in a way that anticipates many later studies.

Crawford, Robert, *Devolving English Literature*, 2nd edn, Edinburgh: Edinburgh University Press, 2000.
Crawford pioneers the argument that what came to be called English Literature arose largely from Scottish contexts.

Daiches, David, *The Paradox of Scottish Culture: The Eighteenth Century Experience*, Oxford: Oxford University Press, 1964.
A classic account of the nationalist/unionist split in Scottish literary consciousness.

Davis, Leith, *Acts of Union*, Stanford: Stanford University Press, 1998.
A scholarly study of how Scotland negotiated its position in eighteenth-century writing.

Crawford, Robert and Mick Imlah (eds), *The New Penguin Book of Scottish Verse*, London: Penguin, 2001.
A good place to start, and a full and powerful collection.

Dunn, Douglas (ed.), *The Oxford Book of Scottish Short Stories*, Oxford: Oxford University Press, 2001.
Perhaps the most interesting selection; read this then go on to journals for more contemporary work.

Finlay, Ian Hamilton, ed. Yves Abrioux, *Ian Hamilton Finlay: A Visual Primer*, London: Reaktion, 1985.
Art-book-style collection of Finlay's work up to the mid-1980s; usefully divided into themes and periods, and beautifully illustrated.

Galloway, Janice, *The Trick is to Keep Breathing*, London: Vintage, 1999, first published 1989.
Galloway's first novel; it interestingly sets personal breakdown within the breakdown of the welfare state.

Gibbon, Lewis Grassic, *A Scots Quair*, Edinburgh: Canongate, 1995, first published 1932–4.
Trilogy concerning an Aberdeenshire family; it is important both thematically and linguistically.

Gifford, Douglas, Sarah Dunnigan and Alan MacGillivray (eds), *Scottish Literature*, Edinburgh: Edinburgh University Press, 2002.
An enormous and exhaustive anthology with very useful contextualising notes.

Gray, Alasdair, *Lanark – A Life in Four Books*, Edinburgh: Canongate, 2002, first published 1981.
Gray's epic, semi-autobiographical tale of an imaginary Glasgow; start reading here before moving to the smaller novels.

Gunn, Neil M., *The Silver Darlings*, Edinburgh: Canongate, 1999, first published 1941.
Or start with *Highland River* (1937)

Hogg, James, *The Private Memoirs and Confessions of a Justified Sinner*, Oxford: Oxford University Press, 1999, first published 1824.
Classic Calvinist account of good and evil; start here before tackling the rest of Hogg's large *oeuvre*.

Kelman, James, *How late it was, how late*, London: Secker and Warburg, 1994.
One of Kelman's philosophically richest works, but you could start with short stories – *Not not while the giro* (1983), or *The Good Times* (1998); *Translated Accounts* (2001) represents a serious departure.

Kennedy, A. L., *Looking for the Possible Dance*, London: Minerva, 1994.
Highly rated as a Scottish version of magic realism.

Leonard, Tom, *Intimate Voices: Selected Work, 1965–1983*, London: Vintage, 1995.
A collection of poetry by one of the earliest exponents of Glasgow dialect in a new orthography.

Lindsay, Maurice, *History of Scottish Literature*, London: Robert Hale, 1977.
Periodised and systematic, moving from medieval to Renaissance (including mid-century); an excellent reference book.

MacDiarmid, Hugh, *Collected Poems*, 2 Vols, Manchester: Carcanet, 1993–4.
These cover the whole range of poems from early lyrics, through overtly marxist work, to more jagged later pieces.

MacDiarmid, Hugh, *Contemporary Scottish Studies*, Manchester: Carcanet, 1995, first published c. 1926.
First written for an educational journal at the height of MacDiarmid's profligacy, it attempts to work back through and modernise a vast range of Scottish cultural material.

Maclean, Sorley, *From Wood to Ridge: Collected Poems in Gaelic and in English Translation*, Manchester and Edinburgh: Carcanet and Birlinn, 1999.
MacLean is typically rated as the most important Gaelic poet to date; this would be the place to start.

Morgan, Edwin, *Collected Poems*, Manchester: Carcanet, 1990.
Already dated, this is nevertheless an invaluable and handsome collection of Morgan's work through the decades.

Morgan, Edwin, *Crossing the Border: Essays on Scottish Literature*, Manchester: Carcanet, 1990.
A collection of Morgan's 'critical' work; it would be interesting to compare this with MacDiarmid's *Contemporary Scottish Studies*, above.

Morgan, Edwin, *Collected Translations*, Manchester: Carcanet, 1996.
The breadth of Morgan's translations is vast, and has significantly increased since this volume, which is nevertheless quite exhaustive and the place to start.

Muir, Edwin, *Scottish Journey*, London: Fontana, 1985, first published 1935.
In part a reply to J. B. Priestley's *English Journey* (1926); comes at the nadir of Scottish confidence and tends to dwell on the country's industrial wastelands. Muir is an important poet on his own and, with Willa Muir, the main translator of Franz Kafka.

Ryan, Ray, *Ireland and Scotland: Literature and Culture, State and Nation, 1966–2000*, Oxford: Clarendon, 2002.
A celebrated post-devolution account of some of the two nations' contemporary writers, and their cultural contexts.

Scott, Walter, *Heart of Midlothian*, London: Penguin, 1994, first published 1818.
Start here or with *Waverley* (1814); see above.

Smith, Ian Crichton, *Collected Poems*, Manchester, Carcanet, 1992.
One of the vital poets of his generation; comparable to, though not as experimental as, Edwin Morgan.

Smith, C. Gregory, *Scottish Literature: Character and Influence*, London: Macmillan, 1919.
Smith identifies the division between Britishness and Scottishness and to an extent the Renaissance; he coins the term 'Caledonian antisyzygy'.

Smollet, Tobias, *The Expedition of Humphry Clinker*, Oxford: Oxford University Press, 1984, first published 1771.
Classic Scoto-British scene-setter.

Spark, Muriel, *The Prime of Miss Jean Brodie*, London: Penguin, 2000, first published 1961.
Brilliantly ironic puncturing of middle-class Edinburgh's tendency to be pompous, and a serious connection of the ideas of the Scottish Enlightenment to fascism.

Spark, Muriel, *All the Stories of Muriel Spark*, New York: New Directions, 2001.
Spark has been central to modern Scottish literary production; her wry voice often comes out best in her stories, all collected here.

Stevenson, Robert Louis, *The Strange Case of Dr Jekyll and Mr Hyde and Other Stories*, London: Penguin, 1979, first published 1886.
This needs little introduction; classic tale of cultural schizophrenia.

Stevenson, Robert Louis, *Kidnapped*, London: Penguin, 1994, first published 1886.
An historical account of the Jacobite movement and its difficulties; it is both more breathtakingly 'adventurous' and more reflective than Scott's account, which was an important model.

Welsh, Irvine, *Trainspotting*, London: Minerva, 1994, first published 1993.
This needs to be taken seriously as literature in terms of its thematics of sectarianism and imperialism, dropped by the film; very highly readable (assuming that you can keep up with the dialect) and acidly intelligent.

Association for Scottish Literary Studies: http://www.arts.gla.ac.uk/ScotLit/ASLS/

Chapman: http://www.chapman-pub.co.uk/

Edinburgh Review: http://www.englit.ed.ac.uk/edinburghreview/

Product: http://www.product.org.uk/

The Scorpion: http:www.thescorpionscotland.com

CHAPTER 12

Visual Arts and Architecture

One of the founding moments of modern Scottish visual art – albeit a negative moment – was the movement against pre-Reformation (that is, older Catholic) art stirred up by the speeches of the radical Protestant John Knox towards the end of the sixteenth century. Pre-Reformation decorativeness would be actively recovered by later generations right up to the twentieth century; a second blow, however, came with the loss of patronage when the royal house moved to London in 1603. Yet Scottish painting remained in touch with Europe: from quite early in the seventeenth century a Flemish influence was evident in architecture – as in Heriot's Hospital in Edinburgh – and an understanding of light in painting. In the latter part of the seventeeth century, William Bruce began to introduce the practices of Christopher Wren, and there was something of a convergence of Scottish and English architecture.

Perhaps unsurprisingly given the need for patronage, the one type of painting that would continue to flourish from this time through the Enlightenment and Victorian periods was portraiture. The renowned portraitist Allan Ramsay (junior) would pave the way for later artists such as Henry Raeburn, who established the domestic genre. And these two have behind them a large number of lesser-known painters who, by the late eighteenth century, would habitually go and study, and frequently live for long periods, in Rome. Together with the landscape painter James Norrie, Ramsay founded the Academy of St Luke, Scotland's first art college, in Edinburgh in 1729. Robert Foulis would attempt to do the same in Glasgow in 1754, but his institute folded as soon as 1775. Despite this, there emerged from Foulis Academy prominent artists like David Allan, who became an illustrator for the works of Robert Burns, including 'Tam o' Shanter' and 'The Cotter's Saturday Night'. Allan also worked closely with George Thomson (who introduced him to Burns; Burns had already seen and admired Thomson's illustration to Ramsay (senior)'s 'The Gentle Shepherd' (1725)).

Ramsay (junior)'s portraits of Enlightenment luminaries (David Hume, Jean-Jacques Rousseau) are well known and often reproduced; most important for Ramsay's own career survival was his work as a painter to George III. He also painted a number of other nobles, most notably John Stuart, Earl of Bute (1758), himself a painter. James Tassie created relief profiles of prominent Enlightenment figures, which, like Ramsay's portraits, have also passed into public memory. Portraiture was nevertheless also at times pressed into pure Jacobite service, in the work of John Michael Wright and John Alexander. Gavin Hamilton also became celebrated as a portraitist, though he hankered after historical painting, and became known in his own time as a facilitator for painters of the Scottish Roman diaspora.

In 1740, in a classic early Enlightenment text, George Turnbull laid out the standards for visual art by describing paintings' *moral* value, calling for an 'aesthetic naturalism' – by which he means the identification of the picturesque *painterly scene* in which the *natural scene* can be seen (a logic not far from the idea that the natural monarch is framed by the art of government). Like Hume, who believed that a skilful critic could guide us towards an *objective* understanding of art, Turnbull argues that good artistic properties can be agreed on, and depend on certain definite laws of proportion.

Rational proportion can be seen in the context of a general move towards 'improvement' throughout the country. Robert Adam, the most influential architect of his age, incorporated Enlightenment ideas such as that of the Sublime (a transcendental elevation of the spirit) into his work (long before better known Romantic poets used similar ideas); he and his brother William drew on *both* Jacobite and Hanoverian motifs. William Adam, ironically, even drew on a Jacobite style while building the roads intended to help General Wade crush 'rebellious Scots'. English architecture of the time was favouring an Augustan, or 'Palladian' – sixteenth-century Italian revivalist – style, and this is also duly reflected in the Adams' neoclassical and opulent rooms.

Figure 12.1 Robert Adam's Gosford House, East Lothian, 1790–1803. (Crown copyright: Royal Commission on the Ancient and Historical Monuments of Scotland.)

Also highly Scoto-British is the concept of the New Town, meaning not just the 1760s and 1770s development of Edinburgh – itself spawning a whole sub-genre of portraits and landscapes – but also various projects up to the twentieth century, based around the idea of a self-contained community with discrete and highly planned quarters for each activity. The Third Duke of Argyll's total re-design of the town of Inverary is a case in point. Edinburgh New Town, and even Robert Owen's utopian experiment of New Lanark (from 1800), despite its liberal intentions, are also *total environments* geared towards anticipating the movements of each individual – in other words, sur-veillance. Surveillance is the down-side of the Enlightenment desire to know and classify; with its later descendent, the British welfare state, the fashion of creating New Towns duly returned after the Second World War along with the National Health Service.

The desire of the progressive Enlightenment thinker to know and place others, whether in encyclopaedias or in institutions, became a general British domestic phenomenon. In England this desire reached a peak with the famous design by the English liberal Jeremy Bentham of a *panopticon*, a prison that maximises the vision of persons from a central viewing point, made famous again by its analysis by the French philosopher Michel Foucault. What is less well known is that the

Figure 12.2   William Stark's Glasgow Asylum, 1804–20. Note the similarity to
Jeremy Bentham's ideal prison, the 'panopticon', and the Enlightenment idea that
power comes from surveillance. (Crown copyright: Royal Commission on the
Ancient and Historical Monuments of Scotland.)

panopticon, as well as drawing on Scottish Enlightenment ideas, also
directly influenced the design of Edinburgh Bridewell prison (Robert
Adam, 1791) and then Glasgow Asylum (William Stark, 1807–20). In
1824 the *Glasgow Mechanics Magazine* openly suggested that the city
undergo panoptical total surveillance, so that 'the necessity of sending
out emissaries to reconnoitre the conduct of the lieges would be
superceded, since everything would then take place, as it were, under
the eye of the Police'. In November 1992, the first town in Britain to
have CCTV cameras installed in its streets was the working–class
Glasgow satellite town of Airdrie. This is all, in a sense, a result of the
Enlightenment's obsession with seeing–knowing, and goes in tandem
with colonial organisation – in India after the 'Sepoy Rebellion' of
1857, Lord Napier restructured Delhi and Lucknow, building systems
of wide boulevards and terraces which had a sense of British opulence
but also lent themselves to easy surveillance.

In the later eighteenth century, as we might expect of a country
with Scotland's literary production (in the wide sense of 'literary' –
see Chapter 10), paintings frequently featured themes from books.
From the 1760s Ossianic motifs were used by Robert Adam and others
in architecture and by a number or painters; themes from Walter
Scott's novels and Robert Burns's poetry would later be commonly

portrayed. William Quiller Orchardson would portray European Enlightenment figures with a lighting that made their opulent rooms strangely spatial, as in his *Voltaire* (1883). Scottish artists also became known for illustrating the products of a flourishing publishing industry. This tradition survived through to Talwin Morris and other etchers of the early twentieth century, and even to Alasdair Gray, whose immediately recognisable work decorates not only his own literary work but various contemporary projects, for example the *Edinburgh Review*.

So it was not all portraits. Alexander Nasmyth and David Wilkie took up a historical/narrative idiom, to document the changing face, so to speak, of the country. From the 1780s, Nasmyth painted not only rural landscapes but also urban ones, showing the effects of the country's growing tradition of science and engineering. The fascination with both the power and the damage of technology remains a concern of artists like Ken Currie and David Mach today. Wilkie consolidated some of the scientific innovations of the Enlightenment,

Figure 12.3   *Edinburgh from Calton Hill*, Alexander Nasmyth, 1825. (Courtesy of Clydesdale Bank.)

drawing on a range of the new 'human sciences', from anatomy to sociology. His work is also often quite social-realist (and I am going to go ahead and use this anachronistic term), and is comparable to the kind of cultural commentary that would later become familiar with Victorian English fiction. Nasmyth was responsible for some of the most familiar images to remain from the turn of the nineteenth century, including his early portrait of his friend Robert Burns (1787), and the pair of paintings *Edinburgh from Princes Street* and *Edinburgh from Calton Hill* (both 1825). (The latter was used, appropriately, for the cover of the reissue of G. E. Davie's *The Democratic Intellect* – see Chapter 4.) For many, Wilkie is the most significant painter of the early nineteenth century, following his interest in detailed scenes from everyday life, including festivals and fairs. He turned to historical art around 1806, including painting a picture of the battle of Waterloo commissioned by the Duke of Wellington (1816). In 1818 he painted Walter Scott and in 1822 covered the fatefully Unionist Nationalist entry of George IV to Holyrood in *Reception of the King at the entrance of Holyrood Palace.*

By the turn of the nineteenth century, workplace and home were becoming increasingly separated and the home increasingly subject to *design*. The now-familiar 'palace' look of the Scottish terraced house, for example, dates from about the 1790s, and can still be seen throughout Glasgow. The nineteenth-century expansion of Glasgow called for a rapid increase of housing, mostly in the form of terrace-style tenements, some of which, via overcrowding and disrepair, would become the slums of the mid-twentieth century. The later nineteenth century saw a rapid growth in the more exclusive villa and, via a partially imperial logic of social engineering, the suburb. In tune with the Victorian ethic of the family, many architects shifted their concentration to the individual home.

In Glasgow neoclassicism, or Grecianism, was modified by an eclecticism associated with David Hamilton, while the east coast became more purely 'Grecian': Aberdeen's main street, symptomatically called Union Street, began to take its present shape in 1801 and was broadly neoclassicist, following Edinburgh. In the early nineteenth century there was a pan-European standardisation of the architectural Great Styles backed up by a growing abundance of art and architecture textbooks; these were drawn on, for example, by Alexander 'the Greek' Thomson, champion of, as the name suggests,

Grecianism. One of the immediate contexts for this fashion is the way Britain had come to see itself as a 'liberator' after victory against its imperial rival France in 1815 (even though Anglo-British education was taking on a more *Roman* model, which stressed conquest). Thus, Edinburgh became known as the 'Athens of the North', a now-wearied phrase which some tourist guides still find irresistible – though this naming also resonates with Scottish education's determination to hold on to Greek and philosophy, as described by G. E. Davie, and with Adam Smith's earlier Greek-and-English leanings in his *Lectures on Rhetoric*. Grecianism from the first three decades of the nineteenth century still shapes the face of Edinburgh today, most obviously in the Parthenon – designed by William Henry Playfair and built on Calton Hill overlooking the city, but abandoned in 1829 – and in Playfair's Edinburgh Royal High School (1825–9) (the originally proposed site for the new Scottish Parliament).

Scottish painting was now flourishing: the Scottish Academy was founded in 1826, and its founding members would help establish the National Gallery of Scotland in 1859. Mid-Victorian orientalism – decorative, imperial images of 'the East' laid flat for Western consumption – also had its Scottish adherents, for example David Roberts, who travelled widely in the Middle East, and, to an extent, Arthur Melville. In part via a friendship between Walter Scott and J. M. W. Turner, the latter's marbled, Romantic light was gradually transferred to Edinburgh, making the city seem somehow even more British, for example in David Octavius Hill's *A View of Edinburgh from North of the Castle* (c. 1859).

From the 1820s, and in the shadow of the Scott/Turner aesthetic, John Knox began to produce the kind of images of the Highlands as spectacular wilds that would become familiar *as* Victorian Scotland. The Highland image was made even more sugary in the landscapes of Horatio McCulloch, whose bubbling burns and contented sheep (as in *Glencoe* (1864)) would be even further diluted in various reincarnations through the years, to end up on living room walls between Puppy with Big Eyes and Donkey from Majorca – the sort of 'punter art' described by Rab C. Nesbitt as good for hiding stains on living room walls. McCulloch's famous *My Heart's in the Highlands* (1860) appropriates a line from Robert Burns, a habit already established but also ominously prefiguring kailyard fiction (see Chapter 10).

Biblical themes also became common around the mid-nineteenth century, as in the extraordinary work of William Dyce, whose strangely modernist-looking accounts of Christ's trials, it has been suggested, also reflect the trials of Scottish presbyterianism at the time of the Disruption (see Chapter 5). Much of Dyce's work was influenced by the English school of pre-Raphaelitism, which otherwise never really took hold in Scotland. It features lone Romantic and melancholic figures gazing meaningfully into the middle distance, and is strongly allegorical, directly narrating episodes from the Bible. 'Literary' painting, arguably of Unionist Nationalist flavour, remained strong in the work of David Scott, Noel Paton and James Drummond; Drummond's *The Porteous Mob* (1855) recently covered the Penguin edition of Walter Scott's *Heart of Midlothian*, from which yarn the story is taken.

In the building of the individual country house, as we might expect, Walter Scott again pioneered a Unionist Nationalist tone of *nostalgic* Jacobite excess in his Abbotsford (1817–23); this style would be honed down to 'Scotch Baronial' and would become common amongst the moneyed Anglo-Scottish mid-century. Again, the confident Britishing of Scottish cultural nationalism can be seen in the fact that John Steell's monument to Walter Scott on Edinburgh's Princes Street (1840–1) is Gothic (spiky and Scotch-looking); and in the rise of the 'Scotch Baronial' style for country houses, peaking with Queen Victoria's retreat at Balmoral (1853–6), the design of which was overseen by Prince Albert. Even more spiky Gothic Free Church designs (after the Disruption of 1843) were exported to the colonies for the use of missionaries. Time after time, we find that a Unionist Nationalist version of Scottish culture is exaggerated *in export*.

The high-Unionist mid-century saw an economic expansion throughout Britain coupled with desire for social reform, for example Edinburgh Old Town was partially reconstructed. Empire offered fame to ambitious individual Scots, and visual art reflects this. Steell's public sculptures from the 1830s portray single heroic figures, at the same time as Thomas Carlyle's neo-Enlightenment vision was defining history as a progression of Great Men. Steell's heroic-figure legacy was taken up by David Stevenson, whose Wallace Monument near Stirling (1887) is the best known of Scotland's many Wallace monuments. Singling out individual Scottish heroes was, as I have suggested, a way of showing national pride while remaining politically Unionist. This relatively comfortable environment the 1870s and

1880s generally saw an expansion of exhibitions, and in part to answer the demand for individual heroes, the Scottish National Portrait Gallery was founded in 1889.

At the same time, however, there were Scots who were influenced by continental early modernism; from the 1860s, William McTaggart's work showed the influence of John Millais (who painted in Scotland) as well as John Constable; McTaggart also established a link with French impressionism which would help ease Scotland's way into modernism, and gradually the research diaspora settled in Paris rather than Rome. McTaggart's work is frequently social-realist/historical despite his proto-modernist idiom which tends towards the abstract; he documents themes including the leaving of Clearance emigrants, and depicts migration from the Highlands and Islands as a wider effect of empire.

Another product of this cultural shift was the Edinburgh Social Union, formed in 1885, which went about creating a 'Celtic' revival. The movement is known for its sharp-edged abstraction, its revival of ancient myths, and its association with the Celtic revivalism of Ireland powered by the poet W. B. Yeats. John Duncan is perhaps the best known exponent of the Scottish Celtic revival, his haunting painting *St Bride* (1913) being one of the movement's finest achievements. The movement should not be seen as accompanying any significant political Nationalism, but may have been an important precursor. In Ireland, Yeats was invited to be a member of the Irish Parliament after the independence of the Free State. The Celtic Revival also had an eye towards France and, later in the early twentieth century, French modernism would be imported by Samuel Peploe, John Fergusson and Francis Cadell. Like Henri Matisse, Dorothy Johnstone, G. L. Hunter, Eric Robertson, and later Anne Redpath and Joan Eardley, concentrated on intense patches of colour; they were rediscovered in the 1980s and became collectively known as the Scottish Colourists.

Celtic Revivalism also has links to the Arts and Crafts movement, originally a very English design look (though the stained-glass craftsman Daniel Cottier had worked with William Leiper and Alexander Thomson on the interior decoration of local houses since the 1870s). One of the best known expressions of the Scottish take on Arts and Crafts comes later, in Robert Lorimer's Scottish National War Memorial (1924–7), in Edinburgh Castle; the work of Phoebe

Figure 12.4   *The Progress of a Soul: The Victory*, Phoebe Traquair, 1899–1902. (Courtesy of the National Galleries of Scotland.)

Traquair is also worth finding. George Walton established a decorating company in Glasgow in 1888, showing the direct influence of the English socialist William Morris, and was commissioned to decorate two tearooms in Buchanan Street and Argyle Street. The one in Buchanan Street opened in 1896 but then by that time Walton was trying to move down to London; jobs he had left over he gave to Charles Rennie Mackintosh, who was relatively unknown at the time – although it was in that same year, 1896, that he designed Glasgow School of Art.

The 1890s saw the peak of the fashion for tearooms in the newly-leisured Glasgow, which Celtic Revivalists used as a vehicle for ornate decor. Towards the end of the nineteenth century in general, however, architecture became more purposeful, based on themes rather than Grand Styles, and, later, more client-centred. There was also an increase in public authority architecture, seen for example in the Glasgow municipal buildings (1883–8), which make liberal and opulent use of marble. From the 1870s Glasgow had at least rivalled Edinburgh as a centre of art. James Guthrie, Joseph Crawhill, George Henry and Edward Hornel, known collectively as the 'Glasgow Boys' despite being based in the Royal Scottish Academy in Edinburgh, gained recognition by challenging the classical tone of the art establishment, as well as the obsession with portraits. Moving towards rural as well as urban themes, their social realism would become canonical in the early twentieth century.

The Glasgow School showed the influence of McTaggart and of James Whistler, as well as expanding the industrial aesthetic into a general design theme, to some extent anticipating German Bauhaus. The Glasgow School was consolidated by Patrick Geddes's magazine *The Evergreen*. As well as Celticism, Japanese art was an influence on, for example, George Henry and Edward Hornel, whose clean-lined curving illustrations often appeared in *The Evergreen*. The Celtic-Japanese influence is seen in Mackintosh's design, as well as in his painting, as in the early *Harvest Moon* (1892). Showing a disdain for McCulloch-like nostalgia, as MacDiarmid would for kailyard, *The Evergreen* prefigures the Renaissance of the 1920s in attempting a general cultural rethink.

Mackintosh's un-ornamental import of Art Deco – these days still often marketed as *the* Scottish style – was used in tearooms, resorts, public buildings and, most famously, Glasgow School of Art (1896), a Baronial style made oblique by stark geometrical shapes. What became known as the 'Mackintosh style', a by-word for Scottish modernism, was actually the creation of four people – Herbert MacNair, Frances Macdonald, Margaret Macdonald and Mackintosh himself. They are collectively known as 'the Glasgow four', and their style as

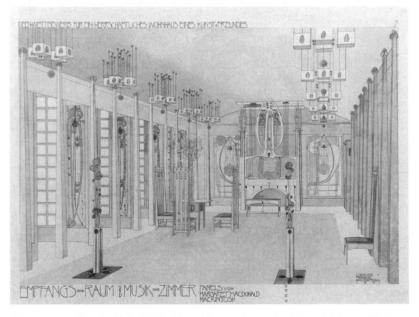

Figure 12.5   Charles Rennie Mackintosh's plan for an Art Lover's House. (Source: *Meister der Innenkunst: Charles Rennie Mackintosh, Glasgow: Haus eines Kunstfreundes*, Darmstadt: A. Koch, 1902.)

'Glasgow style' (and this is so linked with the city as to be still often presented as contemporary).

In the 1920s and 1930s, John Duncan Fergusson's layered landscapes showed a domestication of cubism, as did the work of D. Y. Cameron, William McCance, William Johnstone, to some extent Mackintosh, and later, Robert Colquhon and Robert MacBryde. Stanley Cursiter's lines in motion even point towards futurism. William McCance attempted to carry on Geddes's 1910s aesthetic thought into the 1940s; Johnstone marked a general move towards abstraction. Alan Davie, something like an early beat figure with his interests in jazz and zen, took the call further into abstract expressionism, though abstract expressionism never became widespread in Scotland. James Cowie's fragmented neoclassical style influenced James McIntosh Patrick and Edward Baird, who also seem touched by surrealism. Eduardo Paolozzi is known as a creator of jagged-lined public art and murals to be seen at various places in Glasgow; he was also influenced by surrealism and had a hand in the collage techniques which would later feed into pop art.

Mid-century the utilitarian impulse re-intervened in welfare state architecture, and architecture became more client-led in the private field, and more starkly practical in the public field. John James Burnet, and, even more so, Thomas Tait, often used bare, pyramidal, 'stepped' designs of the kind to be seen in Tait's Scottish Office building, St Andrew's House, in Edinburgh (1932). Tait was also responsible for the 1938 'Tower of Empire' for the Glasgow Empire Exhibition, during a period of broad unionist consensus. Such a consensus would last post-war to the regeneration of Glasgow, largely via the tower block, championed by Housing Committee Convenor David Gibson. Gibson praised the Red Road flats, which later became notoriously dangerous – like so many housing schemes – after they had been run down through lack of infrastructure, something Gibson could not have anticipated. Robert Matthew and Basil Spence redeveloped the Gorbals area of Glasgow; Matthew also created Edinburgh University's spartan David Hume Tower (1960–7) – something of a shock to the 'historical' city, though retaining the unionist nomenclature. Matthew became architect to London County Council and was therefore responsible for London's Royal Festival Hall, for example; Spence designed Sussex University (1960–) and other functionalist structures. To an extent – perhaps in part because of the fate of tower

Figure 12.6   Thomas Tait's St Andrew's House, home of the British government's pre-1999 Scottish Office. Note the various 'Grecian' monuments surrounding it in this picture. (Crown copyright: Royal Commission on the Ancient and Historical Monuments of Scotland.)

blocks under later governments, and perhaps in part because of the failed devolution campaign – Scottish architecture lost some confidence during the 1970s and 1980s. Somewhat in line with the times, one of the few areas to benefit from renewal during this time was the 'Merchant City' in Glasgow.

Ian Hamilton Finlay is usually described as a sculptor, but he has experimented with a number of materials including text; his 'neopresocratic' aesthetics, for example in classical-looking scupltures set in the Scottish countryside, are strongly post-Enlightenment in setting nature against culture, or showing how culture does *not* always follow nature. His Little Sparta garden is an exercise in setting nature against culture, and does so in a Scottish environment that troubles the aesthetic order of the English garden. Until recently, the received wisdom was that Finlay was better known outside Scotland than inside, since he received commissions from around the world while living quietly at Little Sparta. But if this was true once, it is no longer: Finlay is now frequently discussed. His canonisation coincided with an aggressive rebirth of social realism in the work of Ken Currie and Stephen Campbell; high-modernist and caricatured, their pictures often take key moments in the history of the Scottish labour movement as their themes. David Mach is also neo-industrial in his use of welded steel, as in *Big Heids* (1999).

Calum Colvin, whose work is used for the cover of Cairns Craig's *The Modern Scottish Novel* (1999), appropriates everyday objects in an over-formalised style comparable to postmodernism. In 1996 Douglas Gordon won the Turner Prize (two years after James Kelman won the Booker Prize); the next year Christine Borland was shortlisted. Glasgow is now a major player in the UK art scene as a whole, with both Borland and Gordon studying there (the latter under Bruce McLean), and artists self-running projects such as Transmission Gallery. Dundee Contemporary Arts Centre opened in March 1999 and, despite the unglamorous image of the city, has become an important venue across a range of arts. In Edinburgh, the Museum of Scotland designed by Benson and Forsyth (1995–8) marked a new expectation of a greater measure of self-determination – and a look round the museum will illustrate some of the themes of this book. The Scottish Parliament at Holyrood, hugely late and over budget (see Chapter 9) but nevertheless an epochal structure, was completed in 2004 and was the work of Enric Miralles, Benedetta Tagliabue and their Edinburgh partners with a circular debating chamber (sides do not 'oppose' one another as in the mock-adversorial Westminster chambers). It represents some of the hopes of a small nation, and its policy takes culture more seriously than has the UK Parliament in London.

SUMMARY

- The move of the royal court to London robbed Scottish art of many of its local patrons; there is an architectural convergence, however, with the import of Wren and the unionist loyalties of some architects.
- In the early to mid-eighteenth century, Scottish painting and architecture suffered from a double pressure from Jacobitism on one hand, and Unionism on the other; many artists combined both.
- The Enlightenment saw a move towards 'improvement' in architecture, and 'perfect proportion' in painting.
- After the quietening of Jacobites, a central style of country houses in the nineteenth century was 'Scotch Baronial'; Queen Victoria's Balmoral is typical of this.

- Portraits and statues of great historical figures, reflecting the individualist times, became common in the mid– to late nineteenth century.
- 'Mackintosh style' is the product of four people, and is only one of many Scottish moves towards modernism, though it has become strongly associated with the image of Glasgow. Glasgow also had its share of later modernists, and is now a force in the UK art world.
- Much Scottish architecture after the Second World War shows an impulse that is both utilitarian and socialist; though some of the tower blocks are despised now, this is largely due to neglect by later governments.

QUESTIONS FOR FURTHER RESEARCH AND THOUGHT

- What does it mean to say that Edinburgh is an 'Athenian' city?
- In what kinds of contexts or publications are Ramsay's and Raeburn's portraits used today?
- How was the English 'Arts and Crafts' movement received in Scotland?
- Why has the figure of Charles Rennie Mackintosh remained so strong in public memory?
- Are there any styles of modernism that flourished in England but not in Scotland?
- How did most Glasgow people feel about moving from the old tenements to tower blocks or New Towns?
- Is the link between the artist and the academy stronger or weaker than it was 200 years ago?

FURTHER READING

Glendinning, Miles, and Aonghus MacKechnie, *Scottish Architecture*, Thames and Hudson, 2004.
A thorough and well illustrated guide to the history of buildings from ancient times to the new Scottish Parliament.

Macmillan, Duncan, *Scottish Art 1460–2000*, Edinburgh: Mainstream, 2000.
A weighty survey which attempts to locate Scottish Art within a European tradition.

Macmillan, Duncan, *Scottish Art in the Twentieth Century*, Edinburgh: Mainstream, 2001.
This is more relevant to our purposes because of its timescale; it convincingly draws paths via various modernisms and comes almost right up to the present.

Turnbull, George, *A Treatise on Ancient Painting*, London: A. Millar, 1740.
A classic Enlightenment account of the idea of perfect proportion; only a few copies exist.

National Galleries of Scotland: http://www.natgalscot.ac.uk/ (includes all the National Galleries)

The Centre for Contemporary Arts: www.cca-glasgow.com

Dundee Contemporary Arts Centre: http://www.dca.org.uk/

CHAPTER 13

Mass Media

Television, the most influential of the mass media, grew from a particularly Scoto-British context: its technology was developed largely by one Scot, John Logie Baird, and given its role as a vehicle of public education by another Scot, John Reith, the first Director General of the BBC. Reith had high hopes for the BBC as a carrier of mass education, and that has remained, on paper at least, its remit. ITV began broadcasting in 1955, with advertising and no such lofty ambitions, amounting to a deregulation of what had been conceived as a national body. BBC2, the 'alternative' BBC channel, started in 1964, and Channel Four in 1982. In the 1980s and early 1990s Channel Four would shake up TV significantly by making brave commissions, including films from or about Scotland. The fifth terrestrial channel, Channel Five, consists mostly of B-movies and shock-horror enter-tainment.

The BBC is ready-devolved, or networked to Britain's 'regions'. The year 1984 is sometimes seen as a watershed, when Bill Bryden came to head BBC Scotland, and his dynamism in nationalising content is viewed as one reason for an increased sense of media inde-pendence in Scotland (to add to all the other 1980s cultural move-ments we have seen). Cast in terms of the high culture/popular culture split of the inter-war period, Reith was thinking of the BBC at least in part as a vehicle of high culture, which it was for its first few decades, though over recent years British TV as a whole has justifiably come under attack for 'dumbing down' and for thematic repetition. The 'house makeover' show is a notorious example: as *Scotch and*

Wry's Reverend I. M. Jolly puts it, sometimes you can find yourself literally watching paint dry. As well as these terrestrial channels, there are a growing number of satellite channels covering various themes with varying quality. But as John Reith might have pointed out, more channels do not necessarily mean a greater diversity of opinions (and for an example, we only need to look at the way in which US journalists were 'embedded' during the Iraq war, reducing it to a single infantile story). 'Interactive' TV is gradually coming online, though as I have argued at length in the online journal *Reconstruction*, the closed circuit of TV and viewer represents a completion of the Enlightenment project of individuation (of which Reith is an inheritor), and a *loss of* choice, if we see choice as the ability to reflect without being overwhelmed by advertisements, banners and other techniques designed to compete for the eye.

Until recently TV made in Scotland had been largely reliant on obvious 'types', made by Scots for Scots laughing (and cringeing) at Scots, as in *Francie and Josie* (Rikki Fulton and Jack Milroy) (1962–5), and the various characters of Stanley Baxter in his *Picture Show* (1972–5), both of which had a music-hall feel. *Para Handy* (1959–60), a comedy series centring on small-time maritime cargo carriers and originally based on the stories of Neil Munro, is these days seen in the same kailyard frame, as is *Doctor Finlay's Casebook* (1962–71). Until at least the 1980s, lived Scottishness seemed abnormal, outside of TV standards – a great irony, given Reith's background. There seemed a vast gulf between tartan-clad stand-up and the popular networked situation comedies which seemed always to be based in detached houses in the English Home Counties, centring round a housewife and a husband in middle-management. They may as well have been set in Istanbul: we Scots had no idea what they were on about. As a child, I often wondered whether Surbiton was a real place, or whether it was some kind of pun made from the idea of a generic suburb (note to others of my generation: it is a real place). Why was the vicar always 'popping round', and what was a vicar anyway? And why did these people all have enormous houses, in empty streets? The point is, during these more unionist times of the 1970s and before, the world of the mass media belonged to some other place; it was only in the 1980s that it seemed to become connected to Scotland at all.

Also easily accused of kailyardism is the BBC's *Hamish Macbeth* (1995–7), starring Robert Carlyle before he started his career playing

James Bond villains, and perched in postmodern fashion between high-tartanry and strategic kitsch. Carlyle as a local policeman uncovers various minor mysteries (the kailyardesque joke being that there is no real crime), and runs us through various themes of small-town Highland life. The kailyard reading may be disingenuous here, however; the series contains scenes touched by brilliance, as in the moment when a good-hearted urchin flees north from the urban hell of Glasgow, depicted as a maze of alleys and grey viaducts recalling the 1930s descriptions of Hugh MacDiarmid or Edwin Muir. An equally ironic vision of Glasgow was evoked by the popular comedy *Rab C. Nesbitt* (1989–99), with Gregor Fisher as an unemployed scheme-dweller, the show itself a spin-off of the Scottish comedy-sketch series *Naked Video* (1986–91). Again the show was often accused of showing the worst side of Scottish urban life, though perhaps the problem was that its caricatures were too accurate for comfort.

There has also been a Scottish tradition of literary TV crime drama stretching from adaptations of Sir Arthur Conan Doyle through the Glasgow hard-men of William McIlvanney, to the sophisticated and popular novels of Ian Rankin, now undergoing dramatisation (2000–). Scottish Television's major long-running addition to the detective series, *Taggart* (1983–), has continued, unprecedentedly, even after the death of its central character. BBC Scotland has also made some high-profile non-crime literary dramatisations, notably *A Scots Quair* (BBC 1971, 1982, 1983), and John Byrne's dramatisation of his own *Slab Boys Trilogy* (1996). Byrne's *Tutti Frutti* (1987), a gently comic tale of itinerant musicians starring Robbie Coltrane and Emma Thompson, was also highly popular, and Byrne followed it up in 1990 with *Your Cheatin' Heart*. In 2004, at the height of Scottish literary confidence, the BBC broadcast a series on Scottish authors entitled *Writing Scotland* (2004).

Chewin' the Fat (1999–2001) is a Scottish comedy useful for an illustration of the 'ned' phenomenon (aimless cropped-haired council-scheme male hooligans), which itself goes a long way towards describing modern Scottish culture. The soap opera *River City* started in 2002, and is set in the fictional Glasgow area of Shieldinch (filmed in Dumbarton), and seems *prima facie* like a devolved version of the BBC's long-running London soap *Eastenders*; ironically, *Eastenders* has been accused of stealing *River*

City's ideas, possibly because *River City* has a longer delay before filming. In any case, the same uninspired pub-centred standard types appear in both. *Monarch of the Glen* (2000–) is a drama series somewhat in the tradition of *Hamish Macbeth*, though with a different kind of irony, and featuring the accomplished English actor Richard Briers. BBC Scotland also runs a gently investigative journalism series *Frontline Scotland*. As it happens, one of the world's most genuinely cutting-edge investigative journalists, Duncan Campbell, is a Scot, working in a number of media.

Radio can be broadly split into three categories: BBC Radio, which is covered by the licence fee and so carries no advertising; independent radio, geared to each region as a kind of rival to the BBC; and community radio, attracting much smaller audiences. On the BBC in Scotland, BBC Radio Scotland and its Gaelic equivalent, Radio Nan Gaidheal, are most listened to nationally, while the usual BBC Radio channels are also available (BBC Radios 1–4, World Service, Asian Network, and so on). Independent radio is region-based, making Radio Clyde (Glasgow) and Radio Forth (Edinburgh) the stations with the largest audiences. BBC Radio Scotland is a mixture of talk and music, with a local/AOR/country/blues feel. Billy Kay, under his company name *Odyssey*, has written and presented a wide range of programmes on Scottish arts themes, and BBC Radio Scotland often features discussions on current events.

Radio has a tiny audience compared to TV. Scots' TV addiction (as in Britain as a whole) can be seen in the extraordinary amount of TV coverage in tabloid newspapers. If you took out TV news, football and gossip from a British tabloid, there would be little left. Scotland's biggest paper is the *Daily Record*, sister paper of the British *Daily Mirror* and by far Scotland's most popular daily tabloid, with a readership of about 730,000; its Sunday version *The Sunday Mail* has about 750,000. The *Evening Times*, useful, as the name suggests, for getting the day's news in the evening, has a readership of 280,000. The competition for the broadsheet ('serious') newspaper reader is between *The Scotsman* in Edinburgh, with a readership of 220,000, and *The Herald*, (until 1992 *The Glasgow Herald*) a daily newspaper since 1859 in Glasgow, with a readership of 274,000. There is little cross-reading (in other words, most of the public choose one or the other) and preference splits pretty much across east/west lines. Both of these Scottish broadsheets go down much better with Scottish readers than the British press (sometimes mistakenly called 'the English press'). British papers like *The Guardian* do have their supporters, and for the right wing who are no longer represented by the Scottish press, there is the *Daily Mail* (tabloid), the *Daily Telegraph* (broadsheet), and the slightly more centrist *The Times* – none of which have anything like the presence in Scotland they have south of the border.

The *Sunday Mail*'s main rival is *The Sunday Post* (claiming a readership of 1,327,000). Although this has been jazzed up and looks much better than it did a couple of decades ago, it still represents a classic latter-day kailyard – sub-literary stories told in the shadows of a Whig British historiography growing from rural Scotland with an eye on the empire, stories whispered with a placating smile so as not to disturb those in power (thus, Tom Nairn's famous comment that Scotland would be free when the last Church of Scotland minister was strangled with the last *Sunday Post*). In Dundee D. C. Thomson also produces a number of other tabloids, such as the unbelievably inane *Weekly News* (214,000) and, apparently stretching back to 1739, *The Scots Magazine* (139,000). This last should not be confused with proper Scottish writing: it is of the babbling brooks and contented sheep of Horatio MacCulloch variety, and reading it is like trying to listen to your gran when you have a hangover. In the late 1930s there was a boom of comics arising from the same publisher: *The Dandy* in 1937 and *The Beano* in 1938, both of which remain to this day, though they are not specifically Scottish in content (in 2004 *The Dandy* underwent a painfully-PC facelift). 1936 saw the advent in the *Sunday Post* of *Oor Wullie*, an itinerant and ageless scallywag (according to an unofficial website, he is ten) sitting on a bucket and getting into scrapes by stealing apples and knocking off policemen's helmets. *The Broons*, appearing next to *Oor Wullie*, started out as D. C. Thomson's idea of the typical Scottish family, but they have remained unchanged as the world has changed around them.

The anachronistic nature of these strips has been picked up by later generations of Scottish comic illustrators, largely working underground. In *Electric Soup*, Frank Quitely, who also works in various other 'super-hero' comic modes, parodies *The Broons* in his strip *The Greens* – an easy target, but he does it brilliantly (see the cover of this book). Like the American comic underground, much of the content of Scottish comics, or that which is not of the straight 'superhero' kind, is connected to soft drugs, particularly cannabis (as in *Northern Lightz*); yet amongst this there are moments of biting sarcasm, as in *Electric Soup*.

John Grierson stands in a similar relation to Scottish cinema as does John Reith to the BBC, sharing a timescale, a vision and, in a sense, a unionism. Like Reith's TV, Grierson's documentary film was to be a medium of mass education. His *Drifters* (1929), about a herring fleet setting out from Shetland, influenced 1930s documentaries such as Harry Watt's well known *Night Mail* (1935), which also, tellingly, depicts an Anglo-Scottish journey, as did Alfred Hitchcock's adaptation of John Buchan's novel *The Thirty-Nine Steps* (1935). Thereafter Michael Powell in, for example, *The Edge of the World* (1937) and *I Know Where I'm Going* (1945) used the Scottish Highlands in a more crypto-nationalist sense which subtly stressed resistance to the Clearances, just as the far-western island of St Kilda was being evacuated. Both Reith and Grierson broadly conceived of both union and empire as instruments of social reform, and this comes out strongly in their work of the 1930s.

Cinema took off early in Scotland, with theatres opening in the 1890s and growing in number in the 1900s; by the mid-twentieth century there were more cinema-goers per capita than in England. The first British three-reel feature film was *Rob Roy* in 1911. In the 1940s a number of documentaries on Scotland were funded by the Ministry of Information and by the Scottish Office, recently 'devolved' to Edinburgh (*The Crofters*, 1944; *North East Corner*, 1946). The mid-century also saw a spate of literary adaptations in Hollywood including *The Master of Ballantrae* (1953), which cast Errol Flynn as a swashbuckling Jacobite – another indicator of how romantic-nostalgic the figure of the Jacobite had become; Clarence Elder's version of Neil Gunn's *The Silver Darlings* (1947); and multiple versions of *Kidnapped*, culminating in the 1971 version in which Michael Caine is hilariously miscast as Alan Breck.

From the 1954 set-up of *Films of Scotland*, modern film funding began to come into place; initially, funding bodies exercised a great deal of power, and the films were almost promotional: the Edinburgh Festival, for example, was repeatedly advertised. There were also a number of films on literary figures, such as Neil Gunn, Norman MacCaig and Hugh MacDiarmid. Meanwhile, though, Scotland in its metonymic Highland form was being sold as a land of carefree glories in *Bonnie Prince Charlie* (1948) and the kailyard-on-acid fantasy of *Brigadoon* (1954).

Alexander Mackendrick's domestic *Whisky Galore* (1949) often takes a lot of stick for its nostalgia. The story was based on a Compton Mackenzie novel, in turn based on the real shipwreck of the *SS Politician* in the Western Isles, whose cargo of whisky was partly appropriated by the islanders. *Whisky Galore* is easily misunderstood as a harmless film of the Ealing Comedy variety, but Duncan Petrie notes Charles Barr's demonstration that the film is more ambitious and ambivalent in its portrayals of human motivations. It has also has a lesser-known follow-up in Michael Relph's *Rockets Galore* (1958), which goes back to rural clearance for its theme, this time for a British nuclear base (scarcely a nostalgic topic).

Scottish fictional feature films only began to be made in the late 1960s, in particular Laurence Henson and Eddie McConnell's *Flash the Sheepdog* (1967). Amongst the first Scottish *auteurs* was Mike Alexander, with *The Bodyguard* (1969) and *The Family* (1970). Bill Douglas's trilogy, *My Childhood* (1972), *My Ain Folk* (1973) and *My Way Home* (1978), describes a child growing up in a mining village; it is shot in a melancholy monochrome as if seen from the view of a child, using a steady camera but jumpy narrative, a form of naturalism that would be brought back by Lynne Ramsay's debut film *Ratcatcher* (1999), a story set in the same period. (Ramsay followed *Ratcatcher* with *Morven Callar* (2002), very loosely based on the popular novel by Alan Warner.)

In general (the likes of Bill Douglas notwithstanding), what had been happening was that Scotland in film had been more or less shrunk down to the Highlands, whereas mid-twentieth century Scotland had become, by European standards, exceptionally urbanised. In 1982 the collection of essays *Scotch Reels* critiqued kailyard-type images in the depiction of Scotland. *Scotch Reels* set a tone of suspicion of Scottish 'heritage' (a favourite term, remember, of Margaret Thatcher), which would trigger a re-reading of the presentation of Scottishness in the 1980s and 1990s. Nevertheless, a kind of Glasgow social realism in film might perhaps be dated back to *The Gorbals Story* (1949). This was an adaptation of Robert McLeish's stage play, performed by the Glasgow Citizens' Theatre Company, itself founded by James Bridie in 1943 and inspiring John McGrath's 7:84 company set up in the early 1970s (the numbers 7:84 refer to the

Figure 13.1   Citizens' Theatre, Glasgow. (Photograph: Michael Gardiner.)

division of wealth). *The Brave Don't Cry* (Philip Leacock, 1952) is based on a true story of Ayrshire miners trapped down a shaft, and marks another move to naturalism; the film was partly funded by the National Film Finance Company, of which Grierson was the executive producer.

Already in place, additionally, was 'Clydesidism' – a naturalistic and mostly unionist documentary celebration of shipbuilding, as in *Red Ensign* (1934), *The Shipbuilders* (1943), and their Hollywood counterpart, *Rulers of the Sea* (1939). The Clydeside satellite town of Greenock has also featured throughout Scottish film as a microcosm of the rise and fall of west-coast employment and morale (though not in the same unionist sense) from Peter McDougall's *Just Your Luck* (1972), *Just a Boy's Game* (1979), and *Down Where the Buffalo Go* (1988) – set on the nuclear base at Holy Loch – through to Ken Loach's *Sweet Sixteen* (2002). Glasgow Clydesidism went on as late as *Seawards the Great Ships* (1960), and should be regarded as a celebration of how the war had revived shipbuilding on the Clyde.

The other side of this British coin is sectarianism, and as Scottish national consciousness increases, so do films showing Scotland's religious tensions. McDougall's *Just Another Saturday* (1975) follows a young Orange Marcher (see Chapter 5) coming to terms with his role. He also made *A Sense of Freedom* (1981), on the notorious gangster Jimmy Boyle, *Dreaming* (1990), and *Shoot for the Sun* (1987) – one of a long line of films and TV dramas depicting an urban hard-drugs scene, long before more famous examples. *The Big Man* (1990), written by William McIlvanney and directed by David Leland, and featuring Billy Connolly and Liam Neeson, combines gangsterism and family drama, as an ex-miner is drawn into a world of illegal boxing, posing some of the problems that would be explored by the later outright socialism of the English director Ken Loach. The disturbing *Silent Scream* (David Hayman, 1990), based on the imprisonment of the murderer Larry Winters, follows the path of the urban crime/drugs maze, as does John MacKenzie's *Looking After Jojo* (1997). It is arguable that English crime/drugs/prison features of the same 'stylish' mode, yet much lighter in content, have been influenced by similar Scottish films immediately before.

In 1976 the 'Film Bang' attacked the problem of funding, and tried to cohere Scottish film into an industry capable of making feature films. One of the first it helped make, on a micro-budget of £2000, was Bill Forsyth's *That Sinking Feeling* (1979), a comedy about Glasgow teenagers stealing kitchen sinks. This film is remarkable not only for its success, but also because it established the Scottish *auteur* feature film. Forsyth went on to make the much higher-budget *Gregory's Girl* (1981), a story of adolescent love acted almost entirely by teenagers in a New Town. His *Local Hero* (1983) returns to the Highlands, and gives the culture-of-place an ecological twist when a beach cabin-dweller played by Fulton McKay refuses to sell his stretch of beach to an American oil company. *Comfort and Joy* (1984) was loosely based on the Glasgow 'ice-cream wars', with Bill Paterson as a radio DJ caught up in the rivalry between ice-cream vans. Forsyth's gentle comedies set the tone for a Scottish feature movement in the 1980s, including *Restless Natives* (Michael Hoffman, 1985), *Heavenly Pursuits* (Charles Gormley, 1985), and *The Girl in the Picture* (Cary Parker, 1986). *Heavenly Pursuits* signalled another step-up in funding scale and the use of known stars.

In the late 1970s and early 1980s a number of local film workshops were set up, and it was from these grassroots that the Scottish film boom of the late 1990s would grow. From 1982 the new Channel Four committed itself to funding 'diverse' film via the 'Film on Four' series, and it did fund four such features in 1982–3. As in the case of Reith, Channel Four's first chief executive, Jeremy Isaacs, was Scottish. Channel Four would continue to commission series, including John McGrath's *Blood Red Roses* (1986), until 1991, when its policy changed to a more entrepreneurial stance of one-off commissions. The British Film Institute was also active in commissioning in the early 1990s, including Ian Sellar's *Venus Peter* (1990), an elegiac tale of a young boy (young boys being common in Scottish film) growing up in Orkney surrounded by sea and poetry. In 1989 Timothy Neat's version of John Berger's *Play Me Something* moved flittingly between the Western Isles and mainland Europe, its narrative cuts seeming to fit the place of the 'small nation'.

It was in the mid-1990s that Scottish cinema became much more self-sufficient and, famously, more fashionable. In 1993 the Scottish Film Production Fund and BBC Scotland inaugurated the 'Tartan Shorts' series, which would provide a step from the film festival circuit to the feature film for new directors. In 1996 'Prime Cuts' was started by British Screen and Scottish Television, as well as 'Gear Ghear', a Gaelic version of Tartan Shorts. National Lottery money is also 'devolved' to the Scottish Arts Council, meaning that the SAC is able to use the money as it chooses.

There was a huge increase in the number of films made in and *about* Scotland in the mid-1990s. Lars von Trier's powerful *Breaking the Waves* (1996) stars Emily Watson as a young woman whose sexual identity is tortured by the Free Kirk in a small island community. In 1997 Coky Giedroyc directed A. L. Kennedy's story *Stella Does Tricks*, describing a Scottish prostitute and representing, like Lynne Ramsay, another form of enhanced localism (Kennedy's fiction has often been described as a kind of Scottish magic realism). David Kane also had major successes with *Ruffian Hearts* (1995) and *This Year's Love* (1999); in 1996 Gillies Mackinnon directed *Small Faces* (1996), one of many films concerned with urban gangsterism.

Ken Loach had been interested in Glasgow since *Riff Raff* (1991), starring Robert Carlyle as a construction worker down south, which continues with *Carla's Song* (1997), in which Carlyle (again) is a Glasgow bus driver who persuades a Nicaraguan refugee to return home to face her problems. Loach's Scottish fascination had until *Sweet Sixteen* centred on Glasgow, and with *Ae Fond Kiss* (2004) he returned to Glasgow; perhaps Loach's finest moment is his second collaboration with Scottish writer Paul Laverty, *My Name is Joe* (1998), in which a recovering alcoholic gets caught up in drug smuggling, and is faced with insoluble ethical and economic problems, Loach's narrative stock-in-trade. Loach's undogmatic direction draws a brilliant

188 MODERN SCOTTISH CULTURE

performance from Peter Mullan, who then made his directorial debut in *Orphans* (1999), a story of four siblings trying to reach their mother's funeral. Mullan followed his debut with *The Magdalene Sisters* (2002), on the treatment of 'fallen women' by the Irish Catholic church.

The major breakthrough in *scale* in cinema in Scotland came with the success of *Shallow Grave* (1995), the first recipient of Glasgow Film Fund money, made by the soon-to-be-famous team of director Danny Boyle, producer Andrew McDonald and writer John Hodge. Set in Edinburgh's New Town, it seems to signal a new and young independence, though there seems something of the yuppie in most of this team's heroes. They followed up their success with a version of Irvine Welsh's *Trainspotting* (ironically, largely shot in Glasgow), which shows a new market awareness in flattening out the book's ambivalence over sectarianism and imperialism. In many ways, Paul McGuigan's rendering of Welsh's short stories *The Acid House* (1999) is a more challenging film, made on less than a tenth of the budget. As well as using rapid cuts and 'scratches' and point-of-view shots (and letting Ewan Bremner do some proper acting, denied by the comedic sidekick made of his character in the film version of *Trainspotting*), it also retains the book's most provocative themes. Thus, dissenting voices such as that of Colin McArthur began to question the way in which Scottish films were becoming market-led. Instead, argued McArthur, there should be a place for *low-budget* Scottish films to maintain integrity.

All of *Trainspotting*'s central actors were soon in great demand. Ewan MacGregor was soon schmaltzing with Cameron Diaz in *A Life Less Ordinary* (1997), and became a previous incarnation of the ultra-English Alec Guinness in *Star Wars: Episode One* (1999). He also starred in *Complicity* (2000), based on the novel by fellow-Scot Iain Banks, and then in *Young Adam* (2003), by fellow-Scot Alexander Trocchi. Robert Carlyle's acting career was celebrated but took peculiar turns: he became a Bond villain in *The World is Not Enough* (1999), with Judi Dench as Bond's handler – an interesting reversal of Scots' historical complicity with imperial intelligence, and a far cry from the times of Sean Connery as 007 (his Scottish Nationalist tattoo is briefly visible in *Dr No* (1962)). Carlyle has also starred in films of dubious quality since then (*Formula 51*, 2001; *Hitler: Rise of Evil* 2003). Of the *Trainspotting* actors, it is perhaps Ewan Bremner's output that has been the most interesting, not only in *The Acid House* (1999), or his well-known and brilliant cameo as Archie in Mike Leigh's *Naked*

(1993) but also in his work with Harmony Korine in the extraordinary *Julien Donkey-Boy* (1999).

From the Hollywood side of things, Mel Gibson's *Braveheart* was released in the same year as *Shallow Grave*, much to the benefit of the Scottish Tourist Board (it directly and strongly influenced the number of visitors to Scotland, despite being filmed largely in Ireland). What annoys scholars of Scottish Studies is not that the film is silly or that it is historically 'wrong', but that it harks back to a mid-Victorian moment of Unionist Nationalism, when Wallace was commemorated by numerous monuments *within* an environment of unionism and imperialism (or in Gibson's case, globalisation), and Scotland's complex place in the UK was reduced to an anti-English 'ethnic' pride. Similar comments could be made about *Rob Roy*, Michael Caton Jones's addition to the many *Rob Roys* already produced by Hollywood. Both of these films have heroes who are impossibly heroic, maverick figures who are difficult to relate to the world outside the cinema in other than ethnocentric terms. Billy Connolly's gruff ghillie to Judi 'the spy master' Dench in *Mrs Brown* (John Madden, 1997) could be cast in a similar Unionist-Nationalist-Masculinist frame. Figures like Connolly's ghillie or Gibson's Wallace are fantastic figures, super-human, super-ethnic, and super-masculine, and ultimately a bit absurd. As Duncan Petrie points out, the kilt-raising scene in *Braveheart* uncannily resembles the kilt-raising scene in *Carry On Up the Khyber* (1968).

SUMMARY

- Both BBC television and early British documentary film have very strong Scottish connections; originally they had a unionist, liberal remit, intended to educate.
- BBC1 and ITV, the latter featuring programmes by Scottish Television, are the most popular television channels.
- As well as the usual British radio channels, the BBC 'regionally' broadcasts BBC Radio Scotland; independent radio from each Scottish region represent rivals to this.
- There is a rich tradition of Scottish film documentary, made for various purposes and with various sources of funding.
- The first Scottish *fictional* feature films were not made until the late 1960s.

- From the late 1980s, Scottish media became more distinctive.
- In the mid-1990s, the scale and nature of the funding of Scottish film, and its audience reach, changed dramatically.

QUESTIONS FOR FURTHER RESEARCH AND THOUGHT

- Why did *Oor Wullie* and *The Broons* become popular?
- Given John Reith's original hopes for the BBC, does BBC Scotland still have a duty to public education?
- What made Grierson and Reith so confidently unionist?
- Where are the women narrators of Scottish film?
- To what extent was the mid-1990s success of Danny Boyle's *Shallow Grave* and *Trainspotting* related to the earlier work of Bill Douglas and Bill Forsyth?
- The message of Ken Loach's *Ae Fond Kiss* (2004) is that no religious community can be maintained in its original purity today; true or false?

FURTHER READING

Dick, Eddie (ed.), *From Limelight to Satellite*, London: BFI, 1990.
A collection of essays on *auteurs* and contexts making up a history of Scottish cinema (before, of course, the 1990s boom).

Hardy, Forsyth, *Scotland in Film*, Edinburgh: Edinburgh University Press, 1990.
A comprehensive survey of depictions of Scotland in film, their historical contexts and budgetary restraints. Has been overtaken to an extent by more recent events.

McArthur, Colin (ed.), *Scotch Reels*, London: BFI, 1982.
A turning-point in recognising how depictions of Scotland in film had been stereotyped and kailyard-based; as such, a movement towards a more naturalistic cinema.

Petrie, Duncan, *Screening Scotland*, London: BFI, 2000.
A authoritative and highly-readable history of Scottish film; it shows an awareness of archive material you are unlikely to find anywhere else.

Petrie, Duncan, *Contemporary Scottish Fictions – Film, Television, and the Novel*, Edinburgh: Edinburgh University Press, 2004. This builds on Petrie's knowledge of film, and merges picture and language in a highly readable and timely account of Scottish 'stories'.

BBC Scotland: http://www.bbc.co.uk/scotland/tv/

The Scotsman: http://www.scotsman.com/

The Herald: http://www.theherald.co.uk/

Daily Record: http://www.dailyrecord.co.uk/

BBC Radio Scotland: http://www.bbc.co.uk/scotland/radioscotland/

BBC Radio 1: http://www.bbc.co.uk/scotland/radioscotland/

BBC Radio 4: http://www.bbc.co.uk/radio4/

Radio Clyde; http://www.radioclyde.co.uk/

Radio Forth 1: http://www.forth1.com/

Edinburgh International Film Festival: http://www.edfilmfest.org.uk/

CHAPTER 14

Scottish Music

It used to be thought that modern Scottish music suffered from a debilitating split between a native folk tradition on the one hand, and a foreign classical tradition on the other, and that this division prevented the emergence of a Scottish Ralph Vaughan Williams or an Edward Elgar. If this was once a worry, today the situation looks almost the opposite – generic anxiety between folk/popular and classical traditions is notable by its absence, and 'traditional' and 'art' musics feed into one another constantly. The 'Seriously Scottish' series of CDs produced by the Scottish Music Information Centre (SMIC) positively ignores any generic distinctions at all. To an extent, this is a Britain-wide phenomenon, at a time when Squarepusher is liable to be played alongside Phillip Glass in London concert halls; in Scotland, however, the pulling together of apparently separate threads has been even more vigorous, in part to answer this old idea that the folk idiom is naturally limiting.

Why this need to be vigorous? Because there still exists ethnocentrism, the idea that the nation equals a particular people at a particular time. If you find Scottish music sold as 'ethnic' or 'world' music, its focus may turn out to be extremely narrow: in 2003 *The Rough Guide to Scottish Music* ignored classical, rock, pop and electronica, in favour of 100 per cent folk music, reducing Scotland to the ethnic 'flavour' meaning of the national adjective, as we saw in the Introduction. For *The Rough Guide*, bagpipes, fiddles and drums are 'Scottish Music' but tabla, bass guitars and laptops, are not. Fortunately, Scottish music itself provides the antidote to this nonsense, and all you have to do is listen to it.

Despite the older received wisdom that the Scottish folk idiom was severed at the root from the classical, a growth of classical music in Edinburgh from the 1770s was noted throughout Europe, and classical concerts were regularly performed in the city. The Edinburgh Musical Society had been formally established as early as 1728, building its own venue, St Cecilia's Hall, in 1762. By the 1770s the Society was enthusiastically adapting baroque and rococo, it was attracting some of Europe's best known musicians, and was involved in the European interchange of musical ideas. The composer Thomas Erskine, for example, is known to have made an impression on Mozart. Nevertheless, most ambitious Scottish composers followed the familiar road to London, especially after the Society folded in 1798, leading to something like the hiatus we have seen in mid-nineteenth-century Scottish literature.

Meanwhile, the folk tradition thrived before *and* after the Edinburgh Music Society, and, as we now realise, the idioms *did* mix normally (except for the problem of notation relative to the harmonic scale now 'globalised' via the classical canon, something common to most folk musics). For example, the use of that most 'Celtic' of instruments, the fiddle/violin, was an import from European classical music. Many musicians, then as now, worked within 'both' idioms: Neil Gow, the renowned folk fiddler, earned a living by playing classical – the reverse of what we might expect. The mid-eighteenth-century composer James Oswald, later chamber composer to George III, grew up within a folk tradition that is audible in his compositions, for example *Airs for the Seasons* (various dates). Oswald's work is these days sometimes put together on CD with that of David Foulis, also learned in European classical but immersed in folk, born in the same year and a fellow-member of the Society.

The 'classical' Oswald was a keen collector of folk tunes, and the Enlightenment, with its encyclopaedic desire to know-and-classify in music as in every other field, gave birth to a boom of publications of folk tunes, comparable to the Ossianic tendency in literature. Allan Ramsay, not surprisingly, was involved early with his *Tea Table Miscellany* (1724–37) collection of songs, begun just before William Thomson's *Orpheus Caledonius* (1725). Both collections came under criticism for their 'legitimacy', as would Macpherson's Ossianic variations, but later the folksong-collecting ethic was given more credibility by Robert Burns, who contributed to the six-volume *Scots Musical Museum* (1787–1803). And Burns, as we now realise, was really a

Figure 14.1   Henry Raeburn's portrait of the celebrated fiddler Neil Gow, 1793.
(Courtesy of the National Galleries of Scotland.)

Europhile radical, and a vernacular inventor of the 'protest song'. Also often forgotten are Carolina Oliphant, a prolific writer of Jacobite songs, and Scott Skinner, who composed almost 600 songs in the nineteenth century.

After an Enlightenment start would come the question of whether music after the demise of the Edinburgh Musical Society would go on to Romanticism and, by implication, a consciously *national* art music. By the early nineteenth century, George Thomson was using harmonies indebted to Beethoven, and thus, arguably, to German Romanticism. But this was only a start: indeed the length and centrality of the Romantic musical style in Scotland, from early nineteenth to early twentieth century, might pose a problem for the theory (associated with Tom Nairn) that Victorian Scotland failed to develop a proper nationalist culture as did, for example, Germany. Thomson commissioned well-known European composers to write piano accompaniments to 'traditional' songs. These were nevertheless largely unloved, since the composers usually had little idea of the original context; the attempt led, however, to Thomson's *Select Collection of Original Scottish Airs* (1793–1841).

By the latter part of the nineteenth century something like a national school of orchestral and operatic music seemed to be in place: the composers John B. McEwen, Learmont Drysdale, William Wallace (an extraordinarily versatile figure who was also a poet, a classicist and an eye surgeon) and Hamish MacCunn were all active and widely known. MacCunn's work has fared much better than the rest in the national memory; but typically for the period, all four spent most of their working lives in London. The work of both MacCunn and McEwen was perhaps once seen as sentimental, but has more recently been rescued and re-evaluated within the context of European Romanticism, especially MacCunn's operas. His overture *Land of the Mountain and the Flood* (1887), written when he was still at college, has regained popularity; so too have his *Six Scotch Dances* (1896), which, as their name suggests, can be likened to the work of Béla Bartok in their formalising native rhythm and harmony.

After writing the 1888 orchestral ballad *The Ship o' the Fiend*, MacCunn began a series of choral works on Scottish subjects, which were well received by critics in Europe and America. During the 1890s he produced two important operas, *Jeanie Deans* and *Diarmid*, but he succumbed to British jingoism at the turn of the twentieth century, with *The Masque of War Peace* produced at Her Majesty's Theatre in 1900 for the benefit of the Guards' War Fund, *The Golden Girl* in 1905 and The *Wreck of the Hesperus* for chorus and orchestra, and in 1908 *The Pageant of Darkness and Light.* Like other Scottish classical composers, MacCunn advocated the formation of a Scottish College of Music in Edinburgh, but died before he could help realise one.

Both A. C. Mackenzie and John McEwen were appointed principal of the Royal Academy of Music (not at the same time) but though they are often grouped together with MacCunn on CD, they have remained less known than him. McEwen has sometimes been likened to Mendelssohn (whose 'Fingal's Cave' (1829), from the *Hebridean Overture,* is one of the best known pieces of music *about* Scotland); McEwen's adaptation of the concerto form in *Scottish Concerto for Piano* (1897) follows the experimental format of the German composer. A violinist himself, A. C. Mackenzie is best known for his violin concertos and early orchestral work such as *Scotch Rhapsodies* (1879–80). In 1884 his *The Rose of Sharon* enjoyed great critical success; he became principal of the Royal Academy of Music in 1888, and from 1892 to 1899 he conducted the Philharmonic Concerts, as would John McEwen from 1924. McEwen was less Romantic-nationalist than MacCunn, though his orchestral works also incorporated Scottish folk melodies, as in the *Border Ballads* (1908) and the *Solway Symphony* (1911). His suite *Pibroch* (1889), chosen to head the *Seriously Scottish* sample CD, shows how, even during these most kailyard years, it was possible to identify a highly classical, yet highly 'native' Scottish classical music.

The pibroch (traditional piping) form was traditionally used for a clan gathering, and can still be heard at Highland games and similar events. It is based on a theme, or *urlar* – ground – and variations are made on notes using 'cuttings', or ornaments. Originally military, the pibroch has tonally evolved away from the strict military pattern, but still has an ethnic and warlike image – and there remains the problem of claiming as Scottish a musical tradition that became known partly via an aggressively British context. For colonised people in the nineteenth century, the pibroch was associated with imperial violence; for Scottish descendents of this colonised people in the twenty-first century, a form of violence continues in the sense that the racks of 'Scottish music' in record shops, *Rough Guide*-style, often refuse them admittance into the national tradition. Furthermore, although Scotland exported pipe band music to the British empire, the instrument itself is not exclusively Scottish, but common from Ireland to Northern France; for some people then, this 'pan-Celticism' holds the pipes' real socio-political meaning.

The pianist and composer Ronald Stevenson, born in Lancashire but constantly preoccupied with national themes, has followed the earlier triumvirate in building classical music from the tonality of folk, preparing treatments of folk songs amongst other projects, including concertos for his own instrument, the piano (1966, 1972). His modernist take, within the era of the 'Second Renaissance' when 1920s literary figures were being reread in a socialist-and-nationalist context, perhaps comes out best in his piano music and songs, where he adapts Hugh MacDiarmid, Sorley MacLean and William Soutar, and in the song cycle *Border Boyhood* (1971). His work, like that of MacDiarmid, is fiercely modernist, the initials on his important eighty-minute piano work *Passacaglia on D-S-C-H* (1963) referring to its dedicatee, Dmitri Shostakovich.

Similar claims may be made of Robin Orr and Cedric Thorpe Davie, who match high modernism to native cadences. Erik Chisholm also modernised high tradition, as can be heard in works such as his *Pibroch Piano Concerto* (1930), the *Straloch Suite for Orchestra* (1933), and the sonata *An Riobhan Dearg* (1939). In 1928 Chisholm founded the Scottish Ballet Society (later the Celtic Ballet), and with the choreographer Margaret Morris created several ballets, most famously perhaps *The Forsaken Mermaid* (1940). Another major achievement was the foundation of the Active Society for the Propagation of Contemporary Music (1930–40), for which Chisholm brought leading composers to Glasgow to perform their work.

Edward McGuire has several large-scale works that have won critical acclaim, including a chamber opera *The Loving of Etain* (1990), and concerti for guitar, trombone, viola, violin and (most recently) double bass. Following the 'doubling' tradition, McGuire also plays flute with, and writes for, the Scottish folk group The Whistlebinkies.

Both Stevenson and his collaborator Frances George Scott wrote twelve-tone modernism. William Sweeney, widely commissioned by the BBC and the Royal Scottish Academy of Music and Drama, was influenced early by the atonality of Stockhausen, but returned to a tonal folk idiom. Iain Hamilton, Thea Musgrave and Thomas Wilson have all worked in the post-Schoenberg idiom of serialism – repetition with difference, often based on environmental factors – though they have largely moved away from this with the times. More recently, the celebrated Craig Armstrong, conversant with a range of contemporary musics, has been responsible for a number of film soundtracks including *The Bone Collector* (1999), Peter Mullan's *Orphans* (2000), and *Moulin Rouge* (2001). Though his arrangement is classical, Armstrong's unit is the *song* – in an era when many 'popular' electronica artists would not dream of making a CD of twelve songs of five minutes or so each. Armstrong has worked with Liz Fraser of the Cocteau Twins and Massive Attack, amongst others, and is no stranger to the uniform percussion of techno. His *The Space Between Us* (1998) is a good place to start listening.

Another of Scotland's major contemporary composers, James Macmillan, was influenced early on by Polish experimentalism, which he brought to bear on contemporary Scottish issues as a committed socialist. His angular high modernism benefits from Scottish folk elements both harmonically and rhythmically, as in the orchestral *The Confession of Isobel Gowdie* (1990), describing the burning of a seventeenth-century witch. His *Veni, Veni Emmanuel* (1992) was written for the internationally renowned Scottish percussionist Evelyn Glennie. He continues to mix the atonal and the very tonal in striking ways, in opera and in his first symphony, *Vigil* (1997), perhaps the best known of his work and also perhaps the best place to start.

Today, the Royal Scottish National Orchestra, the Scottish Chamber Orchestra, the BBC Scottish Orchestra, Scottish Opera, the Scottish Dance Theatre and Scottish Ballet all perform regularly, remarkably for a small nation. Also remarkable is the continued tradition against the odds to reject generic pigeonholing, as in Edward McGuire's work for the Scottish Symphony Orchestra, the Royal National Scottish Opera and The Whistlebinkies. This brings us to the question of the folk 'revival', the term suggesting that folk disappeared until the 1960s, whereas it is probably more the case that folk music as such lacked the confidence to declare itself until the 1960s.

There was certainly a growing *awareness* of folk tradition after the Second World War. Ewan MacColl, the composer of 'Dirty Old Town', later famously covered by the Irish band The Pogues, was one of the key figures behind the revival, collecting ballads, as later would Norman Buchan and Hamish Henderson. The 1960s and then 1970s were served by a large number of specialist folk record shops and magazines including *Living Tradition*. Largely associated with Glasgow, the ongoing 'folk revival' stretches as far as Shetland, and its national festival; influences include Irish music, the popular/classical cross-over, and the good old protest song turned against, for example, the installation of nuclear weapons. The folk music tradition indeed helped to crystallise a popular tradition of protest which fed into the second devolution campaign.

The 'Scottish Tradition' series of recordings, based on musical collections spanning a number of decades, was produced by Edinburgh University School of Scottish Studies; they run from Outer Hebridean folk musics including 'waulking songs' available commercially for the first time, to pibroch and other more familiar forms, and taken together were another motor of the folk revival. The series is available through the label Greentrax, which probably has the fullest list of folk and 'traditional' (this is the last time I will use that word) music, with some fascinating fusions as well as 'purer' song (though some fusions are best avoided, especially the cringeworthy 'Keltic Elektric' series, which overlays traditional playing with bog-standard late-1980s electronic drums). In Greentrax-esque vein there are also the labels Highlander Records, Moidart, Temple, Tradition Bearers, and Fence Records; Offbeat Scotland seems to keep folk in a singer/songwritery idiom. 'Celtic' music appears on Foot Stompin', Mill Records, and Scotland's Music. Established and respected bands including Shooglenifty and Capercaillie are on the Vertical Records label; Aly Bain and Phil Cunningham record for Whirlie Records in Edinburgh. A much more popular version of 'Scottish country dance music' (Jimmy Shand, The Clydesiders) is represented by the REL label; similarly Sandy Reid, Jim MacLeod and others are on Ross Records. Now almost silenced are Harry Lauder and his later incarnation Andy Stewart, tartan-clad Liberaces whom Billy Connolly has described as 'singing shortbread tins'.

Folk musicians to start listening to include Dick Gaughan, an Edinburgh-based singer and guitarist who takes joy in the protest song in the best 'folk revival' traditions, the Battlefield Band (named after a suburb of Glasgow, not a warlike sentiment), Blazin Fiddles, Shooglenifty, the Kitchen Band, and Jock Tamson's Bairns. Dougie MacLean is an influential folk-rock singer-songwriter who was once a member of folk band Silly Wizard. 'Gaelic rock' comes a bit after the folk revival and perhaps feeds on its visible Scottishness: Runrig were the first popular band to perform their own songs in Gaelic when their *Play Gaelic* broke through in 1978; Capercaillie, singing in Gaelic and the Scots of the western Highlands, are Gaelic rock's main other superstars, though they are too musically flexible and outward-looking to be classed this narrowly – they continue to experiment with other musics with great bravery. Pan-'Celtic' music is now celebrated in the annual festival Celtic Connections, in Glasgow.

Scotland also has its share of jazz musicians, most famously Kevin MacKenzie and Tommy Smith. The Scottish National Jazz Orchestra was formed in 1995, latterly directed by Smith, and commissions original work. The Glasgow Jazz Festival, around the end of June and the start of July, has attracted enormous names in the world of jazz including Dizzy Gillespie, Taj Mahal, Oscar Peterson, Art Blakey, the Kronos Quartet, and Horace Silver, and takes place at a range of venues in the city. The record label Linn (as in the makers of top-end music systems) represents a range of classical and jazz artists including Tommy Smith. Jazz is also to be found on Caber Music, Hep Records, and Spartacus Records. It may be that jazz in Scotland is more likely to slide towards blues, country and singer-songwriterism, as in the folk/blues sound of Eric Bogle or Michael Marra, than its more metropolitan and more strictly 'modern jazz' equivalent in London. Once we reach the pubs, a huge array of bluesists, singer-songwriters and country singers are to be found. Glasgow's Centre for Contemporary Arts is a multimedia space which also caters for visual arts, talks and film, and has a restaurant and bar. Other now-traditional and world-renowned festivals include the Edinburgh International Festival in August/September, which has a large musical element, and Glasgow's Mayfest. The TripTych festival, held at various venues throughout Scotland at the end of April and beginning of May, has attracted an amazing international line-up of artists in the fields of dance, electronica, dub and modern composition.

By the time the folk revival had kicked off, Scots were already active in popular music. Lonnie Donegan was largely responsible for the popularisation of skiffle in the 1950s, from which grew the 'group sound', making the guitar common in pop music, thus feeding into bands like The Beatles. In 1959 the Glaswegian Lulu had a hit with her annoying song 'Shout' (originally by the Isley Brothers), and she went on to appear on *Top of the Pops* in every decade till the 1990s; in 2000 she played at the 'Scottish Glastonbury', the T in the Park festival. Her 'girl-at-Tesco' image was briefly echoed in the 1980s by Sheena Easton. Around the turn of the 1970s the Sensational Alex Harvey Band worked a heavy rock akin to Black Sabbath. In similar vein, Nazareth came to prominence after their self-named album in 1971. After working with the Rolling Stones, John McLaughlin and others, Jack Bruce became one of the trio Cream, who recorded the ground-breaking *Wheels of Fire* (1968). The singer Rod Stewart's success began as early as 1968 with the Jeff Beck Group; on becoming a megastar, he relocated to Los Angeles, got more highlights in his hair, and continued to support Celtic FC.

The now world-famous comedian/actor Billy Connolly started out as a folk musician in The Humblebums, a band which also included Gerry Rafferty. The latter went on to musical fame after Connolly's comedy monologues seemed to take centre stage and the band split in 1971. Rafferty's more rocky *City to City* (1978) includes 'Baker Street', and surely one of the most memorable saxophone riffs ever. In the mid-1970s the Bay City Rollers entered the charts with an über-tartanry which steamrollered the cultural cringe; they have recently, unsurprisingly, been exhumed as 'retro' in celebration of their shameless use of Scotch kitsch. Less well known are Pilot, active at the same time, and even featuring ex-members of the Rollers, but 'quieter' in their image. Also peaking in the early 1970s were the Average White Band, based around average white Scot Hamish Stuart, but including black members, and much 'blacker' than the Black Sabbath bands.

In 1976 the Edinburgh Art College band The Rezillos signalled the arrival of punk in the nation, and were accompanied by too many other punk acts to mention. The next year a Dunfermline band formed by Richard Jobson and Bill Simpson expanded to become The Skids, who would go down in punk history with their anthemic 'Into the Valley'. Stuart Adamson left in 1981 to form the stadium-rock band Big Country, a slightly more Celtic-feeling, angular and less long-winded version of Simple Minds, who also packed out stadia in the 1980s. From 1986 Wet Wet Wet were the most successful exponents of a Scottish white-soul pop movement which, arguably, also took in Deacon Blue, Hipsway, Texas, Del Amitri, Aztec Camera, and Orange Juice. Wet Wet Wet had a chain of hits and contributed to the cheesy hit movie *Four Weddings and a Funeral* (1994). Altered Images, largely as a result of the excessive pop energy of Clare Grogan, had a number of hits; Grogan then went back to the acting career which had seen her as Gregory's last date in *Gregory's Girl* (see Chapter 11), to appear on *Eastenders* and elsewhere. The Eurythmics made use of the strong character of Aberdeen's Annie Lennox, and provided the (not terribly fitting) soundtrack for Michael Radford's film rendition of George Orwell's *Nineteen Eighty-Four* (1984). Unquantifiable by any of these standards, the Cocteau Twins (of whom there were three members), hailing from the un-beautiful location of Grangemouth, spun extraordinary and magical songs around the circling guitar of Robin Guthrie and the vocals of Liz Fraser 'in a language she made up all by herself', becoming the flagship act of the label 4AD. EPs 'Tiny Dynamine' and 'Echoes in Shallow Bay' (1985) are extraordinary; you could also start with *Garlands* (1982), *Treasure* (1984), or *Victorialand* (1986).

'Indie' of the 1980s often took on an ironically 'cute' sound and image, sometimes concealing a warped sexuality (BMX Bandits, The Vaselines, Shop Assistants), using the fanzine and the flexidisc, and genuinely independent until Alan McGee's label Creation made it big. Some of these bands have broken recently, for example Eugenius (ex-Vaselines) and The Pastels, who seemed finally to come to international attention via the film *The Last Great Wilderness* (2002). In 1985 The Jesus and Mary Chain released their groundbreaking album *Psychocandy*; their drummer Bobby Gillespie afterwards formed Primal Scream, who moved from 1960s guitar pop to spearhead the indie/dance crossover *Screamadelica* (1991), produced by Andy Weatherall and incorporating elements from gospel to psychedelica, and arguably defining the moment of the rock/dance crossover better than anything that emerged from Manchester. Teenage Fanclub came from the same scene a bit later.

Alan McGee has more recently started again with the label Poptones (presumably named after the tune by Public Image Limited), signing bands including Beachbuggy (who seem to have borrowed heavily from The Fall), The Bell Rays, and (briefly) The Hives. Glasgow's Chemikal Underground Records represent artists including Arab Strap, whose dry humour is always good value, Bis, pitched somewhere between Stereolab and Luke Vibert, yet retaining something of the Scottish indie look (and hugely successful in Japan, for some reason), Aerogramme, Mogwai – now internationally known and the subject of an interesting CD of remixes – and the Delgados, tirelessly championed by the late Radio One DJ John Peel. Belle and Sebastian add some style to the Scottish indie sound, and have been highly applauded by critics. They belong to Glasgow's Electric Honey records, as do the indie rockers Snow Patrol, suddenly very successful. Human Condition Records from Edinburgh have an interesting range of indie and electroacoustic, and the capital city is also home to Susan Lawly, the label of Whitehouse and other extreme noisemerchants (and this does mean extreme). Daniel Patrick Quinn, equally unqiue but not nearly as disturbing, is on Edinburgh's Suilven Recordings, and ploughs a lonely furrow with a kind of layered folk New Age influenced by Brian Eno but sounding more like Robyn Hitchcock. The Pleasantly Surprised label have represented Dif Juz and Test Dept.

Glasgow's Travis recorded their first album in 1997, and were soon supporting the English band Oasis on tour; ultimately, they emerge from a similar background to Mogwai and Teenage Fanclub. Mount Florida, a combination of an installation artist and a DJ, make a music which is extraordinarily eclectic, sounding in turns like Cabaret Voltaire, European electro and the Butthole Surfers. Momus (Nick Currie) is a Paisley-born pop singer-songwriter stylishly plying his own personal kinks. Adventures in Stereo involve ex-Primal Screamer Jim Beattie and are on Creeping Bent records, who also represent Alan Vega and The Nectarine No. 9. Mull Historical Society (Colin MacIntyre) writes strong pop songs which have begun to be recognised. Franz Ferdinand, who are almost always preceded by the epithet 'art rock', perfectly reconstruct 1979 as if everyone in 1979 had been listening to angular and intelligent pop (Wire, Gang of Four, Television), for a generation only just too young to remember the rest of the rubbish which was also around in 1979.

There is also a fairly healthy bhangra scene in Scotland, though it tends to remain underground, except for the Mela Festival in Edinburgh. Asian dance clubs are not as common as Ken Loach makes them seem in *Ae Fond Kiss* (beware also the hero of that film describing himself as a 'DJ', when he is only playing records). Scottish dance music has also absorbed the lessons of Jamaican dub, and we have reached a period when these styles cross over rapidly, as in the Asian/dub/rap mix of Future Pilot AKA. Not all crossover styles, however, have had such rosy results: Glasgow's take on early 1990s rave was, as Simon Reynolds and others have pointed out, grim, and most of it ranged from gabba at worst (a brutal high-speed techno developed in Holland) to 'happy hardcore' at best.

There was also a chemical difference: though the English soon recognised that 'ecstasy' meant MDMA, in Scotland 'ecstasy' remained a generic term containing amphetamine plus anything from gravel to strychnine to low-grade heroin. MDMA is usually described as 'unpredictable' (its possible effects include dehydration and psychological addiction), but it has been around since the 1910s, and much more is known about it than some drugs GPs prescribe, like Prozac. On the other hand the generic cocktail *described as* ecstasy is undoubtedly harmful and abused by neds, as are a range of other cheap and harmful drugs (as reflected in the terrible choice of name for the dance label Soma – in *Brave New World*, Aldous Huxley's imaginary drug induces a personal 'vacation' *away from* the crowd, whereas ecstasy *creates* a crowd). The question of MDMA is an important one; firstly, unlike alcohol, it decreases the likelihood of violence; secondly, it prioritises the tactile over the visual and is therefore readable in terms of the Scottish tradition of thought described in Chapter 3; thirdly, it encourages people to inter-relate rather than splitting into couples (which was what the government of the early 1990s disliked about it most).

To an extent the rave phenomenon in its festival-like sense passed Scots by (the London M25 'orbital' scene is not, for example, the same kind of rave written about by Irvine Welsh). One popular high point came in the form of the KLF – comprising Jimmy Caulty, ex-Killing Joke, and Bill Drummond – who were justifiably described in terms of French Situationism, a political movement that encouraged spontaneous political surprises. The KLF's wheezes included firing fake machine-guns at record company bosses during the 1992 Brit Awards, establishing an anti-Turner Prize for art, and, most famously of all, burning money. Today, however, there *is* a thriving and healthy techno and electronica scene, mainly associated with Glasgow and at various levels of the underground. Glasgow techno/electronica labels include Gdansk, Lost Dog, Royal Jelly, Stuff, Soma, Glowin', Red Monkey, Five2oEast, Debunk, Emoticon, and Subplate; elsewhere in Scotland there are the electronica labels UTI, Incorporeal, Injun Ears, T&B Vinyl, Yummi, Aural Addiction, Psychiatric, Mouthmoth, and Benbecula.

Aside from the talented and versatile Howie B from Edinburgh (start listening with his *Folk* or his collaboration with Sly and Robbie),

Figure 14.2   Cover of Boards of Canada's *Music Has The Right To Children*.
(Courtesy of Boards of Canada and Theo Seffusatti at Warp Records.)

the neglected and now-dated Finitribe also from Edinburgh, and the more esoteric Christ, Scottish electronica probably found its first *auteurs* in Boards of Canada. They are a 'reclusive' (music business jargon meaning that they don't live in London) duo from Pentland in the far north of Scotland; they seem to dredge up sounds from somewhere deep in the shared cultural memory – many of the sounds they use, bouncy yet muffled, could have come from 1970s children's TV cartoons or feature films (compare them to the score of *Gregory's Girl* – see Chapter 11). Boards of Canada understand the importance of the analogue crackle or glitch is a way that puts them closer to Oval than Autechre, with a sound so oddly friendly and familiar that it cannot simply be described as 'experimental' in the usual electronica sense.

They are an apt image for where Scottish culture as a whole might be going: they see their 'decentred' status as a plus rather than a minus, staying close to the land – 'a beautiful place in the country'; they are reflective in a way that seems to make a local mythscape powerful – as in another of their samples, 'the past inside the present'.

SUMMARY

- The idea that Scottish folk tunes couldn't adapt to classical was once overstated, but has been rethought recently.
- During the Enlightenment, there was a boom of collections of folk songs.
- Scotland's three best-remembered, late nineteenth-century composers, Hamish MacCunn, John McEwen and A. C. Mackenzie, all had a Romantic turn, all successfully used folk idioms, and all lived for long periods outside of Scotland.
- Amongst others, Ronald Stevenson, Robin Orr and Erik Chisholm have taken forwards the folk–classical sound of the above three composers.
- Craig Armstrong has composed the scores of a number of well-known films, domestic and Hollywood; he could be described as a classical composer working in a popular idiom.
- Of the pop and rock music you know, much more than you think has come from Scotland.

QUESTIONS FOR FURTHER RESEARCH AND THOUGHT

- What does it mean to say that the early eighteenth-century collections of Allan Ramsay and William Thomson are 'inauthentic'?
- What are the cultural politics of the early nineteenth-century 'folk-song collection' tradition?
- Are the trio of late nineteenth-century composers McEwan MacCunn, and Mackenzie identifiable as 'Unionist Nationalist' in a similar way to Walter Scott?
- Have any Scottish composers experimented with electronic composition in a similar way to Karlheinz Stockhausen, Pierre Henry or Luc Ferrari?

- Was the 'folk revival' of the 1960s really a revival in the sense of a multiplication of bands and a rediscovery of tunes, or had these always been there? If so, *where* was the music played and heard before the 1960s?
- In his 2002 novel *Porno*, Irvine Welsh strikes a chord with many Scots by making the homophobic psychopath Francis Begbie a fan of Rod Stewart. Yet in the film *Breaking the Waves* (1996), Lars von Trier overlays a tune of Stewart's on an island landscape to great effect. Which of these is the real Rod Stewart?
- Alan McGee's label Poptones claims on its homepage to be Situationist, a claim also made by Tony Wilson for his Factory label two decades before. Do the Poptones label's practices really resemble those of Situationism?

FURTHER READING

Collinson, Francis M., *The Traditional and National Music of Scotland*, **London: Routledge and Kegan Paul, 1966.**
Now inevitably a bit dated but a highly readable guide.

Coutts, W. G., *Scottish versus Classic Music, in an Ethical and Aesthetical Aspect*, **Edinburgh: H. B. Higgins, 1887.**
Not easy to find, but an interesting addition to the popular supposition of a folk/classical rift, with which theme I began the chapter.

Henderson, Hamish, *Alias MacAlias*, **Edinburgh: Birlinn, 2004, first published 1992.**
A large collection of writing on folksongs, literature and politics, from one of the twentieth century's most celebrated men of letters.

Johnson, James and Robert Burns, ed. Donald A. Low, *The Scots Musical Museum, 1787–1803*, **2 vols, Aldershot: Scolar Press, 1991, first published in different form c. 1809.**
The collection to crown the Enlightenment song-collecting boom; it stood in a relation to later Romanticism as did Macpherson's Ossianic variations.

Scottish Arts Council, *Music Strategy, 2002–2007*, **Edinburgh: SAC, 2002.**

Scottish Music Centre, *Scottish Music Handbook*, Glasgow: SMC, annual.

Strong, Martin C., *The Great Scots Musicography: The Complete Guide to Scotland's Music Makers*, Edinburgh: Mercat, 2002.
Like the name says, a useful reference book.

Scottish Music Centre: http://www.scottishmusiccentre.com/

Scottish Opera: http://www.scottishopera.org.uk/

Scottish Chamber Orchestra: http://www.sco.org.uk/

Scottish Dance Theatre: http://www.scottishdancetheatre.com/home/

Glasgow Royal Concert Hall: http://www.grch.com/grch/index.cfm

Glasgow Jazz Festival: http://www.jazzfest.co.uk/

Centre for Contemporary Arts: http://www.cca-glasgow.com/

Dundee Rep Theatre (including dance events): http://www.dundeereptheatre.co.uk/

The Lemon Tree, Aberdeen: http://www.lemontree.org/

Edinburgh International Festival: http://www.eif.co.uk/

Shetland Folk Festival: http://www.shetlandfolkfestival.com/

MayFest: http://www.mayfest.org.uk/

T in the Park: http://www.tinthepark.com

Mela Festival: http://www.edinburgh-mela.co.uk/

Triptych festival (2004 site): http://www.triptycho4.com/

Chemikal Underground Records: http://www.chemikal.co.uk/

Greentrax Records (including 'Scottish Tradition' recordings): http://www.greentrax.com/

Scottish and Irish Records: http://www.scottish-irish.com/asp/

Macmeanmna Records' generic Gaelic music site: http://www.gaelicmusic.com/

Jockrock online magazine: http://vacant.org.uk/jockrock/index. html

First Foot online magazine: http://www.firstfoot.com/

Miso (dance and electronica): http://www.ilovemiso.com/

Kill Your Timid Notion: http://www.killyourtimidnotion.org/

Index